Lecture Notes in Computer Science   10195

Commenced Publication in 1973
Founding and Former Series Editors:
Gerhard Goos, Juris Hartmanis, and Jan van Leeuwen

More information about this series at http://www.springer.com/series/7409

Spyros Blanas · Rajesh Bordawekar
Tirthankar Lahiri · Justin Levandoski
Andrew Pavlo (Eds.)

Data Management on New Hardware

7th International Workshop on Accelerating
Data Analysis and Data Management Systems Using
Modern Processor and Storage Architectures, ADMS 2016
and 4th International Workshop on In-Memory Data
Management and Analytics, IMDM 2016
New Delhi, India, September 1, 2016
Revised Selected Papers

 Springer

Editors
Spyros Blanas
Ohio State University
Columbus, OH
USA

Rajesh Bordawekar
IBM Thomas J Watson Research Center
Yorktown Heights, NY
USA

Tirthankar Lahiri
Oracle Cor.
Redwood Shores, CA
USA

Justin Levandoski
Microsoft Corporation
Redmond, WA
USA

Andrew Pavlo
Computer Science Department
Carnegie Mellon University
Pittsburgh, PA
USA

ISSN 0302-9743   ISSN 1611-3349   (electronic)
Lecture Notes in Computer Science
ISBN 978-3-319-56110-3   ISBN 978-3-319-56111-0   (eBook)
DOI 10.1007/978-3-319-56111-0

Library of Congress Control Number: 2017935567

LNCS Sublibrary: SL3 – Information Systems and Applications, incl. Internet/Web, and HCI

Printed on acid-free paper

This Springer imprint is published by Springer Nature
The registered company is Springer International Publishing AG
The registered company address is: Gewerbestrasse 11, 6330 Cham, Switzerland

Preface

The International Workshop on Accelerating Analytics and Data Management Systems Using Modern Processor and Storage Architectures (ADMS) and the International Workshop on In-Memory Data Management (IMDM) were held jointly this year.

The objective of this workshop is to investigate opportunities in accelerating analytics/data management systems and workloads (which include traditional OLTP, data warehousing/OLAP, ETL, streaming/real-time, business analytics, and XML/RDF processing) running in memory-only environments, using processors (e.g., commodity and specialized multi-core, GPUs, and FPGAs), storage systems (e.g., storage-class memories like SSDs and phase-change memory), and hybrid programming models such as CUDA, OpenCL, and OpenACC. The workshop hopes to explore the interplay between overall system design, core algorithms, query optimization strategies, programming approaches, as well as performance modeling and evaluation, from the perspective of data management applications.

In addition, over the past 30 years, memory prices have been dropping by a factor of 10 every 5 years. Main memory is the "new disk" for data storage. The number of I/O operations per second (IOPS) in DRAM is far greater than other storage media such as hard disks and SSDs. DRAM is readily available in the market at a better price point in comparison with DRAM alternatives. These trends make DRAM a better storage media for latency-sensitive database applications, large-scale Web applications, and future applications such as wearable devices. The International Workshop on In-Memory Memory Data Management and Analytics (IMDM) aims to bring together researchers and practitioners interested in the proliferation of in-memory data management and analytics infrastructures.

These proceedings contain papers from the joint ADMS/IMDM workshop that was co-located with VLDB 2016 in New Delhi, India. The workshops were well-attended and sparked interesting technical discussions.

All papers in these proceedings were peer-reviewed by an expert Program Committee comprising experts from both industry and academia. We would like to thank these committee members as well as the authors for contributing high-quality work.

February 2017

Spyros Blanas
Rajesh Bordawekar
Tirthankar Lahiri
Justin Levandoski
Andrew Pavlo

Organization

Workshop Organizers

Spyros Blanas	Ohio State University, USA
Rajesh Bordawekar	IBM T.J. Watson Research Center, USA
Tirthankar Lahiri	Oracle, USA
Justin Levandoski	Microsoft Research, USA
Andrew Pavlo	Carnegie Mellon University, USA

Program Committee

Reza Azimi	Huawei, China
Nipun Agarwal	Oracle Labs, USA
Christoph Dubach	University of Edinburgh, UK
Qiong Luo	Hong Kong University of Science and Technology (HKUST), Hong Kong
Sina Merji	IBM Toronto, Canada
Mohammad Sadoghi	IBM T.J. Watson Research, USA
Nadathur Satish	Intel, USA
Sudhakar Yalamanchili	Georgia Tech, USA
David Schwalb	Hasso-Plattner Institute (HPI), Germany
Viktor Rosenfeld	TU Berlin, Germany
Shirish Tatikonda	Target, USA
Christian Lang	Acelot, USA
Vincent Kulandaisamy	IBM Analytics, USA
Eric Boutin	MemSQL, USA
Badrish Chandramouli	Microsoft Research, USA
Martin Grund	Amazon, USA
Ryan Johnson	LogicBlox, USA
Hideaki Kimura	Hewlett Packard Enterprise, USA
Viktor Leis	TU Munich, Germany
Ippokratis Pandis	Amazon, USA
Evangelia Sitaridi	Columbia University, USA
Ryan Stutsman	University of Utah, USA
Sandeep Tata	Google, USA
Pinar Tozun	IBM Research, USA
Oded Shmueli	Technion, Israel

Contents

Cache-Sensitive Skip List: Efficient Range Queries on Modern CPUs

Stefan Sprenger$^{(\boxtimes)}$, Steffen Zeuch, and Ulf Leser

Institute for Computer Science, Humboldt-Universität zu Berlin,
Unter den Linden 6, 10099 Berlin, Germany
{sprengsz,zeuchste,leser}@informatik.hu-berlin.de

Abstract. Due to ever falling prices and advancements in chip technologies, many of today's databases can be entirely kept in main memory. However, reusing existing disk-based index structures for managing data in memory leads to suboptimal performance due to inefficient cache usage and negligence of the capabilities of modern CPUs. Accordingly, a number of main-memory optimized index structures have been proposed, yet most of them focus entirely on single-key lookups, neglecting the equally important range queries. We present Cache-Sensitive Skip Lists (CSSL) as a novel index structure that is optimized for range queries and exploits modern CPUs. CSSL is based on a cache-friendly data layout and traversal algorithm that minimizes cache misses, branch mispredictions, and allows to exploit SIMD instructions for search. In our experiments, CSSL's range query performance surpasses all competitors significantly. Even for lookups, it is only surpassed by the recently presented ART index structure. We therefore see CSSL as a serious alternative for mixed key/range workloads on main-memory databases.

Keywords: Index structures · Main-memory databases · Scientific databases

1 Introduction

Over the last years, various index structures were designed for fast and space-efficient execution of search operations in main memory, like the adaptive radix tree (ART) [13] or Cache-Sensitive B$^+$-tree (CSB$^+$) [18]. By reducing cache misses, improving cache line utilization, and exploiting vectorized instructions, they outperform conventional database index structures, like B-trees [5], which were mostly designed to reduce disk accesses. Most of these novel index methods focus on single-key lookups and show suboptimal performance for range queries, despite their importance in many applications. Use cases for range queries are numerous, such as: queries in a data warehouse that ask for sales in a certain price range, analysis of meteorological data that considers certain yearly time periods in long time series, and Bioinformaticians who build databases of hundreds of millions of mutations in the human genome that are analyzed by ranges defined by genes [9].

© Springer International Publishing AG 2017
S. Blanas et al. (Eds.): ADMS 2016/IMDM 2016, LNCS 10195, pp. 1–17, 2017.
DOI: 10.1007/978-3-319-56111-0_1

In this paper, we introduce the Cache-Sensitive Skip List (CSSL), a novel main-memory index structure specifically developed for efficient range queries on modern CPUs. CSSL is based on skip lists as described in [16], yet uses a very different memory layout to take maximal advantage of modern CPU features like CPU-near cache lines, SIMD instructions, and pipelined execution. In this work, we focus on read performance but provide a technique for handling updates, too. Besides many other use cases, we see CSSL as perfectly suited for scientific databases that prefer fast reads over fast writes and need range queries in many cases. Especially the bioinformatics community, which is confronted with an exponentially growing amount of genomic data that is mostly analyzed with range queries to investigate certain genomic regions [20], may benefit from our approach.

We evaluated CSSL on data sets of various sizes and properties and compared its performance to CSB$^+$-tree [18], ART [13], B$^+$-tree [7], and binary search on a static array. We also include experiments with real-world data from the bioinformatics domain to investigate performance on non-synthetic key distributions. For range queries and mixed workloads, CSSL is consistently faster than all state-of-the-art approaches, often by an order of magnitude; also its lookup performance is way ahead of all competitors except ART.

The remaining paper is structured as follows. The next section introduces skip lists, the index structure that CSSL is based on. Section 3 presents the Cache-Sensitive Skip List as our main contribution. Section 4 describes algorithms for executing lookups and range queries on CSSL. In Sect. 5, we compare CSSL against other state-of-the-art index structures using synthetic as well as non-synthetic data. Section 6 discusses related work, and Sect. 7 concludes this paper.

2   Preliminaries

Skip lists were originally presented as a probabilistic data structure similar to B-trees [16]. Skip lists consist of multiple lanes of keys organized in a hierarchical fashion (see Fig. 1). At the highest level of granularity, a skip list contains a linked list of all keys in sorted order. In addition to this so-called *data list*, skip lists maintain *fast lanes* at different levels. A fast lane at level i contains $n * p^i$ elements on average, where n is the number of keys to be stored and $0 < p < 1$ is a parameter. Skip lists were originally proposed as probabilistic data structures, as the elements to be stored in higher lanes are randomly chosen from those at lower lanes: Every element of fast lane i appears in fast lane $i + 1$ with probability p. This scheme allows for efficient updates and inserts, yet makes the data structure less predictable.

In our work, we use a deterministic variant of skip lists, so-called *perfectly balanced skip lists* [15]. In balanced skip lists, the fast lane at level $i + 1$ contains every $1/p$'th element of the fast lane at level i. Accordingly, for $p = 0.5$ a lane at level $i + 1$ contains every second element of level i, in which case a skip list resembles a balanced binary search tree. Figure 1 shows a balanced skip list over nine integer keys with two fast lanes for $p = 0.5$.

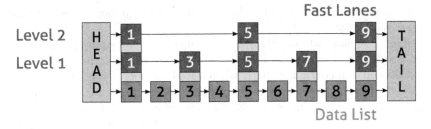

Fig. 1. A balanced skip list that manages nine keys and two fast lanes; each fast lane skips over two elements ($p = 1/2$).

In case of a low p value, fast lanes skip over many elements, therefore, fast lanes can be considered sparse. In case of a high p value, fast lanes skip over few elements, therefore, fast lanes can be considered dense. Fast lanes are used to narrow down the data list segment that may contain the searched element to avoid a full scan. For instance, a search for key 6 would traverse the skip list of Fig. 1 as follows. First, search determines the first element of the highest fast lane at level 2 by using the head element. Second, the fast lane will be traversed until the subsequent element is either equal to the searched element, in which case search terminates, or greater than the searched element. In this example, search stops at element 5. Third, search moves down to the next fast lane. In this example, traversal jumps to element 5 of the fast lane at level 1. Fourth, steps two and three are repeated until the data list is reached. Fifth, the data list is scanned until the searched element is found or proven to be non-existing. In a fully built balanced skip list for $p = 0.5$, search requires $O(log(n))$ key comparisons in the worst case. Parameter p directly influences the structure of the fast lane hierarchy and should be chosen depending on the expected number of keys. If p is too high, only few keys need to be compared per fast lane when searching, but a lot of fast lane levels are required to fully build a balanced skip list. If p is too low, a lot of keys need to be compared per fast lane when searching, but only few fast lane levels are required to fully build a balanced skip list.

Besides single-key lookups, skip lists also offer very efficient range queries. Since the data list is kept in sorted order, implementing a range query requires two steps: (1) Search the first element that satisfies the queried range, and (2) traverse the data list to collect all elements that match the range boundaries.

In the original paper [16], skip lists are implemented using so-called *fat keys*. A fat key is a record that contains a key and an array, which holds pointers to subsequent elements for every fast lane and for the data list. The advantage of this approach is that all nodes are uniform, which simplifies the implementation. Furthermore, if a key is found in an upper lane, search immediately stops as all instances of a key are kept in the same record. On the other hand, such an implementation is space inefficient, because it requires space for $O(m * n)$

pointers (if m is the number of fast lane levels), although most values in higher levels are padded with NULL.

Searching in skip lists using fat keys requires to follow many pointers. This layout is suboptimal on modern CPUs, as it incurs many cache misses due to jumps between non-contiguous parts of allocated memory. Even when searching the data list, cache utilization is suboptimal due to the *fatness* of keys. For instance, in a skip list that stores 32-bit integer keys and maintains five fast lanes in addition to the data list, each node takes $4\,bytes + 6 * 8\,bytes = 52\,bytes$ of memory on a 64-bit architecture. Given that a cache line is typically $64\,bytes$, each traversal step fills almost an entire cache line although only a small part of it is used. Typically, traversal steps just need the key and one pointer to find the subsequent element on a certain fast lane, i.e., $4\,bytes + 8\,bytes = 12\,bytes$.

3   Cache-Sensitive Skip List

In this paper, we present Cache-Sensitive Skip List as alternative implementation for balanced skip lists, which uses a radically different memory layout that leads to much higher efficiency in today's CPU architectures. The first and most obvious idea is to keep fast lanes as separate entities in dense arrays. This leads to less cache misses, improves the utilization of cache lines, and allows to use SIMD instructions. Figure 2 shows a Cache-Sensitive Skip List that manages 32 integer keys with two fast lanes for $p = 0.5$. The traversal path, which search would take to find key 7, is highlighted in red.

CSSL's main contributions are threefold: First, fast lanes are linearized and managed in one dense array, which is called *Linearized Fast Lane Array*, instead

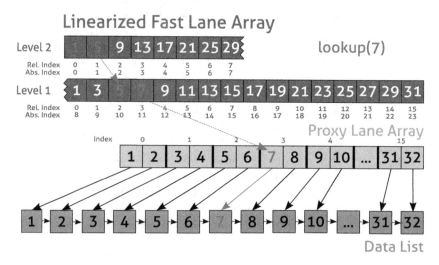

Fig. 2. A cache-sensitive skip list that manages 32 keys with two fast lanes ($p = 1/2$). (Color figure online)

of being kept in data list nodes. This improves utilization of cache lines when executing a lookup or range query. Second, by linearizing fast lanes we eliminate the need to store and follow pointers. For a given n, the number of fast lane elements is known a-priori since we build on balanced skip lists. Thus, we can simply compute the position of follow-up elements within the array, making pointers completely superfluous. In Fig. 2, pointerless traversal over fast lanes is indicated by dotted arrows. In our current implementation, we always preallocate a certain amount of memory per fast lane based on a hypothetical maximum t of keys. As long as $n < t$, all inserts can be managed inside the data structure; as soon as n exceeds t, we rebuild fast lanes and increase t by a fixed fraction (see Sect. 3.2 for details on an update strategy). Third, CSSL uses SIMD instructions to iterate over matching keys when executing range queries, which is especially useful in the case of large ranges. We exploit the lowest fast lane, i.e., the fast lane at level 1, to search for the last key that satisfies the queried range. To the best of our knowledge, CSSL is the first index structure that can make significant use of SIMD instructions when executing range queries.

Our approach to linearization of fast lanes has the following benefits compared to conventional skip lists: First, CSSL need less memory. Let k be the size of a key and r be the size of a pointer. Ignoring space requirements for data objects, which is equal in both layouts, conventional skip lists require $n * (m * r + r + k)$ space, whereas CSSL only require $n * (r + k) + \sum_{i=1}^{m} p^i * n * k$. Second, traversing linearized fast lanes has a better cache line utilization because we always use the whole cache line content until we abort search and jump to a lower layer. In the case of 32-bit keys, 16 fast lane elements fit into one 64-byte cache line while only one fat key of a conventional skip list fits into it. Third, since traversal of linearized fast lanes accesses successive array positions, we can make use of prefetched cache lines. Fourth, array-based storage of fast lane elements allows the usage of SIMD instructions and enables data-level parallelism. Given that s is the size of a SIMD register and k is the key size, $\frac{s}{k}$ fast lane elements can be compared in parallel. Modern CPUs usually feature SIMD registers having a size of 128 or 256 bits, thus four or eight 32-bit integers can be processed per instruction. For the implementation of CSSL, we use Intel's AVX instructions [2] that support 256-bit SIMD registers.

3.1 Optimizations

Besides these main concepts, we apply a number of further optimizations to fully exploit modern CPUs. First, we always tailor the size of fast lanes as multiples of the CPU cache line size (see Fig. 3). This especially affects the highest fast lane level. Second, we introduce an additional lane, called *proxy lane*, between the lowest fast lane and the data list (see Fig. 2). For each key, the proxy lane maintains a pointer to its corresponding data object. Connections between the proxy lane, which is implemented as an array of structs, and the fast lane at level 1 are implicit: The i'th fast lane element is part of the struct that can be found at index $i - 1$ of the proxy lane. We use the proxy lane to connect the lowest fast lane with the data list. Third, in practice we observed that searching

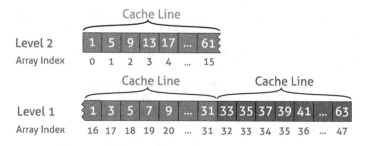

Fig. 3. Linearized fast lane array of a CSSL that indexes all 32-bit integers in $\{1, .., 64\}$ with two levels ($p = 1/2$).

the highest fast lane is very expensive in terms of CPU cycles if it contains lots of elements. This is especially the case if the number of fast lanes is kept small and the highest fast lane contains a lot more than $1/p$ elements. In the worst case, we have to scan the whole lane, while searching the remaining fast lanes can never require more than $1/p$ comparisons per lane. We accelerate searching the highest fast lane by using a binary search instead of sticking to a sequential scan.

3.2 Updates

In our implementation, a CSSL is initialized with a sorted set of keys. Nonetheless, we still want to support *online updates*. In the following, we describe techniques for inserting new keys, updating existing keys, and removing keys.

Inserting Keys: Since CSSL employs dense arrays for managing fast lanes, directly inserting keys into fast lanes would require a lot of shift operations to preserve the order of fast lane elements. For this reason, new keys are only inserted into the data list, which is implemented as a common linked list. We create a new node and add it at the proper position. As soon as the fast lane array gets rebuilt to allocate more space, new keys are also reflected in the fast lane hierarchy. Nonetheless, we can find new keys in the meantime. If search does not find a key in the fast lanes, it moves down to the data list and scans it until the key is found or proven to be non-existing. The insert algorithm can be implemented latch-free by using an atomic compare-and-swap instruction for changing pointers in the data list.

Deleting Keys: In contrast to insertions, we cannot delete keys from the data list but leave fast lanes untouched, because this would lead to invalid search results. In the first step of deleting a key from CSSL, we need to eliminate it from the fast lane array. Just changing the corresponding entry to $NULL$ would require reshift operations to close gaps in the array. Therefore, we replace to-be-deleted entries with a copy of the successive fast lane element. This allows fast deletes but leaves the fast lane structure intact. We end up with duplicates in the fast lane array that are removed as soon as the array gets rebuilt. As last step, the *next* pointer of the preceding node in the data list is changed to point to the successor of the to-be-removed-node and the node is deleted.

Updating Keys: Updates are basically implemented as an insert operation followed by a deletion.

Though being based on balanced skip lists, which leads to less flexibility compared to common skip lists, CSSL is able to handle online updates. By limiting in-place updates on the fast lane array, we can keep the number of cache invalidations small.

4   Algorithms

In this section, we describe in detail algorithms for executing lookups and range queries using CSSL. We start by presenting the lookup algorithm, because the execution of range queries is based on it.

Lookups: Pseudocode for lookups is shown in Algorithm 1. If search is successful the element's key will be returned, if not INT_MAX will be returned. The algorithm can be split into multiple parts. First, the highest fast lane is processed with a binary search (see Line 1). Second, the remaining fast lanes are searched hierarchically to narrow down the data list segment that may hold the search key (see Lines 2–8). We scan each fast lane sequentially instead of employing a binary search, because we need to compare only $1/p$ elements per fast lane level. Third, if the last fast lane contains the searched element, it is immediately returned (see Line 9); otherwise the associated proxy node is loaded and all keys of the data list are compared with the searched element (see Lines 10–12). INT_MAX is returned if no matching element is found (see Line 13).

Algorithm 1: lookup(key)

```
 1: pos = binary_search_top_lane(flanes, key);
 2: for (level = MAX_LEVEL - 1; level > 0; level--) {
 3:    rPos = pos - level_start_pos[level];
 4:    while (key >= flanes[++pos])
 5:       rPos++;
 6:    if (level == 1) break;
 7:    pos = level_start_pos[level-1] + 1/p * rPos;
 8: }
 9: if (key == flanes[--pos]) return key;
10: proxy = proxy_nodes[pos - level_start_pos \cite{bib1}];
11: for (i = 1; i < 1/p; i++)
12:    if (key == proxy->keys[i]) return key;
13: return INT_MAX;
```

Range Queries: Pseudocode for range queries is shown in Algorithm 2. Search returns pointers to the first and last data list element that match the given range defined by *start* and *end*, i.e., it returns a linked list that can be used for further processing. Execution of range queries is implemented as follows.

First, the first matching element is searched similar to executing a lookup (see Lines 1–16 of Algorithm 2). Second, the algorithm jumps back to the lowest fast lane and scans it using vectorized instructions to find the last element that satisfies the queried range. Using AVX, CSSL can process eight 32-bit integer keys in parallel (see Lines 17–25). Third, the proxy node, which is associated with the matching fast lane entry, is loaded and compared with the range end to determine the last matching element (see Lines 29–35). Fourth, range search returns a struct that provides pointers to the first and last matching element in the data list (see Line 36).

Algorithm 2: searchRange(start, end)

```
 1: RangeSearchResult res;
 2: pos = binary_search_top_lane(flanes, start);
 3: for (level = MAX_LEVEL - 1; level > 0; level--) {
 4:    rPos = pos - level_start_pos[level];
 5:    while (start >= flanes[++pos])
 6:       rPos++;
 7:    if (level == 1) break;
 8:    pos = level_start_pos[level-1] + 1/p * rPos;
 9: }
10: proxy = proxy_nodes[rPos];
11: res.start = proxy->pointers[1/p - 1]->next;
12: for (i=0; i < 1/p; i++) {
13:    if (start <= proxy->keys[i]) {
14:       res.start = proxy->pointers[i]; break;
15:    }
16: }
17: sreg = _mm256_castsi256_ps(_mm256_set1_epi32(end));
18: while (rPos < level_items \cite{bib1} - 8) {
19:    creg = _mm256_castsi256_ps(
20:       _mm256_loadu_si256((__m256i const *) &flanes[pos]));
21:    res = _mm256_cmp_ps(sreg, creg, 30);
22:    bitmask = _mm256_movemask_ps(res);
23:    if (bitmask < 0xff) break;
24:    pos += 8; rPos += 8;
25: }
26: pos--; rPos--;
27: while (end >= flanes[++pos] && rPos < level_items \cite{bib1})
28:    rPos++;
29: proxy = proxy_nodes[rPos];
30: res.end = proxy->pointers[1/p - 1];
31: for (i=1; i < 1/p; i++) {
32:    if (end < proxy->keys[i]) {
```

```
33:      res.end = proxy->pointers[i - 1]; break;
34:    }
35:  }
36: return res;
```

5 Evaluation

We compare CSSL to other index structures optimized for in-memory storage. We also include B$^+$-tree [7] as baseline approach, though we note that it is designed to be stored on disk. We compare competitors w.r.t. performance of range queries (see Sect. 5.1), performance of lookups (see Sect. 5.2), performance on a mixed workload (see Sect. 5.3), and space consumption (see Sect. 5.5). An evaluation with real-world data from the bioinformatics domain can be found in Sect. 5.4; results are very similar to those for synthetic data sets. Search performance is measured in throughput, i.e., how many queries are processed per second. For our main evaluation, we use n 32-bit integer keys with dense and sparse distribution. For dense distribution, every key in $[1, n]$ is indexed; for sparse distribution n random keys from $[1, 2^{31})$ are indexed. We evaluate CSSL with two configurations, CSSL$_2$ with $p = 1/2$ and CSSL$_5$ with $p = 1/5$, to investigate effects on dense and sparse fast lanes. In both cases, we use nine fast lanes, because this setting results in a balanced number of inter- and intra-fast lane traversals in our experiments.

We compare to the following approaches:

- the adaptive radix tree (ART) [13], a recent radix tree variant designed for main memory,
- the CSB$^+$-tree [18], a cache-sensitive variant of the B$^+$-tree,
- a binary search (BS) on a static array,
- and a B$^+$-tree [1] as baseline approach.

For ART and CSB$^+$, we used implementations provided by the authors. For CSB$^+$, we had to implement range queries. We consider BS as the only index structure that is read-only by design.

Our test system consists of the following hardware: a Intel Xeon E5-2620 CPU with 6 cores, 12 threads, 15 MB Level 3 Cache, 256-bit SIMD registers (AVX) and a clock speed of 2 GHz. The evaluation system runs Linux and has 32 GB RAM. All experiments are single-threaded. All competitors including CSSL were compiled with GCC 4.8.4 using optimization $-O3$. We use PAPI [3] to collect performance counters.

5.1 Range Queries

The goal of CSSL is to achieve high range query performance by employing a data layout tailored to the cache hierarchy of modern CPUs, which also can be traversed using SIMD instructions. In this section, we evaluate all approaches for

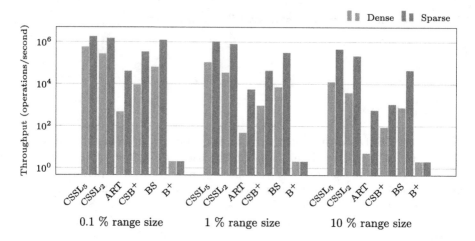

Fig. 4. Range query throughput for 16 M 32-bit integer keys w.r.t. different range sizes (logarithmic scale).

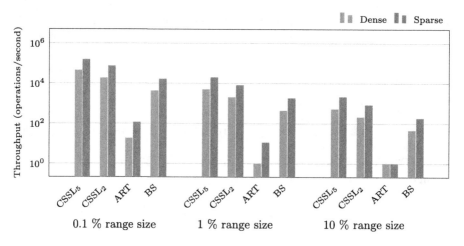

Fig. 5. Range query throughput for 256 M 32-bit integer keys w.r.t. different range sizes (logarithmic scale).

range queries on 16 M and 256 M 32-bit integer keys w.r.t. different range sizes (0.1%, 1%, and 10% of n). We determine to-be-evaluated ranges by selecting a random key from the set of indexed elements as lower bound and adding the range size to define the upper bound. For dense distribution, this creates a range covering $|upper\_bound - lower\_bound|$ elements. For sparse distribution, ranges are created in the same way, yet contain less elements, which usually leads to higher throughput.

Figure 4 shows results for executing range queries on 16 M keys. Both CSSL configurations outperform all contestants for both key distributions and all

Performance Counter	CSSL$_5$	CSSL$_2$	ART	CSB$^+$	BS	B$^+$
Dense						
CPU Cycles	**202k**	661k	501M	27M	3.4M	1,070M
Branch Mispredictions	**12**	15	813k	46	13	1.4k
Level 3 Cache Hits	**8k**	24k	1.3M	49k	21k	1.6k
Level 3 Cache Misses	**21**	7.3k	2.7M	243k	7.4k	7.8M
TLB Misses	**5**	13	1.6M	99	24	381k
Sparse						
CPU Cycles	**5k**	13k	4.5M	620k	59k	1,095M
Branch Mispredictions	**13**	16	16k	4.6k	13	832
Level 3 Cache Hits	**139**	373	14k	364	325	1.8k
Level 3 Cache Misses	**23**	165	28k	5.7k	278	7.4M
TLB Misses	**3**	5	19k	958	10	369k

Fig. 6. Performance counters per range query on 16M 32-bit integer keys (10% range size).

evaluated range sizes. In contrast to all competitors, CSSL does not need to follow pointers when iterating over matching keys but can use SIMD instructions to traverse the fast lane array, which results in an outstanding performance. The usage of SIMD instructions accelerates the performance of CSSL by a factor between 2 to 3. CSSL$_5$ is faster than CSSL$_2$, which is due to the fact that fast lanes skip over five instead of only two elements, thus less keys have to be compared when searching for the range end (see Lines 17–28 of Algorithm 2). The sequential access pattern of CSSL has several benefits as revealed by analyzing performance counters (see Fig. 6). CSSL utilizes most prefetched cache lines, which leads to only few cache misses. Furthermore, CSSL generates less branch mispredictions than the contestants, because it processes mostly consecutive positions of the fast lane array. This benefits the number of CPU cycles needed to execute a range query.

For this experiment, BS is the second best competitor followed by CSB$^+$, ART and B$^+$. By eliminating pointer accesses and taking cache line sizes into account, CSB$^+$ is able to reduce cache misses significantly compared to B$^+$-tree as shown in Fig. 6.

For 16 M dense keys, CSSL$_5$ is up to 16.8X faster (10.4X for sparse data) than the second best competitor BS. Compared to all competitors, CSSL achieves the best relative performance for large range sizes, i.e., the speedup factor is the highest for large ranges, because it can traverse matching keys without chasing pointers. Figure 5 shows results for executing range queries on 256 M keys. Both CSB$^+$ and B$^+$ were not able to index this amount of data, because they ran out of memory. Again, CSSL outperforms BS and ART significantly.

5.2   Lookups

We evaluate the execution of single-key lookups. Lookups are a common operation in database management systems and needed for various use cases. Figure 7 shows our evaluation results concerning lookup performance on 16 M 32-bit integer keys for all contestants. ART achieves the best performance for both distributions. Furthermore, ART is the only competitor that can boost performance on dense keys, for instance by using lazy expansion; the remaining competitors show identical results on both distributions. CSSL achieves the second best performance, closely followed by BS and CSB$^+$. B$^+$ shows the worst performance. The density of fast lanes has almost no influence on executing lookups as CSSL$_2$ and CSSL$_5$ show an identical performance. ART is 4.4X faster than CSSL for dense keys, and 2.4X faster than CSSL for sparse keys.

In Fig. 8, we present performance counters per lookup on 16 M 32-bit integer keys for all competitors. ART produces no branch mispredictions and only few level 3 cache misses, while B$^+$-tree shows the worst performance parameters. As in the case of range queries, CSSL produces only few cache and TLB misses. Though being optimized for range queries, CSSL is able to achieve a lookup throughput that outperforms BS, CSB$^+$ and B$^+$ and is almost as fast as ART in the case of sparse keys.

5.3   Mixed Workload

Many real-world applications do neither use lookups nor range queries exclusively, but employ a mix of both. We investigate the throughput when executing a mixed workload consisting of an equal number of lookups and range queries. In this experiment, we run a benchmark of 1 M randomly generated queries, i.e., 500 k lookups and 500 k range queries, on 16 M dense and sparse 32-bit integer

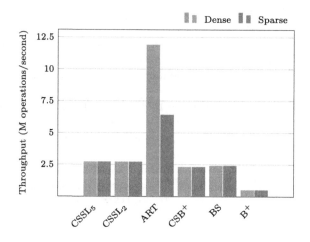

Fig. 7. Lookup throughput for 16M 32-bit integer keys.

Performance Counter	CSSL$_5$	CSSL$_2$	ART	CSB$^+$	BS	B$^+$
Dense						
CPU Cycles	927	956	**209**	1,068	1,036	5,889
Branch Mispredictions	9	13	**0**	1	12	12
Level 3 Cache Hits	11	8	**2**	3	21	28
Level 3 Cache Misses	5	8	**2**	5	9	39
TLB Misses	**1**	3	2	3	4	20
Sparse						
CPU Cycles	926	951	**383**	1,054	1,029	5,789
Branch Mispredictions	9	13	**0**	3	12	12
Level 3 Cache Hits	11	8	5	**3**	20	29
Level 3 Cache Misses	5	8	**3**	4	10	38
TLB Misses	**1**	3	4	5	4	20

Fig. 8. Performance counters per lookup on 16M 32-bit integer keys.

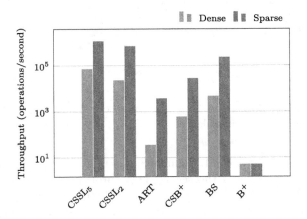

Fig. 9. Throughput for a mixed lookup/range query workload on 16 M 32-bit integer keys (logarithmic scale).

keys. For range queries, we always use a range size of 500 k. Figure 9 shows the results of this experiment.

CSSL shows the best performance across all competitors when confronted with a mixed workload. As in the case of the range query benchmark, it is followed by BS, CSB$^+$, ART and B$^+$. Although ART shows the best single-key lookup performance, CSSL is magnitude faster when running a workload that also includes range queries besides lookups. This emphasizes the need for a fast range query implementation in index structures.

5.4   Evaluation with Genomic Data

We evaluate all competitors on real-world data from the bioinformatics domain to investigate their performance when managing data that features a non-synthetic key distribution. As data source, we used the 1000 Genomes Project [19] that sequenced the whole genomes of 2,504 people from across the world. Data is provided in text files and can be downloaded from the project website for free. We indexed the genomic locations of all mutations that were found on chromosomes 1 and 2, i.e., 13,571,394 mutations in total, and queried them using randomly generated ranges of different sizes (0.1%, 1%, and 10% of the featured genomic interval). Figure 10 shows results of this benchmark.

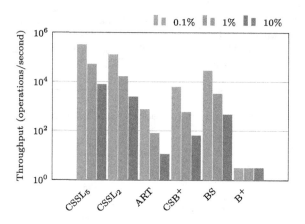

Fig. 10. Range query throughput for genomic data (13,571,394 mutations) w.r.t. different range sizes (logarithmic scale).

As for synthetic data, CSSL dominates all competitors in executing range queries. Again, BS achieves the second best throughput, followed by CSB^+, ART and B^+. All competitors, except B^+, show better performance for smaller range sizes, which is due to the fact that less mutations are covered, i.e., less keys need to be compared. For a range size of 10%, $CSSL_5$ is 16.7X faster than BS, 121.6X faster than CSB^+, and 696X faster than ART.

5.5   Space Consumption

We compare the space consumption of all competitors for storing 16 M 32-bit integer keys, i.e., 64 MB of raw data (see Fig. 11). As already seen in the evaluation of search performance, ART is better suited for managing dense data than sparse data. For a dense key distribution, ART requires the least space followed by BS and CSSL. The tree-based approaches B^+ and CSB^+ show the worst memory consumption. For a sparse key distribution, BS achieves the best result followed by $CSSL_5$ and ART. Again, B^+ and CSB^+ achieve the worst results. For 16M keys, $CSSL_2$ requires 1.8X more memory than $CSSL_5$, because fast lanes hold more entries.

ART's space efficiency would probably grow for larger keys. Then, ART is able to employ further optimization techniques, e.g., path compression, that are not beneficial for small keys [13].

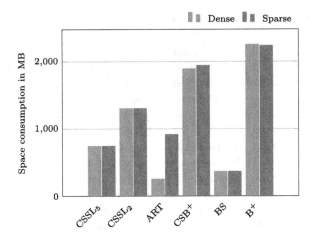

Fig. 11. Space consumption for 16 M 32-bit integer keys (lower is better).

6   Related Work

Although concepts like tailored data layouts, index traversal with SIMD instructions, and pointer elimination have been investigated before [11,17,18], to the best of our knowledge, we are the first to combine these to accelerate range queries. Skip lists [16] were proposed as a probabilistic alternative to B-trees [5]. In the last years, they have been applied in multiple areas and have been adapted to different purposes, e.g., lock-free skip list [8], deterministic skip list [15], or concurrent skip list [10]. In [21], Xie et al. present a parallel skip list-based main-memory index, *PI*, that processes query batches using multiple threads. CSSL is based on [15], but employs a cache-friendly data layout that is tailored to modern CPUs.

There are several others approaches addressing in-memory indexing [6,11–13,17,18], yet few specifically target range queries. CSS-trees [17] build a tree-based dictionary on top of a sorted array that is tailored to cache hierarchy and can be used to search in logarithmic time. CSS-trees are static by design and need to be completely rebuilt when running updates. Rao and Ross [18] introduce the CSB$^+$-tree, a cache-conscious B$^+$-tree [7] variant, which minimizes pointer accesses and reduces space consumption. As shown in Sect. 5, CSSL outperforms CSB$^+$-tree significantly for all workloads. Masstree [14] is an in-memory database that employs a trie of B$^+$-trees as index structure. It supports arbitrary-length keys, which may be useful when indexing strings. We did not include Masstree in our evaluation, because its implementation is multi-threaded, which prevents a fair comparison. Instead, we considered its base index structure, the B$^+$-tree, as competitor. In [22], Zhang et al. introduce a hybrid two-stage index that can be built on top of existing index structures like B-trees or skip lists. They also propose a paged-based skip list implementation that is tailored to main memory.

In contrast to CSSL, it is completely static by design and does not exploit SIMD instructions.

The adaptive radix tree [13] is a main-memory index structure based on radix trees. ART employs adaptive node sizes and makes use of CPU features like SIMD instructions to boost search performance. While it achieves high lookup performance currently only superseded by hash tables [4], its support for range queries is much less efficient since these require traversing over the tree by chasing pointers. As shown in Sect. 5, CSSL outperforms ART significantly for range queries. We assume that the results of our comparison between CSSL and ART would carry over to other index structures based on prefix trees, such as generalized prefix trees [6], or KISS-Tree [12]. Another recent data structure is FAST [11], a binary search tree tuned to the underlying hardware by taking architecture parameters like page or cache line size into account. It achieves both thread-level and data-level parallelism, the latter by using SIMD instructions. Similar to CSSL, FAST does not need to access pointers when traversing the tree. However, FAST is optimized for lookup queries only, where it is clearly outperformed by ART [13]. Therefore, we did not include it in our evaluation.

7 Conclusions

We presented the Cache-Sensitive Skip List (CSSL), a main-memory index structure for efficiently executing range queries on modern processors. CSSL linearizes fast lanes to achieve a CPU-friendly data layout, to reduce cache misses, and to enable the usage of SIMD instructions. We compared CSSL with three main-memory index structures, the adaptive radix tree, a CSB$^+$-tree, and binary search, and one baseline, a B$^+$-tree. CSSL outperforms all competitors when executing range queries on synthetic and real data sets. Even when confronted with a mixed key/range workload, CSSL achieves the best results in our evaluation. CSSL's search performance and memory consumption is influenced by the number of elements each fast lane skips over $(1/p)$. Sparse fast lanes show better results regarding memory consumption and range query execution.

In future work, we will add multithreaded query execution to further accelerate read performance. We plan to work on both inter- and intra-query parallelism.

Acknowledgments. Stefan Sprenger and Steffen Zeuch are funded by the Deutsche Forschungsgemeinschaft through graduate school SOAMED (GRK 1651).

References

1. B+ tree source code (C 1999). http://www.amittai.com/prose/bpt.c
2. Introduction to inteladvanced vector extensions. https://software.intel.com/en-us/articles/introduction-to-intel-advanced-vector-extensions
3. PAPI. http://icl.cs.utk.edu/papi/

4. Alvarez, V., Richter, S., Chen, X., Dittrich, J.: A comparison of adaptive radix trees and hash tables. In: 31st IEEE International Conference on Data Engineering (2015)
5. Bayer, R., McCreight, E.: Organization and maintenance of large ordered indices. In: SIGFIDET (1970)
6. Boehm, M., Schlegel, B., Volk, P.B., Fischer, U., Habich, D., Lehner, W.: Efficient in-memory indexing with generalized prefix trees. In: BTW (2011)
7. Comer, D.: Ubiquitous B-tree. ACM Comput. Surv. **11**(2), 121–137 (1979)
8. Fomitchev, M., Ruppert, E.: Lock-free linked lists and skip lists. In: Proceedings of 23rd Annual ACM Symposium on Principles of Distributed Computing, pp. 50–59 (2004)
9. Hakenberg, J., Cheng, W.Y., Thomas, P., Wang, Y.C., Uzilov, A.V., Chen, R.: Integrating 400 million variants from 80,000 human samples with extensive annotations: towards a knowledge base to analyze disease cohorts. BMC Bioinf. **17**(1), 1 (2016)
10. Herlihy, M., Lev, Y., Luchangco, V., Shavit, N.: A provably correct scalable concurrent skip list. In: Conference on Principles of Distributed Systems (2006)
11. Kim, C., Chhugani, J., Satish, N., Sedlar, E., Nguyen, A.D., Kaldewey, T., Lee, V.W., Brandt, S.A., Dubey, P.: FAST: fast architecture sensitive tree search on modern CPUs and GPUs. In: Proceedings of the International Conference on Management of Data, pp. 339–350 (2010)
12. Kissinger, T., Schlegel, B., Habich, D., Lehner, W.: KISS-Tree: Smart latch-free in-memory indexing on modern architectures. In: Proceedings of the Eighth International Workshop on Data Management on New Hardware, pp. 16–23 (2012)
13. Leis, V., Kemper, A., Neumann, T.: The adaptive radix tree: ARTful indexing for main-memory databases. In: 29th IEEE International Conference on Data Engineering (2013)
14. Mao, Y., Kohler, E., Morris, R.T.: Cache craftiness for fast multicore key-value storage. In: Proceedings of the Seventh EuroSys Conference, pp. 183–196 (2012)
15. Munro, J.I., Papadakis, T., Sedgewick, R.: Deterministic skip lists. In: Proceedings of the Third Annual ACM-SIAM Symposium on Discrete Algorithms, pp. 367–375 (1992)
16. Pugh, W.: Skip lists: a probabilistic alternative to balanced trees. Commun. ACM **33**(6), 668–676 (1990)
17. Rao, J., Ross, K.A.: Cache conscious indexing for decision-support in main memory. In: Proceedings of 25th International Conference on Very Large Data Bases, pp. 78–89 (1999)
18. Rao, J., Ross, K.A.: Making B$^+$-trees cache conscious in main memory. In: Proceedings of the 2000 ACM SIGMOD International Conference on Management of Data, pp. 475–486 (2000)
19. The 1000 Genomes Project Consortium: A global reference for human genetic variation. Nature **526**(7571), 68–74 (2015)
20. Xie, X., Lu, J., Kulbokas, E., Golub, T.R., Mootha, V., Lindblad-Toh, K., Lander, E.S., Kellis, M.: Systematic discovery of regulatory motifs in human promoters and 3' UTRs by comparison of several mammals. Nature **434**(7031), 338–345 (2005)
21. Xie, Z., Cai, Q., Jagadish, H., Ooi, B.C., Wong, W.F.: PI: a parallel in-memory skip list based index. arXiv preprint (2016). arXiv:1601.00159
22. Zhang, H., Andersen, D.G., Pavlo, A., Kaminsky, M., Ma, L., Shen, R.: Reducing the storage overhead of main-memory OLTP databases with hybrid indexes. In: Proceedings of the International Conference on Management of Data, pp. 1567–1581 (2016)

Exploit Every Cycle: Vectorized Time Series Algorithms on Modern Commodity CPUs

Bo Tang[1]([✉]), Man Lung Yiu[1], Yuhong Li[2], and Leong Hou U[2]

[1] Hong Kong Polytechnic University, Hung Hom, Hong Kong
{csbtang,csmlyiu}@comp.polyu.edu.hk
[2] University of Macau, Av. Padre Tomás Pereira, Taipa, Macau
{yb27407,ryanlhu}@umac.mo

Abstract. Many time series algorithms reduce the computation cost by pruning unpromising candidates with lower-bound distance functions. In this paper, we focus on an orthogonal research direction that further boosts the performance by unlocking the potentials of modern commodity CPUs. First, we conduct a performance profiling on existing algorithms to understand where does time go. Second, we design vectorized implementations for lower-bound and distance functions that can enjoy characteristics (e.g., data parallelism, caching, branch prediction) provided by CPU. Third, our vectorized methods are general and applicable to many time series problems such as subsequence search, motif discovery and kNN classification. Our experimental study on real datasets shows that our proposal can achieve up to 6 times of speedup.

1 Introduction

Time series data has various applications in medical diagnosis, speech processing, climate analysis, financial analysis, etc. It has attracted extensive research in the literature [4,9,14,20–22,25,30]. We illustrate representative problems in Fig. 1: (a) the *subsequence search* problem, which takes a query sequence q and finds its most similar subsequence t_c of a time series t, (b) the *motif discovery* problem, which reports the most similar pair of subsequences in a time series t, and (c) the *kNN classification* problem. These problems typically use the Euclidean Distance (ED) and Dynamic Time Warping (DTW) as the similarity measure.

These problems are computation bound rather than disk I/O bound [22]. Many time series algorithms have been evaluated on commodity CPU [4,9,14, 20–22,25,30] in single machine. These works focus on devising lower-bound distance functions to prune unpromising candidates and thus reduce calling expensive distance computations.

Even with these effective lower bounds, the above time series problems are still computation intensive, especially for increasingly long time series nowadays (e.g., medical physiological signals[1]). For example, the subsequence search on a trillion scale time series [22] would take 3.1 hours (under the Euclidean distance) and 34 hours (under Dynamic Time Warping) on a commodity PC.

---

[1] http://www.physionet.org/physiobank/.

© Springer International Publishing AG 2017
S. Blanas et al. (Eds.): ADMS 2016/IMDM 2016, LNCS 10195, pp. 18–39, 2017.
DOI: 10.1007/978-3-319-56111-0_2

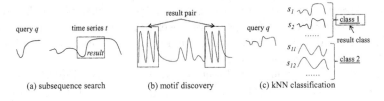

(a) subsequence search   (b) motif discovery   (c) kNN classification

Fig. 1. Problems on time series data

Nevertheless, existing techniques overlook the characteristics of CPU and they have not studied the effect of those characteristics on the CPU time. In general, the CPU time consists of (i) busy cycles, for executing instructions, and (ii) stall cycles, for waiting for instructions or data.

We raise the following questions:

Q1: "In these algorithms, where does time go?"

To answer this question, we profile the performance [3, 27] of existing time-series algorithms (cf. Sect. 3). Surprisingly, most of the CPU time (70%) is spent on stalling.

Q2 "What cause CPU stall cycles?"

According to our performance profiling, the CPU stall is mainly (more than 80%) caused by branch mispredictions, cache misses, and ALU stall in lower-bound and distance functions.

Q3 "How to reduce CPU stall cycles in modern CPUs?"

Modern CPUs have built-in hardware for branch prediction, caching, and processing vector data efficiently (through SIMD instructions). Recent researches have utilized these characteristics to offer speedup on different problems like join [10], sorting [11], set intersection [16]. In this paper, we will design efficient implementations for lower-bound and distance functions by exploiting the characteristics of modern commodity CPUs. Note that our research direction is orthogonal to the development of lower-bound functions [4, 9, 14, 20–22, 25, 30]. Besides, our proposed techniques are also applicable to mobile time series applications (e.g., continuous heart rate monitoring on Apple watch) as Apple mobile processors (e.g., A5) have supported advanced SIMD instructions since 2011[2].

Our proposed techniques achieve performance gain through: (i) reducing branch mispredictions and cache misses, (ii) incorporating parallelism for vector processing in our computations. We then elaborate these issues in the following two paragraphs.

Conditional branches (e.g., if-then-else, case statements) are commonly used in the lower-bound and distance functions on time series. With branch prediction, a CPU can speculatively execute one path of a conditional branch. A correct prediction can improve the performance due to the CPU's instruction pipeline. However, if the prediction is wrong (i.e., *branch misprediction*), then many CPU cycles will be wasted to flush the instruction pipeline, flush and

---

[2] https://en.wikipedia.org/wiki/Apple_mobile_application_processors.

fetch the relevant data, and restart the execution for the other branch. Therefore, it is desirable to rewrite algorithms to use fewer branching statements and avoid cache pollution. Also, we need to reduce non-compulsory cache misses brought by random memory accesses in our algorithms.

Data-intensive functions, like lower-bound and distance functions on time series, execute certain arithmetic operations (e.g., multiplication, division) that incur many CPU cycles and thus cause ALU stall. To reduce ALU stall, we use SIMD instructions to process multiple data values per instruction. For example, a SIMD division instruction takes two vectors of values V_a and V_b as input, and perform division $V_a[i]/V_b[i]$ for each position i simultaneously. In this paper, we present vectorized implementations for lower-bound and distance functions by using SIMD. In addition, our vectorized implementations are designed to avoid using conditional branches.

Besides, our proposed techniques are generic and applicable to many time series problems (e.g., subsequence search, motif discovery, kNN classification). In summary, our contributions are:

- We profile the performance of existing time series algorithms and summarize the key insights (Sect. 3).
- We design vectorized implementations for lower-bound and distance functions. They incur fewer branch mispredictions, cache misses, and ALU stall (Sect. 4).
- We evaluate the efficiency of our proposed techniques for different time series algorithms on different datasets. Our techniques can achieve up to 6 times of speedup (Sect. 5).

The rest of this paper is organized as follows. Section 2 clarifies the preliminaries of our research problem. We present the profiling of existing time series algorithms in Sect. 3. Then, we propose our vectorized implementations in Sect. 4, perform experimental evaluation on existing time series algorithms in Sect. 5. Finally, we discuss the related work in Sect. 6, and conclude this paper in Sect. 7.

2   Preliminaries

2.1   Fundamental Distance Measurement

In this work, we consider two most popular distance functions, i.e., Euclidean Distance (ED) and Dynamic Time Warping (DTW), in time series problems [13, 18,19,21,22,24]. We follow the suggestion from prior literatures [19,22] that every subsequence should be Z-normalized in order to capture the similarity between the shapes of the sequences. Formally, the i-th value of a Z-normalized sequence $\hat{q}$ can be calculated by $\hat{q}[i] = \frac{q[i]-\mu_q}{\sigma_q}$, where μ_q and σ_q are the mean and standard deviation of q, respectively, and $q[i]$ indicates the i-th element of q. For ease of presentation, we use $dist(q,t)$ to denote the distance $dist(\hat{q},\hat{t})$ between Z-normalized subsequences in this paper.

Euclidean Distance: This is the most common similarity metric in time series [13,19,22,25,30] due to its simplicity. We give the definition of squared ED[3] in Eq. 1. It takes $O(m)$ time for a query q of length m.

$$ED(q, t_c) = \sum_{i=1}^{m} (\hat{q}[i] - \hat{t}_c[i])^2 \tag{1}$$

Dynamic Time Warping: DTW can capture the similarity of two sequences which may vary in time or have missing values. It is shown to be effective in time series applications [5,18,24]. DTW aims to find the optimal alignment (i.e., minimum distance) between two sequences, according to the following recursive equation.

$$DTW(q, t_c) = (\hat{q}[1] - \hat{t}_c[1])^2 + \min \begin{cases} DTW(\hat{q}[2...last], \hat{t}_c) \\ DTW(\hat{q}[2...last], \hat{t}_c[2...last]) \\ DTW(\hat{q}, \hat{t}_c[2...last]) \end{cases} \tag{2}$$

where $\hat{q}[2...last]$ denotes the subsequence of $\hat{q}$ containing values from the 2nd to the last offset. To avoid pathological warping (and reduce the computational cost), the literature [22] suggests to limit the warping length r such that $\hat{q}[i]$ can be matched with $\hat{t}_c[j]$ when $|i - j| \leq r$. This reduces the time complexity of DTW from $O(m^2)$ to $O(mr)$.

2.2   Time Series Algorithms

In Table 1, we summarize the computation techniques (e.g., lower-bounds functions and distance functions) that can be used in three representative time series problems: subsequence search, motif discovery, and classification. Where LB prefixed function provides a lower bound of the exact distance.

Table 1. Computation techniques and distance functions used in time series problems

Problem	Technique(s)	Distance
Subsequence search	Early distance stop	ED
Motif discovery	$LB_{Kim\mathbf{FL}}, LB_{Keogh}^{EQ}, LB_{Keogh}^{EC}$	DTW
	LB_{ref} (uses reference indices)	ED
Classification (by kNN)	Early distance stop	ED
	$LB_{Kim\mathbf{FL}}, LB_{Keogh}^{EQ}, LB_{Keogh}^{EC}$	DTW

Subsequence search. Formally, given a time series t of length n, a query q of length m, and a distance function $dist(\cdot)$, the subsequence search problem returns a length-m subsequence $t_c \in t$ such that $dist(q, t_c)$ is the minimum (among all length-m subsequences in t).

---

[3] The squared distance preserves the relative ordering of distances, and it avoids expensive square root calculations.

To the best of our knowledge, UCR Suite [22] is the state-of-the-art solution for the subsequence search problem. It adopts the filter-and-refinement paradigm to reduce exact distance computations. Let bsf be the best-so-far distance obtained during the search process. For ED subsequence search, UCR Suite does not apply any lower-bound function. It accumulates the distance step-by-step and early stops the distance computation $dist(q, t_c)$ as soon as the accumulated value exceeds bsf. For DTW subsequence search, UCR Suite examines each candidate subsequence t_c and applies lower-bound functions on t_c in ascending order of their computation cost: first LB_{KimFL}, then LB_{Keogh}^{EQ} and finally LB_{Keogh}^{EC}. t_c gets pruned as soon as some $LB(q, t_c)$ exceeds bsf. If t_c survives, then UCR Suite executes the distance function on t_c. We proceed to introduce these lower-bound functions as follows.

LB_{KimFL} is derived from the **First** and the **Last** sequence values, taking only $O(1)$ time to compute. It is defined as

$$LB_{KimFL}(q, t_c) = (\hat{q}[1] - \hat{t}_c[1])^2 + (\hat{q}[m] - \hat{t}_c[m])^2 \qquad (3)$$

LB_{Keogh}^{EQ} is derived from the distance between the candidate subsequence $\hat{t}_c$ and the envelop of $\hat{q}$. Given the warping length r, the upper and lower envelop of $\hat{q}$ are defined as $\hat{q}^u[i] = \max_{j=i-r}^{i+r} \hat{q}[j]$ and $\hat{q}^l[i] = \min_{j=i-r}^{i+r} \hat{q}[j]$, respectively, Accordingly, we have

$$LB_{Keogh}^{EQ}(q, t_c) = \sum_{i=1}^{m} \begin{cases} (\hat{t}_c[i] - \hat{q}^u[i])^2 & \text{if } \hat{t}_c[i] > \hat{q}^u[i] \\ (\hat{t}_c[i] - \hat{q}^l[i])^2 & \text{if } \hat{t}_c[i] < \hat{q}^l[i] \\ 0 & \text{otherwise} \end{cases} \qquad (4)$$

LB_{Keogh}^{EC} is derived similarly to LB_{Keogh}^{EQ} but the lower-bound is derived from the distance between the query and the envelop of $\hat{t}_c$ (i.e., switching roles).

Motif Discovery. Formally, given a time series t of length n, and a query length m, the motif discovery problem returns a pair of length-m subsequences $t_c, t_c' \in t$ such that the Euclidean distance $ED(t_c, t_c')$ is the minimum among all pairs.

MK [20] is a representative solution for motif discovery. To avoid examining every subsequence pair, it proposes a reference based lower-bound. Given a set of subsequences and their distances to a set of references R, the lower-bound of two subsequences t_a and t_b can be derived as follows.

$$LB_{ref}(t_a, t_b) = \max_{r_i \in R} |distRef[r_i][t_a] - distRef[r_i][t_b]| \qquad (5)$$

where $distRef[r_i][t] = ED(r_i, t)$.

MK first constructs a sorted list of every subsequence in terms of their distances to a reference. Intuitively, if the lower-bound of every 1st neighbor pair (in terms of their positions in the sorted list) is worse than bsf, then it is not necessary to examine further neighbor pairs (e.g., 2nd neighbor pairs) due to the monotonicity of the sorted list. Thereby, MK iteratively examines the subsequence pairs based on their sorted list positions. At the end of an iteration, the search terminates when no neighbor pair has lower-bound better than bsf.

Classification. ED and DTW are widely accepted for describing the similarity between time series in the classification problem [12]. We can apply the same techniques for subsequence search (i.e., early distance stop for ED and lower-bound techniques for DTW) to boost the classification process.

2.3 Modern Commodity CPUs

Modern commodity CPUs share the following hardware characteristics that can be further exploited in algorithm design.

- (1) **Single instruction multiple data:** Modern commodity CPUs provide vector instructions (SIMD) operating on 256-bit vector registers that allow to perform the same instruction on multiple data values in parallel.
- (2) **Hardware prefetcher:** Modern commodity CPUs have built-in hardware prefetcher. It allows to prefetch additional lines of instruction or data into the L1 or L2 cache in CPU cores.

The modern commodity CPUs also have multiple cores and simultaneous multithreading technique. We leave the study on multi-threading issues for time series algorithms as future work. All algorithms in this paper run in single thread model by default.

3 Profiling of Algorithms

We first describe our experimental platform and then present the profiling result on existing time series algorithms.

3.1 Experimental Setting

In all experiments, we use a machine with a 3.40 GHz Intel(R) Core(TM) i7-4770 CPU based on Haswell micro-architecture, 16 GB main memory, and a SSD (solid state drive, 256 GB capacity, 545 MB/s sequential read throughput). The CPU has 4 physical cores and supports simultaneous multithreading. The machine runs Ubuntu 14.04. All algorithms have been implemented in C++ and compiled by GNU C++ compiler with level 3 optimization.

We use the following real datasets and list their information in Table 2. All datasets are stored in the SSD.

- For the subsequence search problem, we use three datasets. Both **ECG-E**[4] and **ECG-L**[5] are electrocardiography (ECG) recordings, and we use the same query sequences (of length 421) as in [22] as the default query sequences. **EEG-C**[6] contains electroencephalography (EEG) recordings, and we randomly extract query sequences (of length 128) from the epileptic seizure recording as in [26]. For each dataset, we follow the experimental methodology in [22], and obtain a single time series by concatenating all data sequences.

---

[4] http://www.physionet.org/physiobank/database/edb/.

[5] http://www.physionet.org/physiobank/database/ltstdb/.

[6] http://www.physionet.org/pn6/chbmit/.

- For the kNN classification problem, we use **Weather**[7] dataset, which contains the temperature data extracted from weather forecast records. It contains 11,508 sequences, each sequence in Weather corresponds to a one-year time series collected from 5,936 locations. We use the attribute "Country" as the class attribute. We randomly choose data sequences as queries and exclude them from the data.
- For the motif discovery problem, we use two datasets: **EEG-MK**[8] and **TAO-MK** [19].

3.2   Measurement Methodology

Program execution time: According to the Intel performance analysis manual [1], the program execution time (T_R) consists of: computation time (T_C), branch misprediction stall (T_{Br}), backend stall (T_{Be}), and frontend stall (T_{Fe}). The computation time (T_C) is regarded as '*CPU busy*', and the rest as '*CPU stall*'. The backend stall occurs when the requested resource is being held-up in back end. It includes ALU stall (T_{ALU}) and memory stall (T_{Cache}). T_{ALU} is the ALU execution unit stall, which is caused by the execution of arithmetic operations (e.g., divide, square root) that require many cycles. T_{Cache} is the memory-bound stall, which is caused by L1 data cache misses, L2 cache misses, L3 cache misses or TLB cache misses.

Table 2. Dataset information

Dataset	Sequence length	Data size	Problem
ECG-E	$1.60 \cdot 10^8$	611 MB	Subsequence search
ECG-L	$1.89 \cdot 10^9$	7.06 GB	
EEG-C	$1.01 \cdot 10^{10}$	37.5 GB	
EEG-MK	$1.80 \cdot 10^5$	704 KB	Motif discovery
TAO-MK	$7.42 \cdot 10^5$	2.82 MB	
Weather	$1.81 \cdot 10^3,$	19.86 MB	kNN classification

We summarize the breakdown of execution time in a CPU as follows:

$$T_R = T_C + T_{stall}; \text{ where } T_{Stall} = T_{Br} + T_{ALU} + T_{Cache} + T_{Fe}$$

Profiling experiments: To measure the above components of CPU time, we used PAPI [8] to obtain hardware performance counters from CPU, e.g., the number of stall cycles and the number of CPU cycles. In each subsequence search and classification experiment, we report the average CPU time over 10 queries.

---

[7] http://data.gov.uk/metoffice-data-archive.

[8] http://www.cs.ucr.edu/~mueen/OnlineMotif/index.html.

To ensure the confidence level, we repeat running each query until the maximum standard deviation of the important counters (UOPS_RETIRED:RETIRE_SLOTS, CPU_CLK_UNHALTED:THREAD_P) is less than 3%.

Experimental reproducibility: For the sake of experimental reproducibility, we have posted the datasets and source codes at [2][9].

3.3   Identifying the Performance Bottleneck

In this section, we profile the performance of existing solutions and then identify the performance bottleneck. We conduct experiments to profile the performance of representative solutions: (i) UCR Suite [22] for the subsequence search problem, (ii) MK [20] for the motif discovery problem, and (iii) kNN classification [22] for the classification problem.

CPU stall and CPU busy: Figures 2(a) and (b) report the CPU time breakdown of existing solutions into *busy* time and *stall* time, for subsequence search and motif discovery, respectively.

Observation: The majority (65–70%) of the CPU time is spent on stalling (i.e., wasted CPU cycles).

CPU stall breakdown: We then delve into CPU stall and plot the breakdown of CPU stall time in Figs. 2(c) and (d).

Observation: The CPU stall is dominated (more than 80%) by ALU stall, cache misses, and branch mispredictions penalties.

CPU time of different functions: The DTW function and its lower-bound functions ($LB_{Kim\textbf{FL}}, LB_{Keogh}^{EQ}, LB_{Keogh}^{EC}$) are applicable to the subsequence search problem and the classification problem [22]. We profile the performance of [22] on these two problems in Fig. 2(e). Different functions incur different portions of time and pruning ratio (cf. Fig. 2(f)) in different scenarios. For example, lower-bound functions $LB_{Keogh}^{EQ}, LB_{Keogh}^{EC}$ dominate the time for subsequence search. However, the DTW computation incurs more time in kNN classification problems.

Observation: Different time series problems spend very different proportions of time on different functions. Therefore, it is important to optimize the computation of both lower-bound functions $LB_{Keogh}^{EQ}, LB_{Keogh}^{EC}$ and the DTW function.

4   Accelerating Distance Functions with SIMD

As shown in the previous section, the majority of CPU stall is caused by ALU stall, cache misses and branch mispredictions. In this section, we will design vectorized implementations for exact distance and lower-bounds functions to reduce those stalls. We will also evaluate the efficiency of our implementations with experiments.

---

[9] For consistency, we use the 'float' data type to represent time series values in all evaluated methods.

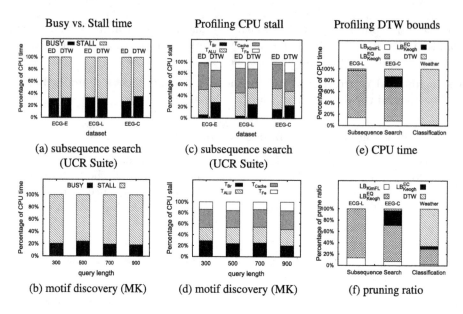

Fig. 2. Profile existing solutions

4.1   How Do SIMD Instructions Reduce Stall?

SIMD Vectorization: Reduce ALU Stall. The ALU stall is caused by the execution of arithmetic operations that require many CPU cycles. For example, the 'division' instruction for two floating-point values takes 24 CPU cycles [1].

Modern CPU provides SIMD instructions to perform the same instruction (e.g., $+, -, \times, /, \min, \max$) on multiple data values in parallel. For instance, Intel i7-4770 and AMD Phenom II support the AVX2 instruction set (SIMD instructions on 256-bit registers). The SIMD instruction simd_div (e.g., _mm256_div_ps in AVX2) performs division on 8 pairs of values in two SIMD registers R_a and R_b simultaneously. It takes only 21 CPU cycles [1], which is much cheaper than executing the 'division' instruction on 8 pairs one-by-one (using $24 * 8 = 192$ cycles). Thus, SIMD instructions help reduce the ALU stall significantly.

Distance computation indeed fits well with SIMD instructions. As we illustrate in Fig. 3, we may divide subsequences into groups of length 8, and then apply SIMD instructions on each group to compute distances for pairs.

Typical SIMD width: Our CPU (Intel i7-4770) is a modern commodity CPU. It supports the following SIMD widths and instruction sets: (i) 64 bits (i.e., MMX instruction set), (ii) 128 bits (i.e., SSE instruction set), (iii) 256 bits (i.e., AVX instruction set). Since the MMX instruction set does not support floating-point values, it cannot be used in time series problems. Thus, we report the results for 128 bits (SIMD-128) and 256 bits (SIMD-256) in following experiments. For simplicity, we set 256 bits (SIMD-256) as default SIMD register.

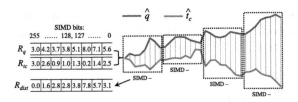

Fig. 3. Using SIMD for distance computation

Hardware Prefetching: Reduce Branch Misprediction. Modern CPU is equipped with a branch prediction unit and it speculatively executes a conditional branch to maximize the utilization of CPU resources. A correct prediction can improve the performance due to the built-in instruction pipeline and hardware prefetching. However, incorrect prediction will bring cache pollution[10] and waste CPU cycles to flush instructions and restart execution.

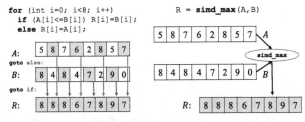

(a) code fragment and schematic   (b) code fragment and schematic
    for if-else statement   for SIMD max instruction

Fig. 4. Example for reducing branching statements

Some SIMD instructions help reduce branch misprediction. For example, for the code fragment in Fig. 4(a), the CPU may incur up to 8 branch mispredictions in the worst case. In contrast, the alternative implementation in Fig. 4(b) has no branch mispredictions because it uses a single instruction `simd_max` instead of conditional branches.

We observe that DTW and its lower-bound functions (cf. Sect. 2) have many conditional branches. Therefore, we need to design SIMD implementations for DTW and its lower-bound functions without using conditional branches.

4.2   Accelerating ED with SIMD

Before presenting our SIMD solutions, we first introduce the existing implementation of Euclidean distance. We call it as SISD-ED (cf. Algorithm 1) because it uses traditional CPU instructions, i.e., *Single Instruction, Single Data* (SISD).

---

[10] http://en.wikipedia.org/wiki/Cache_pollution.

According to Sect. 2, we perform Z-normalization on the subsequence t_c (cf. Line 3). It early stops the computation if the accumulated distance $dist$ exceeds the best-so-far distance bsf (cf. Line 5).

Algorithm 1. SISD-$ED(q, t_c)$

Input: best-so-far bsf, mean μ and stdev. σ of candidate t_c,
Output: squared distance $dist$

1: $dist := 0$
2: **for** $i := 1$ to m **do**
3:     $c := (t_c[i] - \mu)/\sigma$ ▷ Z-normalization
4:     $dist := dist + (c - \hat{q}[idx])^2$ ▷ accumulation
5:     **if** $dist \geq bsf$ **break**   ▷ early stop
6: return $dist$

Next we demonstrate how we employ SIMD to accelerate $ED(\cdot)$ in different steps. The intuition is to compute 8 offsets between q and t_c by batch. In the Z-normalization step, we can normalize 8 offset values simultaneously as follows.

SIMD Z-normalization

1: $R_c := \texttt{simd\_load}(\&t_c[i])$ ▷ load t_c
2: $R_c := \texttt{simd\_sub}(R_c, R_\mu)$ ▷ vectorized $t_c[i] - \mu$
3: $R_c := \texttt{simd\_div}(R_c, R_\sigma)$ ▷ vectorized $(t_c[i] - \mu)/\sigma$

---

where R_c, R_μ, R_σ are the corresponding SIMD registers of variables c, μ and σ, respectively. Note that each register stores 8 floating-point values. In the accumulation step, we can compute the distance of 8 offsets $(\hat{t}[i] - \hat{q}[i])^2$ as follows.

SIMD distance computation

1: $R_{\hat{q}} := \texttt{simd\_load}(\&\hat{q}[i])$ ▷ load $\hat{q}[0]...\hat{q}[7]$
2: $R_d := \texttt{simd\_sub}(R_{\hat{q}}, R_c)$ ▷ vectorized $\hat{t}[i] - \hat{q}[i]$
3: $R_d := \texttt{simd\_mul}(R_d, R_d)$ ▷ vectorized $(\hat{t}[i] - \hat{q}[i])^2$

Before examining the early stop condition (cf. Line 5 of Algorithm 1), we need to accumulate 8 offset distances into $dist$. Since the AVX2 instruction set has no single instruction to accumulate the values of an SIMD register, we accomplish the accumulation by the following sequence of SIMD instructions.

SIMD distance accumulation

1: $R_d := \texttt{simd\_hadd}(R_d, R_d)$ ▷ add horizontal pairs
2: $R_d := \texttt{simd\_hadd}(R_d, R_d)$ ▷ add horizontal pairs
3: $S_d := \texttt{simd\_extractf}(R_d, 1)$
4: $S_d := \texttt{simd\_sadd}(\texttt{simd\_cast}(R_d), S_d)$
5: $dist := dist + \texttt{simd\_scvt}(S_d)$

The accumulation employs instruction $\texttt{simd\_hadd}$ (e.g., $\_\texttt{mm256\_hadd\_ps}$) twice that horizontally adds adjacent pairs of 32-bit floating-point elements in the input registers, and stores the results into an output register. Then decompose the vector into two parts by $\texttt{simd\_extractf}$ and $\texttt{simd\_cast}$. Next, we sum

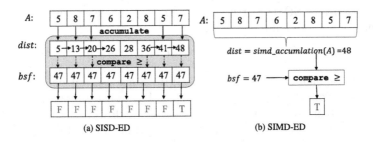

Fig. 5. Example for early stop

the first value of two decomposed vectors (by `simd_sadd`), extract the lower 32-bit floating-point element from the vector (by `simd_scvt`), and accumulate it into *dist*. The accumulation process takes logarithmic cost to the SIMD register length.

Our vectorized implementation reduces CPU cycles by (i) incorporating parallelism for Z-normalization and distance computation, and (ii) reducing branching statements for the early stop condition. Figure 5(a) shows that SISD-ED requires verifying the early stop for every accumulation (i.e., 8 comparisons in total). In SIMD-ED, we only verify the early termination once per 8 accumulations as shown in Fig. 5(b).

4.3 Accelerating DTW with SIMD

For the sake of our discussion, we first present the pseudo code of DTW computation in Algorithm 2. It employs a matrix $C[1..m][1..m]$ whose entry $C[i][j]$ is used to store the DTW value between subsequences $\hat{q}[1..i]$ and $\hat{t}_c[1..j]$. Then, we fill the matrix C by row-by-row ordering (Lines 2–3). Observe that we cannot compute values in the same row (e.g., $C[i][j-1], C[i][j]$) in parallel because $C[i][j]$ depends on $C[i][j-1]$.

Algorithm 2. SISD-$DTW(q, t_c)$

Input: warping constraint length r, normalized query $\hat{q}$ and candidate $\hat{t}_c$
Output: squared distance *dist*
1: Distance array $C[1..m][1..m]$, initialized to $+\infty$
2: **for** $i := 1$ to m **do**
3:     **for** $j := \max(0, i - r)$ to $\min(m, i + r)$ **do**
4:         **if** $i = 1$ and $j = 1$ **then**
5:             $C[1][1] := (\hat{q}[1] - \hat{t}_c[1])^2$
6:         **else**
7:             $C[i][j] := (\hat{q}[i] - \hat{t}_c[j])^2 +$
                 $\min(C[i-1][j], C[i-1][j-1], C[i][j-1])$
8: **return** $C[m][m]$ as *dist*

To better utilize SIMD instructions, we rewrite the equation of $C[i][j]$ into an alternative form as follows.

$$C[i][j] = (\hat{q}[i] - \hat{t}_c[j])^2 + \min(B_{i-1}[j], C[i][j-1]) \tag{6}$$

where $B_{i-1}[j] = \min(C[i-1][j-1], C[i-1][j])$. Since $B_{i-1}[j]$ depends only on values in the previous row of C (i.e., row $i-1$), we can calculate consecutive values of B_{i-1} (e.g., $B_{i-1}[j]$ to $B_{i-1}[j+7]$) in a batch.

The above discussion enables us to rewrite Line 7 in SISD-DTW as the following pseudo code using SIMD instructions.

```
Rewrite inner for-loop (i fixed) in Algorithm 2
1: j_min := max(0, i − r); j_max := min(m, i + r)
2: for j := j_min to j_max, 8 offsets do
3:     load R_x1 with C[i − 1][j, · · · , j + 7]
4:     load R_x2 with C[i − 1][j − 1, · · · , j + 6]
5:     R_B := simd_min(R_x1, R_x2)
6:     B_{i−1}[j, · · · , j + 7] = simd_store(R_B)
7:     C[i][j] := (q̂[i] − t̂_c[j])²
8: C[i][j_min] := C[i][j_min] + B_{i−1}[j_min]
9: for j := j_min + 1 to j_max do
10:    increment C[i][j] by min(C[i][j − 1], B_{i−1}[j])
```

The rewritten code has two nice properties: (i) avoid branch mispredictions by using the simd_min instruction (Lines 3–5), (ii) reduce cache misses by utilizing the data locality of $C[i][j-1]$ and $C[i][j]$ (Line 10). Figure 6 illustrates how our SIMD implementation works (when $i = 4$).

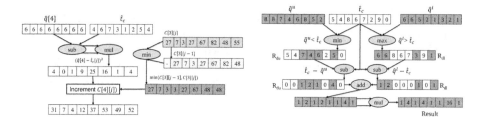

Fig. 6. SIMD DTW illustration, at $i = 4$ **Fig. 7.** LB^{EQ}_{Keogh} SIMD illustration

Optimized implementation: For ease of understanding, we employ $m \times m$ matrices in the above algorithms. An optimized implementation is to use 2 float arrays with size $2r + 1$ (i.e., store $C[i - 1]$ and $C[i]$ in Line 7, Algorithm 2) to compute DTW (for both SISD-DTW and SIMD-DTW). Since these 2 float arrays can fit in low latency cache (e.g., L2 cache rather than L3 cache), we use this optimized implementation for both SISD-DTW and SIMD-DTW in our code.

4.4   Accelerating Lower Bounds for DTW with SIMD

We proceed to present SIMD optimizations for lower-bound functions LB^{EQ}_{Keogh} and LB^{EC}_{Keogh}. Since these two functions are similar, our discussion focuses on LB^{EQ}_{Keogh}.

Algorithm 3. SISD-$LB^{EQ}_{Keogh}(q, t_c)$

Input: best-so-far bsf, mean μ and stdev. σ of candidate t_c, upper and lower envelops $\hat{q}^u$ and $\hat{q}^l$
Output: lower-bound distance lb
1: $lb := 0$
2: **for** $i := 1$ to m **do**
3:     $c := (t_c[i] - \mu)/\sigma$ ▷ Z-normalization
4:     **if** $\hat{q}^u[i] < c$ **then**   ▷ distance of $\hat{t}_c$ and the envelop of $\hat{q}$
5:         $lb := lb + (c - \hat{q}^u[i])^2$
6:     **else if** $\hat{q}^l[i] > c$ **then**
7:         $lb := lb + (\hat{q}^l[i] - c)^2$
8:     **if** $dist \geq bsf$ **break**   ▷ early stop
9: **return** lb

Similar to $ED(\cdot)$, we present the SISD implementation of LB^{EQ}_{Keogh} in Algorithm 3. It derives the lower-bound lb from the candidate subsequence t_c and the envelop of q which is handled by the **if-then-else** statement at Lines 4–7. However, the **if-then-else** statement may cause many branch mispredictions in CPU, leading to high stalling time (e.g., 10–20 clock cycles in modern CPU on average). In addition, as reported in [15], the hardware prefetching (for reducing cache misses) technique becomes less effective in the presence of multiple code paths.

To avoid branch mispredictions and better utilize hardware prefetching, we should remove branching, i.e., the **if-then-else** statement, in Algorithm 3. Lemma 1 shows the alternative form of LB^{EQ}_{Keogh} (cf. Eq. 4 in Sect. 2).

Lemma 1. (Alternative form of LB^{EQ}_{Keogh}).

$$LB^{EQ}_{Keogh} = \sum_{i=1}^{m}((\hat{t_c}[i] - \min\{\hat{t}_c[i], \hat{q}^u[i]\}) + (\max\{\hat{t}_c[i], \hat{q}^l[i]\} - \hat{t}_c[i]))^2$$

Proof. LB^{EQ}_{Keogh} (cf. Eq. 4) consists of three cases.

Case 1: When $\hat{t}_c[i] < \hat{q}^u[i]$, the first part (i.e., $\hat{t}_c[i] - \min\{\hat{t}_c[i], \hat{q}^u[i]\}$) becomes zero so that the equation reduces to $(\hat{q}^l[i] - \hat{t}_c[i])^2$.

Case 2: When $\hat{t}_c[i] > \hat{q}^l[i]$, the second part (i.e., $\max\{\hat{t}_c[i], \hat{q}^l[i]\} - \hat{t}_c[i]$) becomes zero so that the equation reduces to $(\hat{t}_c[i] - \hat{q}^u[i])^2$.

Case 3: Otherwise, none of the first or the second part contributes so the equation returns 0.   □

Since this form uses only $\min, \max, +, -, \times$, we can readily implement them by the corresponding SIMD instructions. Accordingly, the first part and the second part of LB^{EQ}_{Keogh} can be computed as follows. Then, we sum up both parts.

SIMD $\hat{t}_c[i] - \min\{\hat{t}_c[i], \hat{q}^u[i]\}$ **computation, 8 offsets**

1: $R_{\hat{q}^u} := \text{simd\_load}(\&\hat{q}^u[i])$ ▷ vectorized load $\hat{q}^u[i]..\hat{q}^u[i+7]$

2: $R_{du} := \text{simd\_min}(R_{\hat{q}^u}, R_c)$ ▷ vectorized $\min\{\hat{t}_c[i], \hat{q}^u[i]\}$

3: $R_{du} := \text{simd\_sub}(R_c, R_{\hat{q}^u})$ ▷ vectorized $\hat{t}_c[i] - \min\{\hat{t}_c[i], \hat{q}^u[i]\}$

SIMD $\max\{\hat{t}_c[i], \hat{q}^l[i]\} - \hat{t}_c[i]$ **computation, 8 offsets**

1: $R_{\hat{q}^l} := \text{simd\_load}(\&\hat{q}^l[i])$ ▷ vectorized load $\hat{q}^l[i]..\hat{q}^l[i+7]$

2: $R_{dl} := \text{simd\_max}(R_{\hat{q}^l}, R_c)$ ▷ vectorized $\max\{\hat{t}_c[i], \hat{q}^l[i]\}$

3: $R_{dl} := \text{simd\_sub}(R_{\hat{q}^l}, R_c)$ ▷ vectorized $\max\{\hat{t}_c[i], \hat{q}^l[i]\} - \hat{t}_c[i]$

SIMD combining the result of R_{du} **and** R_{dl}**, 8 offsets**

1: $R_d := \text{simd\_add}(R_{du}, R_{dl})$ ▷ vectorized sum

2: $R_d := \text{simd\_mul}(R_d, R_d)$ ▷ vectorized square

We illustrate our idea by a concrete example in Fig. 7. First we extract the *min* values between $\hat{q}^u$ and $\hat{t}_c$ of 8 offsets by simd_min and then store them into R_{du}. Next we subtract R_{du} from t_c to finish the first part computation. The second part is performed similarly where the *max* values are stored into R_{dl}. Next we combine the distance values from R_{du} and R_{dl} to produce R_d. Finally we multiply the values of R_d to generate the squared distance, and then execute SIMD distance accumulation as described in Sect. 4.2.

4.5 Cost Analysis

We proceed to analyze the cost of the SISD and SIMD implementations based on the latency cycle information given in the Intel architecture optimization manual [1].

ED: Our analysis covers four steps in ED: (i) Z-normalization, (ii) distance computation, (iii) distance accumulation, and (iv) early stop, as shown in Table 3(a). In each step, we list all used instructions and their latency cycles. For SIMD-ED, the denominator in latency is 8 as it processes 8 offset values simultaneously. In summary, SIMD-ED is $41/7 = 5.86$ times faster than SISD-ED.

DTW: We analyze the latency of both SISD and SIMD implementations of DTW in Table 3(b). The speedup of the SIMD implementation over SISD one is: $\frac{48}{14.625} = 3.28$.

LB_{Keogh}^{EQ}**:** We analyze the latency for two implementations of LB_{Keogh}^{EQ}. We only list the detail cost at step (ii) distance computation in Table 3(c) as the other three steps are the same as in SIMD-ED (cf. Table 3(a)). SIMD-LB_{Keogh}^{EQ} outperforms SISD-LB_{Keogh}^{EQ} by $43/9 = 4.78$ times.

4.6 Accelerating Reference Index with SIMD

Before proposing our SIMD solution, we first present the existing implementation of LB_{ref} in Algorithm 4.

As the absolute value computation is not supported by the AVX2 instruction set, we rewrite $|dist_{ref}[i][a] - dist_{ref}[i][b]|$ as:

$$\max(dist_{ref}[i][a], dist_{ref}[i][b]) - \min(dist_{ref}[i][a], dist_{ref}[i][b])$$

Exploit Every Cycle   33

Table 3. Instruction latency of SISD and SIMD functions

(a) ED

Step		SISD-	SIMD-
Z-norm.	op	load, −, /	gat., sub, div
	cost	1+3+24 = 28	(1+3+21)/8 = 25/8
Dist. compu.	op	load, −, ×	load, sub, mul
	cost	1+3+5 = 9	(4+3+5)/8 = 12/8
Accum.	op	+	2·hadd, 2·add, ext., scvt, cast
	cost	3	(2*5+2*3+1*2)/8 = 18/8
Ear. stop	cost	1	1/8
Total	cost	41	7

(b) DTW

Step		SISD-	SIMD-
ED (cf. (a))	cost	28+9+3 = 40	(25+12+18)/8 =55/8
Take	op	3*load, 2*cmp	2*load, min,store
Mini.	cost	3*1+2= 5	(2*4+3+3)/8 = 14/8
Accum.	op	+	2*load, 1*cmp, +
	cost	3	2*1+1+3 = 6
Total	cost	48	14.625

(c) LB_{Keogh}^{EQ}

Step		SISD-	SIMD-
Dist. compu.	op	load 2·cmp, −, ×	2·load, 2·sub, min, mul, max, add
	cost	1+2+3+5 =11	(8+6+3+3+3)/8=28/8
Z-norm. Accum. Ear. stop (cf. (a))	cost	28+3+1	(25+18+1)/8
Total	cost	43	9

Algorithm 4. SISD-$LB_{ref}(t_a, t_b)$

Input: best-so-far bsf, reference distance $dist_{ref}$, # of reference R, two subsequences t_a, t_b
Output: Boolean value
1: **for** $i := 1$ to R **do**
2:     **if** $|dist_{ref}[i][a] - dist_{ref}[i][b]| > bsf$ **then**
3:        **return** true   ▷ can be pruned
4: **return** false   ▷ cannot be pruned

Then, we design the SIMD implementation below for LB_{ref}. It avoids using branching statements for early termination in Lines 7–8. We verify the early stop only once by executing simd_cmp for 8 pairs of candidates.

SIMD LB_{ref}, for 8 offsets
1: $R_a := $ simd_load$(dist_{ref}[i][a], \cdots, dist_{ref}[i+7][a])$
2: $R_b := $ simd_load$(dist_{ref}[i][b], \cdots, dist_{ref}[i+7][b])$
3: $R_{bsf} := $ simd_set1(bsf)
4: $R_{max} := $ simd_max(R_a, R_b)
5: $R_{min} := $ simd_min(R_a, R_b)
6: $R_{sub} := $ simd_sub(R_{max}, R_{min})
7: $R_a := $ simd_cmp$(R_{sub}, R_{bsf}, >)$
8: **return** simd_testz(R_a, R_a)

We can further optimize LB_{ref} by sequentializing the memory access (and reducing CPU cache misses). This requires changing the memory layout of $dist_{ref}$ to $dist_{ref}[a][i]$ (i.e., swapping the role of rows and columns) so that Lines 1–2 have sequential main memory accesses.

Cost analysis: For each reference point i, SISD-LB_{ref} takes 6 cycles and SIMD-LB_{ref} takes 27/8 cycles. We omit the detailed analysis here.

Alternative implementation: Another implementation for $|dist_{ref}[i][a] - dist_{ref}[i][b]|$ is to use simd_sub, simd_set and simd_andnot instructions only. Since this implementation spends the same number of CPU cycles as in the above algorithm, we omit its detail discussion in following experiments.

5 Experimental Study

In this section, we conduct extensive experiments to evaluate our proposed techniques with existing solutions. Unless otherwise stated, we use the experimental platform and measurement methodology in Sect. 3. Note that the execution time includes both disk I/O time and CPU computation time. We denote SISD as the original implementation [20, 22] (for corresponding problems), SIMD as the implementation with our proposed techniques.

5.1   Subsequence Search

UCR-ED: UCR-ED [22] is a representative solution for the ED-based subsequence search. It employs the *early abandoning* technique to accelerate the Euclidean distance computation. We show the performance of SISD-based and SIMD-based UCR-ED in Fig. 8.

First, we investigate the components of CPU stall of the methods on the dataset ECG-E in Fig. 8(a). Since our SIMD-based solutions exploit SIMD vectorization techniques, they incur fewer instructions and ALU stall (T_{ALU}) than the SISD-based solution. The results on other datasets are similar to Fig. 8(a), so we omit them for space reasons.

Second, we compare the CPU time of the methods in Fig. 8(b). We omit the results of SIMD-128, as it is similar to SIMD-256. Clearly, our SIMD-based UCR-ED can reduce CPU stalls significantly (e.g., ∼20%).

UCR-DTW: Regarding the DTW-based subsequence search, UCR-DTW [22] cascades three lower bound techniques (i.e., LB_{KimFL}, LB_{Keogh}^{EQ}, and LB_{Keogh}^{EC}) to pruning unpromising candidates without invoking expensive DTW computations. We breakdown the components of CPU stall of the methods on the dataset ECG-E in Fig. 9(a). Since our SIMD-based UCR-DTW accelerated both the exact distance (cf. Sect. 4.3) and the lower bound computations (cf. Sect. 4.4), SIMD-based UCR-DTW introduces fewer CPU stall cycles than the SISD-based solution. Second, we compared the CPU time of the methods on three datasets in Fig. 9(b). The CPU busy ratio of SIMD-based UCR-DTW is almost 50%, which is much higher than SISD-based UCR-DTW.

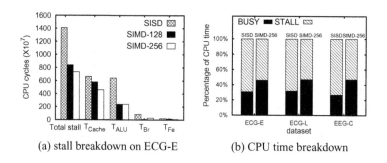

(a) stall breakdown on ECG-E   (b) CPU time breakdown

Fig. 8. SISD-based and SIMD-based UCR-ED

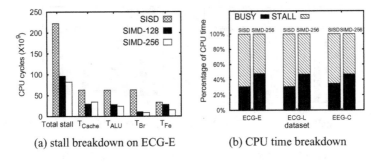

(a) stall breakdown on ECG-E   (b) CPU time breakdown

Fig. 9. SISD-based and SIMD-based UCR-DTW

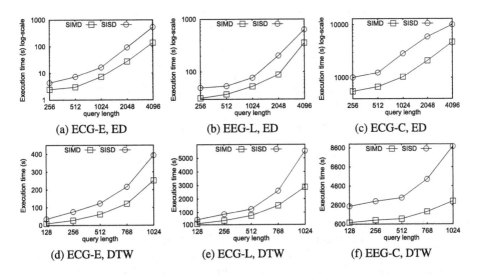

(a) ECG-E, ED   (b) EEG-L, ED   (c) ECG-C, ED

(d) ECG-E, DTW   (e) ECG-L, DTW   (f) EEG-C, DTW

Fig. 10. [Subsequence search] vary query length

Execution Time Speedup: In this set of experiments, we report the execution time of the methods on three time series datasets (i.e., ECG-E, ECG-L, and EEG-C) varying on query lengths in Fig. 10, where the lengths are from 256 to 4096 in UCR-ED and 128 to 1024 in UCR-DTW. Our proposed SIMD-based methods are 1.8–3.8 and 1.5–3.2 times faster than UCR-ED and UCR-DTW, respectively.

5.2   Motif Discovery

MK [20] makes use of (i) the exact distance calculation ED and (ii) the lower-bound calculation LB_{ref}. The SIMD-based implementation of these two functions has been introduced in Sects. 4.2 and 4.6, respectively. Figure 11(a) illustrates the reduced cycles of each CPU stall component in SISD-based and SIMD-based MK. Figure 11(b) shows the improvement of the CPU cycles with

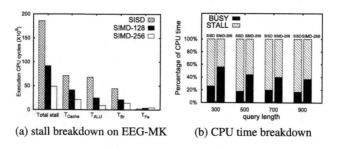

(a) stall breakdown on EEG-MK   (b) CPU time breakdown

Fig. 11. SISD-based and SIMD-based MK, EEG-MK

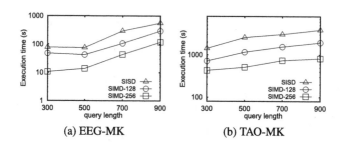

(a) EEG-MK   (b) TAO-MK

Fig. 12. [Motif discovery] vary query length

respect to different query lengths. Again, the SIMD-based solution introduces fewer stall cycles as compared with the SISD-based solution.

We then compare the performance of the methods on the motif discovery problem. Figure 12 plots the execution time (logscale) of the methods with respect to the query length. The performance gap between our methods and SISD widens as the query length increases. The speedup of SIMD over SISD ranges from 2.2 to 6.0.

5.3 kNN Classification

We show the breakdown of CPU stalls of UCR Suite based kNN classification problem on Weather dataset in Fig. 13. We set $k =$ 1 which is the default setting in [12]. This problem is less computational intensive (one candidate per sequence) when compared to the subsequence search problem ($O(n)$ subsequences per sequence) and the motif problem ($O(n^2)$ subsequence pairs per sequence). Even though it is less computational intensive, the SIMD-based solution still saves ∼50% stall cycles for DTW as compared to the SISD-based solution (cf. Fig. 13). Next we show the execution time speedup of the methods on the kNN classification problem in Fig. 13(c). kNN classification problem is less computational intensive, Thus, the speedup by SIMD is lower than before. Nevertheless, SIMD still outperforms all other methods.

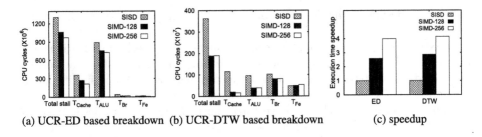

(a) UCR-ED based breakdown   (b) UCR-DTW based breakdown   (c) speedup

Fig. 13. Breakdown of CPU stalls and speedup, kNN Classification

6   Related Work

Time series: The representative problems on time series data are (i) the *subsequence search* problem [9,12,14,21,22,25,30], (ii) the *motif discovery* problem [20] and (iii) the kNN *classification* problem [12,22]. The typical distance functions are the Euclidean distance (ED) and Dynamic Time Warping (DTW). Existing algorithms rely on software-level optimizations such as lower-bound functions and indexing structures [4,13,21,22,30]. However, existing solutions incur high CPU stall times and there are rooms to further improve the efficiency of distance and lower-bound computations. To our best knowledge, our work is the first to exploit data parallelism to speedup the above computations on modern CPU. Our proposed techniques are orthogonal to the above software-level optimizations.

Modern CPU: Modern CPU provides data parallelism via single instruction over multiple data (SIMD) and offer thread parallelism through multiple cores and simultaneous multi-threading (SMT). In the relational database area, SIMD and multi-core CPUs have been used to speedup database operations [29], sorting [11], and joining [6,7,23]. In contrast, we focus on accelerating lower-bound and distance computations on time series data.

Other computing devices: We are aware of methods that accelerate DTW subsequence search on GPUs and FPGAs [24,28]. They aim at parallelizing the computation of DTW, which however is not always the dominant cost as shown in our performance profiling. Note that the performance of GPU degrades if it works on a dataset much larger than its video RAM (2 GB). The typical bandwidth between GPU and the main memory is 15 GB/s, which is much smaller than the bandwidth between CPU and the main memory.

7   Conclusion and Future Work

Summary and Lessons Learnt: In this paper, we conduct performance profiling on existing solutions for time series problems. We find that the performance bottleneck is caused by CPU stalls. We have redesigned vectorized lower-bound and distance functions with SIMD instructions for time series problems. Through our experimental results and analysis, we have two key findings, which will shed light on the design and implementation of time series algorithms on modern commodity CPUs.

Firstly, the performance bottlenecks of different time series applications are different. Even for the same time series algorithm, it may incur different bottlenecks on different datasets, depending on the pruning power of each specific lower bound function. Secondly, the characteristics of modern CPUs (e.g., branch prediction unit, hardware prefetching, vectorization) play important roles in the execution time of an implementation. Frequently-used functions (e.g., lower-bound and exact distance computations) need to be redesigned in order to unlock the full potentials of modern commodity CPUs.

Future Research Directions: Emerging processor architectures have new characteristics and lead to opportunities for further optimization. For example, the 'Many Integrated Core' (MIC) architecture [17] combines a large number cores on a single chip (e.g., Intel Xeon Phi), so that the access time of data items across different cores may depend on the distances between those cores. It becomes important to distribute the workload and transfer data carefully among different cores/threads.

Although our proposed techniques can accelerate existing algorithms by 2–6 times in a single machine, they would take a few hours for very long queries (especially for DTW similarity search). It becomes important to investigate parallel algorithms that run on multiple machines. Some open issues include how to distribute the load among machines, and how to reduce the communication cost among machines.

Acknowledgement. This project was supported by grant GRF 152043/15E from the Hong Kong RGC and grant MYRG2014-00106-FST from UMAC Research Committee and grant NSFC 61502548 from National Natural Science Foundation of China.

References

1. Intel 64 and IA-32 architecutres optimization reference manual. http://www.intel.com/content/dam/www/public/us/en/documents/manuals/64-ia-32-architectures-optimization-manual.pdf. Accessed 20 June 2016
2. Source codes and datasets for experimental study. http://goo.gl/mwDTxP. Accessed 20 June 2016
3. Ailamaki, A., DeWitt, D.J., Hill, M.D., Wood, D.A.: DBMSs on a modern processor: where does time go? In: VLDB, Edinburgh, UK, pp. 266–277 (1999)
4. Assent, I., Krieger, R., Afschari, F., Seidl, T.: The ts-tree: efficient time series search and retrieval. In: EDBT (2008)
5. Athitsos, V., Papapetrou, P., Potamias, M., Kollios, G., Gunopulos, D.: Approximate embedding-based subsequence matching of time series. In: SIGMOD (2008)
6. Balkesen, C., Teubner, J., Alonso, G., Özsu, M.T.: Main-memory hash joins on multi-core cpus: tuning to the underlying hardware. In: ICDE (2013)
7. Blanas, S., Li, Y., Patel, J.M.: Design and evaluation of main memory hash join algorithms for multi-core CPUs. In: SIGMOD (2011)

8. Browne, S., Dongarra, J., Garner, N., Ho, G., Mucci, P.: A portable programming interface for performance evaluation on modern processors. Int. J. High Perform. Comput. Appl. **14**(3), 189–204 (2000)
9. Camerra, A., Palpanas, T., Shieh, J., Keogh, E.J.: iSAX 2.0: Indexing and mining one billion time series. In: ICDM (2010)
10. Chen, S., Ailamaki, A., Gibbons, P.B., Mowry, T.C.: Improving hash join performance through prefetching. TODS **32**(3), 17 (2007)
11. Chhugani, J., Nguyen, A.D., Lee, V.W., Macy, W., Hagog, M., Chen, Y.-K., Baransi, A., Kumar, S., Dubey, P.: Efficient implementation of sorting on multi-core simd CPU architecture. PVLDB **1**(2), 1313–1324 (2008)
12. Ding, H., Trajcevski, G., Scheuermann, P., Wang, X., Keogh, E.J.: Querying and mining of time series data: experimental comparison of representations and distance measures. PVLDB **1**(2), 1542–1552 (2008)
13. Faloutsos, C., Ranganathan, M., Manolopoulos, Y.: Fast subsequence matching in time-series databases. In: SIGMOD (1994)
14. Fu, A.W., Keogh, E.J., Lau, L.Y.H., Ratanamahatana, C.A., Wong, R.C.: Scaling and time warping in time series querying. VLDB J. **17**(4), 899–921 (2008)
15. Hennessy, J.L., Patterson, D.A.: Computer Architecture - A Quantitative Approach, 5th edn. Morgan Kaufmann, San Francisco (2012)
16. Inoue, H., Ohara, M., Taura, K.: Faster set intersection with simd instructions by reducing branch mispredictions. Proc. VLDB Endowment **8**(3), 293–304 (2014)
17. Jha, S., He, B., Lu, M., Cheng, X., Huynh, H.P.: Improving main memory hash joins on intel xeon phi processors: an experimental approach. PVLDB **8**(6), 642–653 (2015)
18. Keogh, E., Ratanamahatana, C.A.: Exact indexing of dynamic time warping. Knowl. Inform. Syst. **7**(3), 358–386 (2005)
19. Li, Y., U, L.H., Yiu, M.L., Gong, Z.: Discovering longest-lasting correlation in sequence databases. PVLDB **6**(14), 1666–1677 (2013)
20. Mueen, A., Keogh, E.J., Zhu, Q., Cash, S., Westover, M.B.: Exact discovery of time series motifs. In: SDM (2009)
21. Papapetrou, P., Athitsos, V., Potamias, M., Kollios, G., Gunopulos, D.: Embedding-based subsequence matching in time-series databases. ACM TODS **36**(3), 17 (2011)
22. Rakthanmanon, T., Campana, B.J.L., Mueen, A., Batista, G.E., Westover, M.B., Zhu, Q., Zakaria, J., Keogh, E.J.: Searching and mining trillions of time series subsequences under dynamic time warping. In: KDD (2012)
23. Ross, K.A.: Efficient hash probes on modern processors. In: ICDE (2007)
24. Sart, D., Mueen, A., Najjar, W.A., Keogh, E.J., Niennattrakul, V.: Accelerating dynamic time warping subsequence search with GPUs and FPGAs. In: ICDM (2010)
25. Shieh, J., Keogh, E.J.: iSAX: indexing and mining terabyte sized time series. In: KDD (2008)
26. Shoeb, A.H., Guttag, J.V.: Application of machine learning to epileptic seizure detection. In: ICML (2010)
27. Sridharan, S., Patel, J.M.: Profiling R on a contemporary processor. Proc. VLDB Endowment **8**(2), 173–184 (2014)
28. Xiao, L., Zheng, Y., Tang, W., Yao, G., Ruan, L.: Parallelizing dynamic time warping algorithm using prefix computations on GPU. In: HPCC/EUC (2013)
29. Zhou, J., Ross, K.A.: Implementing database operations using SIMD instructions. In: SIGMOD (2002)
30. Zhu, H., Kollios, G., Athitsos, V.: A generic framework for efficient and effective subsequence retrieval. PVLDB **5**(11), 1579–1590 (2012)

Compression-Aware In-Memory Query Processing: Vision, System Design and Beyond

Juliana Hildebrandt, Dirk Habich$^{(\boxtimes)}$, Patrick Damme, and Wolfgang Lehner

Database Systems Group, Technische Universität Dresden, Dresden, Germany
{juliana.hildebrandt,dirk.habich,patrick.damme,
wolfgang.lehner}@tu-dresden.de
https://wwwdb.inf.tu-dresden.de

Abstract. In-memory database systems have to keep base data as well as intermediate results generated during query processing in main memory. In addition, the effort to access intermediate results is equivalent to the effort to access the base data. Therefore, the optimization of intermediate results is interesting and has a high impact on the performance of the query execution. For this domain, we propose the continuous use of lightweight compression methods for intermediate results and have the aim of developing a balanced query processing approach based on compressed intermediate results. To minimize the overall query execution time, it is important to find a balance between the reduced transfer times and the increased computational effort. This paper provides an overview and presents a system design for our vision. Our system design addresses the challenge of integrating a large and evolving corpus of lightweight data compression algorithms in an in-memory column store. In detail, we present our model-driven approach and describe ongoing research topics to realize our compression-aware query processing vision.

1 Motivation

In-memory database systems pursue a main memory-centric architecture approach and assume that all relevant data can be fully kept in main memory of a computer or of a computer network (cluster configuration) [1,5]. Lightweight data compression methods play an important role in this approach [2,27]. Aside from reducing the amount of data, compressed data offers several advantages such as less time spent on load and store instructions, a better utilization of the cache hierarchy and less misses in the translation lookaside buffer. Moreover, this approach is characterized by the fact that all performance-critical operations and internal data structures are designed for efficiently accessing the main memory hierarchy (e.g., efficient use of the cache hierarchy) [14,17]. Furthermore, *any access to an intermediate result generated during query processing is just as expensive as access to the base data* [15,19]. Accordingly, the optimization of the intermediate results is extremely important for an efficient query processing.

© Springer International Publishing AG 2017
S. Blanas et al. (Eds.): ADMS 2016/IMDM 2016, LNCS 10195, pp. 40–56, 2017.
DOI: 10.1007/978-3-319-56111-0_3

1.1   Vision of Compression-Aware In-Memory Query Processing

Generally, two orthogonal techniques are possible to optimize the handling of intermediate results. On the one hand, intermediate results should be no longer produced during query processing. Methods to avoid the generation of intermediate results are (i) adopted code generation for query plans [19] or (ii) the usage of cooperative operators [15]. On the other hand, intermediate results—if they cannot be avoided—should be organized so that an efficient further processing is enabled. In this context, we want to utilize lightweight compression techniques for intermediates as for base data. With the explicit compression of all intermediates, we want

1. to increase the efficiency of individual analytical queries or the throughput of an amount of analytical queries since the main memory requirement is reduced for intermediate results and the extra effort for the generation of the compressed form is minimized, and
2. to establish the continuous handling of compression from the base data to the intermediate results during query processing (holistic approach).

This type of query optimization has been already discussed [6], but not examined in detail since the computational effort for compression and decompression exceeded the benefits of a reduced transfer cost between CPU and main memory. Due to the ever-increasing gap between computing power and main memory bandwidth in modern multiprocessor systems [20] and the recent developments in the domain of efficient lightweight compression methods [18,22,25,27], this argument loses increasingly its validity. Nevertheless, to minimize the overall query execution time, it is important to find a balance between the reduced transfer times and the increased computational effort. To achieve such a balance, not only the query processing but also the necessary part of the query optimization has to be addressed (*compression-aware query processing*).

1.2   System Design Challenge for Compression-Aware Processing

In-memory database systems usually store data according to the decomposition storage model (DSM) [7] to efficiently support analytical and long-running queries. For DSM compression, a large corpus of lightweight data compression algorithms has been developed to efficiently support different data characteristics. Examples are: dictionary compression [2,27], run-length encoding [2,21], and null suppression [2,18,21]. The optimal compression method depends on the properties of the data. If we look at intermediate results, we observe that their properties usually change dramatically during the processing of a single query. Consequently, the compression for intermediate results have to be decided and changed during query processing. For example, a selection might get dictionary-compressed data as input and let only small values pass, such that afterwards a null suppression scheme would be more appropriate.

In order to realize our vision, we require an appropriate in-memory system supporting the large corpus of lightweight data compression algorithms. To best of our knowledge, there is no in-memory database system available providing this large corpus of compression algorithms. Therefore, the most challenging task is now to define a system design allowing us to integrate the large and evolving corpus of data compression algorithms.

1.3   Our Contribution and Outline of the Paper

In this paper, we are primarily focusing on the system design challenge as a fundamental basis for our vision. The naïve approach would be to natively implement the compression algorithms in the DSM storage layer of an in-memory database system as done today. However, this naïve approach has several drawbacks, e.g., (1) massive effort to implement every possible lightweight compression algorithm as well as (2) the integration of new and specific algorithms is time consuming. Therefore, we propose a novel and model-based approach for the integration in this paper. In detail our contributions are:

1. We start with a system design overview in Sect. 2. As we are going to introduce, our solution consists of two components: (i) the unified conceptual model for lightweight compression algorithms and (iii) the transformation of model instances to executable storage layer code.
2. We present our unified conceptual model in detail. We begin with a systematic treatment of the lightweight compression aspect and present a derived system description in Sect. 3. Afterwards, we propose our novel conceptual model *COLLATE* in Sect. 4.
3. We show the applicability of *COLLATE* model by describing two algorithms as model instances in Sect. 5. Then, we highlight our transformation approach to derive efficient executable code out of the model instances.

Furthermore, we close the paper with a description of our ongoing research topics realize our vision of compression-aware in-memory query processing. Finally, we conclude the paper in Sect. 7.

2   System Design Overview

Without loss of generality, we restrict our attention to in-memory column stores, because they are perfectly suited for complex analytical queries from a performance perspective [2,27]. The left side of Fig. 1 shows an abstract architecture of a typical in-memory column-store consisting of three layers: *durability, storage*, and *processing layer*. While the *durability layer* guarantees data persistence on non-volatile medium, the *storage* and *processing layer* are the main layers and they are responsible for storing and processing data in main-memory. The *storage layer* itself maintains relational data using the decomposition storage model (DSM) [7]. That means, each attribute is separately stored and the storage equals to a value-based storage model in form of a sequence of values. For the

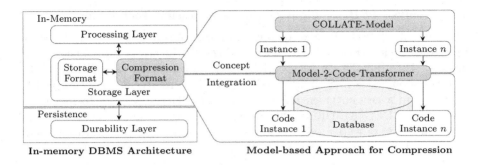

Fig. 1. Model-driven approach for the integration of data compression algorithms.

compression of sequences of values, a large variety of algorithms has been developed [2–4,11,18,21–24,27]. The landscape evolves further because it is impossible to design an algorithm that always produces optimal results for any kind of data.

To avoid the naïve approach by natively implementing each single compression algorithm, we pursue a model-driven approach. Fundamentally, the model-driven architecture (MDA) is a software design approach for the development of software systems [16]. In this approach, the system functionality is defined with a platform-independent model (PIM) using an appropriate domain-specific language [16]. Then, the PIM is automatically translated into one or more platform-specific models (PSM) [16]. The MDA paradigm is widely used in the area of database applications for database creations. On the one hand, the model-driven data modeling and the generation of normalized database schemas should be mentioned. On the other hand, there is the generation of full database applications, including the data schema as well as data layer code, business logic layer code, and even user interface code [12].

In this paper, we propose to use the MDA paradigm for the system-internal domain of lightweight data compression algorithms as illustrated at the right side of Fig. 1. To achieve this, we defined a conceptual model called *COLLATE* for this specific domain. The aim of *COLLATE* is to provide a holistic, abstract and platform-independent view of necessary concepts including all aspects of data, behavior, and interaction. Based on that, a specific compression algorithm can be expressed as model instance. To transform a model instance to executable code, we pursue a generator approach. The generated and optimized code can be used in a column store in a straightforward way.

3   Survey of Lightweight Data Compression Algorithms

Before we present our novel model in the following section, we start with a comparison of basic compression techniques, followed by specific algorithms, and conclude with a system description in this section.

3.1   Analysis of Basic Lightweight Compression Techniques

The basis of lightweight data compression algorithms are six basic techniques: frame-of-reference (FOR) [11, 27], delta coding (DELTA) [18, 21], dictionary compression (DICT) [2, 27], bit vectors (BV) [26], run-length encoding (RLE) [2, 21], and null suppression (NS) [2, 21]. FOR and DELTA represent each value as the difference to a certain given reference value (FOR) respectively to its predecessor value (DELTA). DICT replaces each value by its unique key given by a dictionary. The objective of these three well-known techniques is to represent the original data as a sequence of small integers, which is then suited for actual compression using the NS technique. NS is the most well-studied kind of lightweight compression techniques. Its basic idea is the omission of leading zeros in the bit representation of small integers. In contrast to DICT, the technique BV replaces each input value with a bit vector representation in the output. Finally, RLE tackles uninterrupted sequences of occurrences of the same value, so called runs. In its compressed format, each run is represented by its value and length. Therefore, the compressed data is a sequence of such pairs.

If we analyze these techniques without their application in specific algorithms, we observe the following characteristics:

1. The techniques address different data levels. While FOR, DELTA, DICT, BV, and RLE consider the logical data level, NS addresses the bit or byte level. Therefore, it is clear why algorithms usually combine techniques from the logical level with NS.
2. We are able to distinguish two approaches how input values are mapped to output values. FOR, DELTA, DICT, and BV map each input value to exactly one integer as output value (*1:1 mapping*). The goal is to achieve smaller numbers which can be better compressed on bit level. In RLE, not every input value is necessarily mapped to an encoded output value, because a successive subsequence of equal values is encoded in the output as a pair of run value and run length (*N:1 mapping*). The NS technique is either a 1:1 mapping or an N:1 mapping depending on the concrete expression.
3. The techniques are either *parameter-dependent* or *data-dependent*. Most of the 1:1 mapping techniques except DELTA are *parameter-dependent*. That means, each input value is independently encoded from other values within the input sequence to an output representation, but the encoding depends on some parameter, i.e., the reference value in FOR or the bit width for NS. DELTA is a *data-dependent technique*, because it encodes the values in dependency of their predecessor. The same is valid for RLE, therefore we define RLE as *data-dependent* technique.

Each technique has its own characteristics and objectives, which are applied in the algorithms in different ways. In particular, the algorithms precisely define some open questions regarding the application. For example, one open question is how the parameter values for *parameter-dependent* techniques are determined. A second open question is whether the whole input sequence is processed with the same parameter value, or if the sequence is partitioned and for each subsequence a separate parameter value is used.

3.2   Analysis of Lightweight Compression Algorithms

Without claiming completeness, we analyzed a large variety of algorithms and classified the algorithms in families as follows:

Algorithms in the family of **Byte-oriented Encodings** rely on the basic technique NS [24]. They map uncompressed values to codewords of a bit length that is a multiple of eight. These algorithms implement NS according to a 1:1 mapping, whereas the corresponding parameter for encoding is determined for each single input value (number of essential bytes). That means, byte-oriented encodings compute the parameters for the *parameter-dependent* NS technique *data-dependent* by computing one parameter per input data value. For decoding, it is necessary to store the length of a codeword as a parameter. The algorithms have a lot of similarities. The only difference between two algorithms is the arrangement of bits and they also differ in the encoding of the length value.

Simple-based Algorithms apply only the NS technique, again [3]. Here, the algorithms try to pack as many binary encoded integer values in a 32 resp. 64 bit codeword by suppressing leading zeros. In contrast to the previous family, the algorithms follow an N:1 mapping for NS. The algorithms subdivide the input sequence in subsequences depending on the size of the input values. In each codeword of a fixed length, several descriptor bits serve as parameters to determine the bit width for all values that are encoded with this codeword. The remaining bits are filled with NS compressed data values. Simple-based algorithms apply the *parameter-dependent* NS technique in a *data-dependent* fashion with one parameter per input data subsequence.

PFOR-based Algorithms implement the FOR technique [27] in combination with NS. They subdivide the input in subsequences of a fix length and calculate two parameters per subsequence: a reference value for the FOR technique and a common bit width for NS. Each subsequence is encoded using their specific parameters, thereby the parameters are data-dependently derived. The values that cannot be encoded with the given bit width are stored separately with a greater bit width.

Adaptive FOR algorithms [10,23] bundle a lot of NS algorithms, but they focus on the problem of how to optimize the subdividing of a finite sequence of integer values in subsequences, such that every value in a subsequence is encoded with the same bit width. These algorithms use the *parameter-dependent* technique NS in a data-dependent fashion with a N:1 mapping approach.

All described families apply one or more basic lightweight compression techniques, but the application is different. For the last three families, data subdivision into subsequences plays an important role. Also the calculation of parameter values that are related to all values within a subsequence like a common bit width is a core part of the algorithms. In general, this aspect influences the encoding of the values in each subsequence differently. That is not addressed on the level of basic techniques, but on the level of the algorithms. Furthermore, the parameters for each subsequence have to be included in the encoded output sequences for decompression purposes. Generally, the *parameter-dependent* basic techniques are applied in a *data-dependent* fashion in algorithms by computing the parameters based on the input data sequence.

3.3   Derived System Description and Properties

Based on the decomposition storage model [7], the **input** for every lightweight data compression algorithm is a finite *sequence* of (integer) values. The **output** is a sequence of codewords and parameters representing the compressed data. The parameters like bit width or run length are required for decoding/decompression or are part of an access path within the compressed data format. Input and output data have a *logical representation* (semantic level) and a *physical representation* (bit or encoding level). While for some compression techniques it is useful to focus on the semantic level (FOR and DELTA), for other techniques the physical level is more important (NS).

For the transformation from input to output, two further characteristics play an important role for every algorithm. First, most of the basic lightweight compression techniques are *parameter-dependent*. Within the algorithms, a number of parameter values has to be calculated. Second, the basic techniques and algorithms differ in their mapping cardinalities as described above. For *parameter-dependent* N:1 mappings, parameters are calculated for each subsequence of N values. In general, a lot of algorithms *subdivide input data hierarchically* in subsequences (i.e. PFOR) for which the parameters can be calculated. Moreover, the further data processing of a subsequence depends on the subsequence itself. That means, **data subdivision** and **parameter calculation** are important and the application of the basic techniques is then straightforward. Finally, for an exact algorithm description, the **combination** and arrangement of codewords and parameters have to be defined. Here, the algorithms also differ widely.

4   *COLLATE* Model

We now introduce our novel conceptual and platform-independent model called *COLLATE* for the domain of lightweight data compression algorithms. As described in Sect. 3.3, input is a *sequence* of (integer) values and output is a sequence of codewords and parameters representing the compressed data. To convert input data to its compressed output data, several functional concepts with regard to our system description are necessary. Fundamentally, our model consists of the following five main concepts (functional components):

Recursion: This concept is responsible for the hierarchical data subdivision and for applying the included concepts in the `Recursion` on each data subsequence. Each modeled algorithm is a `Recursion`.

Tokenizer: This concept is responsible for dividing an input sequence into finite subsequences or single values.

Parameter Calculator: The concept `Parameter Calculator` determines parameter values for finite subsequences or single values. The specification of the parameter values is done using parameter definitions.

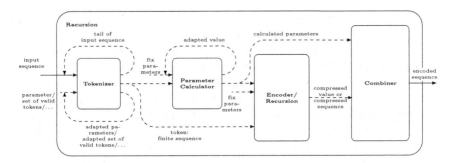

Fig. 2. Interaction and data flow of our *COLLATE* model.

Encoder: The third concept determines the encoded form for values to be compressed at bit level. Again, the concrete encoding is specified using functions representing the basic techniques.

Combiner: The `Combiner` is essential to arrange the encoded values and the calculated parameters for the output representation.

Figure 2 illustrates the interactions of our concepts and the data flow through the concepts for lightweight data compression for a simple case with only one pair of `Parameter Calculator` and `Encoder`. In general, this arrangement can be used as blueprint for lightweight compression algorithms as we will show in the next section. The dashed lines highlight several properties of the concepts. The properties of the concepts `Tokenizer`, `Parameter Calculator` and `Encoder` are as follows:

For the `Tokenizer` concept, we identified three classifying characteristics. The first one is the *data dependency*. A *data independent* `Tokenizer` outputs a special number of values without regarding the value itself, while a *data dependent* `Tokenizer` is used if the decision how many values to output is led by the knowledge of the concrete values. A second characteristic is the *adaptivity*. A `Tokenizer` is adaptive if the calculation rule changes depending on previously read data. The third property is the *necessary input for decisions*. Most `Tokenizers` need only a finite prefix of a data sequence to decide how many values to output. The rest of the sequence is used as further input for the `Tokenizer` and processed in the same manner. Only those `Tokenizers` are able to process data streams with potentially infinite data sequences. There are also `Tokenizers` needing the whole (finite) input sequence to decide how to subdivide it.

All of these eight combinations are possible. Some of them occur more frequently than others in existing algorithms. Some analyzed algorithms are very complex concerning sequence subdivision. It is not sufficient to assume that `Tokenizers` subdivide sequences in a linear way. As an example for PFOR-based algorithms, we also need `Tokenizers` that arrange somehow subsequences, mostly regarding content of single values of the sequence. With such kinds of `Tokenizers` (mostly categorizable as *non adaptive*, *data dependent* and with the need of finite input sequences), we can rearrange the values in a different (data dependent) order than the one of the input sequence.

A second task of the `Tokenizer` is to decide for each output sequence which pair of `Parameter Calculator` and `Encoder` is used for the further data processing. Most algorithms process all data in the same way, some of them distinguish several cases, so that this choice is necessary. The finite output sequence of the `Tokenizer` serves as input for the `Parameter Calculator`.

Parameters are often required for the encoding and decoding. Therefore, we introduce the `Parameter Calculator` concept, which knows special rules (parameter definitions) for the calculation of several parameters. There are different kinds of parameter definitions. We often need single numbers like a common bit width for all values or mapping informations for dictionary based encodings. We call a parameter definition *adaptive*, if the knowledge of a calculated parameter for one token (output of the `Tokenizer`) is needed for the calculation of parameters for further tokens at the same hierarchical level. For example, an adaptive parameter definition is necessary for DELTA. Calculated parameters have a logical representation for further calculations and the encoding of values as well as a representation at bit level, because on the one hand they are needed to calculate the encoding of values, on the other hand they have to be stored additionally to allow the decoding. If an algorithm is characterized by hierarchically calculated parameters, it is possible that a parameter definition depends on other calculated parameters that are additional input for a `Parameter Calculator`.

The `Encoder` processes an atomic input, where the output of the `Parameter Calculator` and other parameters are additional inputs. The input is a token that cannot or shall not be subdivided anymore. In practice the `Encoder` mostly gets a single integer value to be mapped into a binary code (1:1 mapping techniques). An exception is RLE as N:1 mapping technique, where the `Parameter Calculator` maps a sequence of equal values to its run length and the `Encoder` maps the sequence to the special value. Equally to the parameter definitions, the `Encoder` calculates a logical representation of its input value and an encoding at bit level.

5   Transformation of Model Instances

In this section, we deal with the application and the transformation of *COLLATE* model instances into executable code, thereby we focus on algorithms from the class of *Byte-oriented Encodings*. Nevertheless, all algorithms belonging to the algorithm families described in Sect. 2 can be modeled with *COLLATE* as demonstrated on our project website[1]. Due to space constraints, we only highlight the basic feasibility of our transformation approach.

5.1   Model Instances for Byte-oriented Encoding Algorithms

The two simple algorithms *varint-SU* and *varint-PU* belong to the class of *Byte-oriented Encodings* and they are designed to suppress leading zeros [24]. Both

---

[1] *Website* - https://wwwdb.inf.tu-dresden.de/research-projects/projects/collate/.

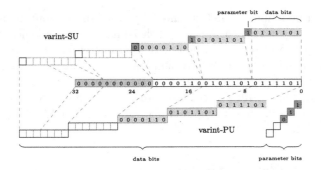

Fig. 3. Example for *varint-SU* (green) and *varint-PU* (blue) (Color figure online).

take 32-bit integer values as input and map them to codewords of variable length. This is shown in Fig. 3 for the binary representation of the value $104,125$. Both algorithms determine the smallest number of 7-bit units that are needed for the binary representation of the value without losing any information. In our example, we need at least three 7-bit units and we are able to suppress 11 leading zero bits. To support the decoding, we have to store the number three—number of necessary 7-bit units—as additional parameter. This is done in a unary way as 011. The algorithm *varint-SU* stores each single parameter bit at the high end of a 7-bit data unit, whereas *varint-PU* stores the complete parameter at one end of the 21 data bits.

Both algorithms are similar, which is also observable in their model instances as depicted in Fig. 4. Both algorithms use a very simple `Tokenizer` subdividing an input sequence of length n into single integer values (indicated by $|_{i=1}^{n} m_i$). For each value, the `Parameter Calculator` determines the number of necessary 7-bit units using an appropriate function ($bw = \lfloor \log_{128}(\max(1, \bullet)) \rfloor + 1$). The determined number is used in the subsequent `Encoder`. This one does not transform the logical value, but it subdivides the bit level representation of the input value into bw 7-bit units (indicated by $|_{j=1}^{bw} \bullet_{7j-1} \cdots \bullet_{7(j-1)}$). Up to now, both algorithms have the same behavior. The only difference between both'

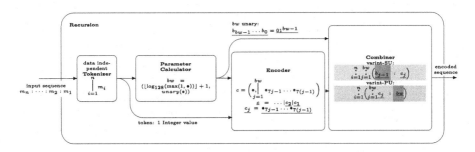

Fig. 4. Model instances for *varint-SU* (green) and *varint-PU* (blue) (Color figure online).

algorithms can be found in the `Combiner`, because only the output is different. The algorithm *varint-SU* concatenates each 7-bit unit of one logical value with one bit of the bit level representation of the parameter bw in a loop (indicated by $:_{j=1}^{bw}$) corresponding to the subdivision inside the `Encoder`. It uses a second loop corresponding to the `Tokenizer` to concatenate all n values (indicated by $:_{i=1}^{n}$). The algorithm *varint-PU* concatenates the whole bit level representation of a parameter bw and all 7-bit units of one value (indicated by $:_{j=1}^{bw}$) as well as all encoded values (indicated by $:_{i=1}^{n}$).

5.2   Transformation to Executable Code

As illustrated above, the algorithms are specified in an abstract way with our novel model approach and appropriate mathematical functions. The next challenge is the transformation in efficient executable code. Figure 5 depicts our developed overall approach for this task, thereby we follow a generator approach. The input of our `Model-2-Code Transformer` are (i) a specification of a model instance in the GNU Octave[2] high-level programming language and (ii) code templates for our model concepts. Our `Model-2-Code Transformer` is written in C and outputs algorithms in C. On the *COLLATE* model level, we have 5 specific concepts and we require one code template for each model concept. The code templates have to be implemented once for each specific database system, e.g., MonetDB [5]. This is necessary to get access to the data on the specific storage layer implementation.

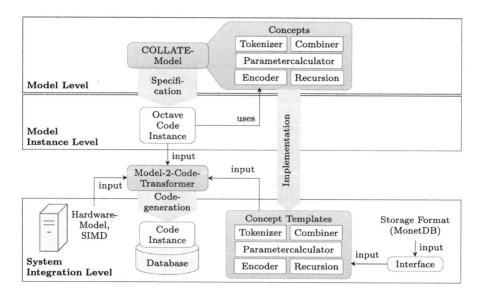

Fig. 5. Transformation of model instances to executable code.

---

[2] https://www.gnu.org/software/octave/.

The transformation is actually a topic for itself, that is why we want to explain here only the core idea of our approach using the *varint-SU* algorithm as shown in Fig. 4. The `Recursion` concept indicates that we iterate over the input sequence, thereby the `Tokenizer` specifies how we iterate over the input data. That means for our templates, the `Recursion` is a loop and `Tokenizer` information is used to concretize the loop. This approach is shown Fig. 6(a) representing the unoptimized output of our `Model-2-Code Transformer` for *varint-SU*. Furthermore, the `Tokenizer` determines which values have to processed in each loop pass. In our example, we process a single integer value in each loop pass. Then, the concept `Parameter Calculator` includes mathematical rules defining which and how parameters values have to be computed. These definitions are translated in a straightforward way. Generally, `Recursion`, `Tokenizer` and `Parameter Calculator` are working on the logical representation of input values. Afterwards, the `Encoder` gets the calculated parameter values and a single integer value as input. Here, we have to distinguish three opportunities. Either the `Encoder` works on the logical level, on the physical level, or on both levels. On the logical level, the encoding rules are translated again in a straightforward way. If the `Encoder` operates at the physical level, the logical value is usually decomposed in bits or bytes. This is represented in our template using a loop iterating over the bit/byte representation. In our example, the integer value is decomposed in *bw* 7-bit units (see corresponding loop in Fig. 6(a)). This decomposition or bit shifting is extracted from the encoder rule. If the `Encoder` works on the logical as well as physical level, we combine both approaches. Then, the `Combiner` works on the output of the `Encoder` and gets also the parameter as additional input. Again, if the `Combiner` works on the physical level, the corresponding template includes a loop iterating over the bit/byte representation.

To summarize, the templates reflect a foundation and the mathematical rules of the concepts are used to concretize the foundation. Figure 6(a) shows our generated C code we obtained with this approach for *varint-SU*. It is easy to see that this code is not optimal since encoder and combiner contain the same loop. To improve the generated code, we are able to optimize the code using well-known compiler techniques. In this case, we are able to fuse the code for the encoding and combining as illustrated in Fig. 6(b) resulting in one loop iterating over the *bw* 7-bit units. The code can be further optimized by unrolling the loop for encoding and decoding as there are maximal 5 7-bit unit opportunities. That means, we have a specific code part for compression a integer value using one 7-bit unit, specific code part for two 7-bit units, etc. The resulting optimized code is depicted in Fig. 6(c). This optimization is currently executed manually, because the automatically determination of code variants is challenging. This optimization has to be investigated more precisely.

Figure 7(a) shows an evaluation based on single threaded versions of *varint-SU* running on a standard server. We compare our generated and optimized codes to an efficient implementation of Lemire [18]. In this experiment, we vary the number of integer values to be compressed, thereby the compressed representations randomly vary between 1 and 5 7-bit units per integer value.

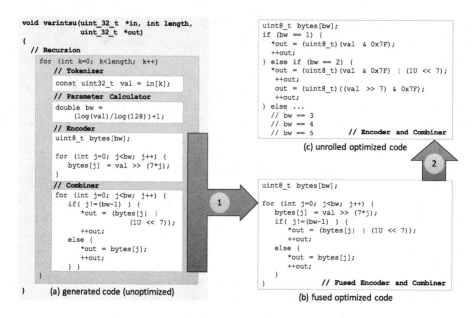

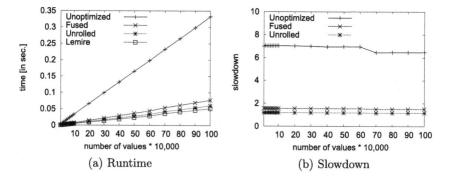

Fig. 6. Generated and optimized code for our *varint-SU* example.

The evaluation is done outside of any column store. As we can see, the unoptimized generated code performs poorly, but with our optimizations, we come close to the native implementation of Lemire. Figure 7(b) indicates the slowdown of our generated and optimized code compared to implementation of Lemire. As we can see, our unoptimized code is around seven times slower than the native code. The fusion of encoder and combiner reduces the slowdown to around 1.5 time, while the unrolling optimization offers the most improvement. Here, our slowdown is around 1.12 compared to the native implementation of Lemire. That means, our generated and optimized code is marginally slower than native code of Lemire.

Fig. 7. Evaluation results for *varint-SU*.

In summary it can be established that we are able generate efficient code with our approach. Nevertheless, the whole code optimization has to be worked out in detail, whereby the SIMD-parallelization must be considered with [22,25].

6 Future Work

As mentioned in the introduction, our central aim is to establish a *compression-aware query processing* concept. With the explicit compression of all intermediates, we want to increase the efficiency of individual analytical queries or the throughput of an amount of analytical queries since the main memory requirement is reduced for intermediate results and the extra effort for the generation of the compressed form is minimized. With our presented system design, we have now an appropriate foundation. Generally, our ongoing research activities cover: (i) the integration and optimization of lightweight compression algorithms (structural aspect) in column stores, (ii) the execution of operators on a compressed data format as far as possible (operational aspect), and (iii) the design of an optimization component to decide depending on the situation which compression method should be used for intermediate results (optimization aspect).

6.1 Structural Aspect

With this paper, we have systematically analyzed classical lightweight data compression algorithms. Furthermore, we have proposed a model-driven approach to efficiently integrate the large corpus of algorithms in a column store, e.g., MonetDB [5]. Here, we have focused on the data compression part. The same applies for decompression using a slightly adjusted conceptual model. Our ongoing research topics in this direction are: (i) simplification of algorithm modeling and (ii) extending the transformation/optimization to enable the utilization of SIMD capabilities of modern CPUs. Especially, the second point is interesting because we do not want to parallelize one specific algorithm, but the entire corpus.

A further interesting topic with regard to our vision is the transformation of compressed data in format X into compressed data in format Y. This is important since the optimal compression format depends on the properties of the data [2]. While the properties of the base data might change only incrementally over time caused by DML operations, the properties of intermediate results usually change dramatically during the processing of a single query. Consequently, operators should be able to output data in another format than their input. For example, a selection might get dictionary-compressed data as input and let only small values pass, such that afterwards a null suppression scheme would be more appropriate. Not adapting the format of the operator's output implies a waste of performance potential. At this point, transformation algorithms are our proposed solution as described here [9]. Our direct transformation techniques convert compressed data in format X to another compression format Y in a direct and interleaved way. They could be applied to the output of an operator or even inside an operator. The transformation algorithms can be also handled with our system design approach.

6.2 Operational Aspect

The operational aspect is another key component for our *compression-aware query processing* aim because physical plan operators have to be designed and implemented, which accept compressed data as an input and provide compressed data as result. The challenge in this task is to ensure that the cost of integrating different combinations of compression formats and operators is as low as possible. There are currently three different strategies for the query execution available which differ in timing and nature of data decompression: *eager decompression* [13], *lazy decompression* [27] and *transient decompression* [6]. In particular, the integration strategy *transient decompression* is very important for our aim. For operators, who can not work on compressed data, the data is decompressed partially and temporarily, however, the compressed representation is used as output. This strategy is intended to form the basis of our approach. However, the fundamental difference is that the intermediate results are transferred in different compression formats in the query plan. This allows changing the optimal compression method in the execution plan, depending on the operators and the data properties.

6.3 Optimization Aspect

At this level, both reduced transfer costs and the overhead of compression and decompression in the search of an optimal execution plan for our compression-aware query processing must be considered. Furthermore, the choice of compression methods for intermediate results and the choice of operator alternatives that can operate on compressed data, are important factors for the query optimization. Our goal is to design a common processing model which includes compression in the query processing as well as optimization. Therefore, further optimization techniques for the compression-sensitive query optimization have to be developed, which can have a major impact on processing times of analytical queries. Our query optimization will be based on a cost model, this cost model has explicit knowledge about the lightweight compression and transformation. This knowledge should be acquired on an empirical evaluation process, thereby we already defined an appropriate benchmark framework [8].

7 Conclusion

In-memory database systems have to keep base data as well as generated intermediate results during query processing in main memory. Furthermore, any access to any intermediate result is just as expensive as access to the base data. Therefore, the intermediate results should be considered separately for an efficient query processing offering two orthogonal optimization approaches:

(i) avoid the generation of intermediate results [15,19] or (ii) organize the intermediate result—if they cannot be avoided—so that an efficient further processing is enabled. In this latter context, we propose to use lightweight compression techniques for intermediates as for base data. In this paper, we explained our overall vision of a compression-aware query processing concept. In particular, we have proposed a model-driven approach to integrate the large and evolving corpus of lightweight data compression algorithms in a column store. Furthermore, we have highlighted our ongoing research activities.

References

1. Abadi, D., Boncz, P.A., Harizopoulos, S., Idreos, S., Madden, S.: The design and implementation of modern column-oriented database systems. Found. Trends Databases **5**(3), 197–280 (2013)
2. Abadi, D.J., Madden, S.R., Ferreira, M.C.: Integrating compression and execution in column-oriented database systems. In: SIGMOD, pp. 671–682 (2006)
3. Anh, V.N., Moffat, A.: Inverted index compression using word-aligned binary codes. Inf. Retr. **8**(1), 151–166 (2005)
4. Arroyuelo, D., González, S., Oyarzún, M., Sepulveda, V.: Document identifier reassignment and run-length-compressed inverted indexes for improved search performance. In: SIGIR, pp. 173–182 (2013)
5. Boncz, P.A., Kersten, M.L., Manegold, S.: Breaking the memory wall in MonetDB. Commun. ACM **51**(12), 77–85 (2008)
6. Chen, Z., Gehrke, J., Korn, F.: Query optimization in compressed database systems. SIGMOD Rec. **30**(2), 271–282 (2001)
7. Copeland, G.P., Khoshafian, S.N.: A decomposition storage model. SIGMOD Rec. **14**(4), 268–279 (1985)
8. Damme, P., Habich, D., Lehner, W.: A benchmark framework for data compression techniques. In: Nambiar, R., Poess, M. (eds.) TPCTC 2015. LNCS, vol. 9508, pp. 77–93. Springer, Cham (2016). doi:10.1007/978-3-319-31409-9_6
9. Damme, P., Habich, D., Lehner, W.: Direct transformation techniques for compressed data: general approach and application scenarios. In: Morzy, T., Valduriez, P., Bellatreche, L. (eds.) ADBIS 2015. LNCS, vol. 9282, pp. 151–165. Springer, Cham (2015). doi:10.1007/978-3-319-23135-8_11
10. Delbru, R., Campinas, S., Samp, K., Tummarello, G., Dangan, L., Delbru, R., Campinas, S., Samp, K., Tummarello, G.: Adaptive frame of reference for compressing inverted lists (2010)
11. Goldstein, J., Ramakrishnan, R., Shaft, U.: Compressing relations and indexes. In: ICDE, pp. 370–379 (1998)
12. Habich, D., Richly, S., Lehner, W.: GignoMDA - exploiting cross-layer optimization for complex database applications. In: VLDB (2006)
13. Iyer, B.R., Wilhite, D.: Data compression support in databases. In: VLDB Conference, pp. 695–704 (1994)
14. Kissinger, T., Schlegel, B., Habich, D., Lehner, W.: KISS-Tree: smart latch-free in-memory indexing on modern architectures. In: DaMoN, pp. 16–23 (2012)
15. Kissinger, T., Schlegel, B., Habich, D., Lehner, W.: QPPT: query processing on prefix trees. In: CIDR 2013 (2013)
16. Kleppe, A., Warmer, J., Bast, W.: MDA Explained. The Model Driven Architecture: Practice and Promise. Addison-Wesley, Massachusetts (2003)

17. Leis, V., Kemper, A., Neumann, T.: The adaptive radix tree: artful indexing for main-memory databases. In: ICDE, pp. 38–49 (2013)
18. Lemire, D., Boytsov, L.: Decoding billions of integers per second through vectorization. Softw. Pract. Exper. **45**(1), 1–29 (2015)
19. Neumann, T.: Efficiently compiling efficient query plans for modern hardware. PVLDB **4**(9), 539–550 (2011)
20. Qiao, L., Raman, V., Reiss, F., Haas, P.J., Lohman, G.M.: Main-memory scan sharing for multi-core cpus. PVLDB **1**, 610–621 (2008)
21. Roth, M.A., Van Horn, S.J.: Database compression. SIGMOD Rec. **22**(3), 31–39 (1993)
22. Schlegel, B., Gemulla, R., Lehner, W.: Fast integer compression using SIMD instructions. In: DaMoN (2010)
23. Silvestri, F., Venturini, R.: Vsencoding: efficient coding and fast decoding of integer lists via dynamic programming. In: CIKM, pp. 1219–1228 (2010)
24. Stepanov, A.A., Gangolli, A.R., Rose, D.E., Ernst, R.J., Oberoi, P.S.: SIMD-based decoding of posting lists. In: CIKM, pp. 317–326 (2011)
25. Willhalm, T., Popovici, N., Boshmaf, Y., Plattner, H., Zeier, A., Schaffner, J.: SIMD-scan: ultra fast in-memory table scan using on-chip vector processing units. PVLDB **2**(1), 385–394 (2009)
26. Williams, R.: Adaptive Data Compression. Kluwer International Series in Engineering and Computer Science: Communications and Information Theory. Springer, US (1991)
27. Zukowski, M., Heman, S., Nes, N., Boncz, P.: Super-scalar RAM-CPU cache compression. In: ICDE, p. 59 (2006)

Overtaking CPU DBMSes with a GPU in Whole-Query Analytic Processing with Parallelism-Friendly Execution Plan Optimization

Adnan Agbaria[1], David Minor[2], Natan Peterfreund[3], Eyal Rozenberg[4(✉)], and Ofer Rosenberg[3]

[1] Intel, Santa Clara, USA
adnan.agbaria@intel.com
[2] GE Global Research, Niskayuna, USA
david.minor1@ge.com
[3] Huawei Research, Ramot Menashe, Israel
natan.peterfreund@huawei.com, oferrose73@gmail.com
[4] CWI Amsterdam, Amsterdam, Netherlands
E.Rozenberg@cwi.nl

Abstract. Existing work on accelerating analytic DB query processing with (discrete) GPUs fails to fully realize their potential for speedup through parallelism: Published results do not achieve significant speedup over more performant CPU-only DBMSes when processing complete queries.

This paper presents a successful effort to better meet this challenge, in the form of a proof-of-concept query processing framework. The framework constitutes a graft onto an existing DBMS, altering some parts of it and replacing its execution engine entirely. It intensively refactors query execution plans, making them better-parallelizable, before executing them on either a CPU or on GPU. This results in a significant speedup even on a CPU, and a further speedup when using a GPU, over the chosen host DBMS (MonetDB) — which itself already bests most published results utilizing a GPU for query processing.

Finally, we outline some concrete future improvements on our results which can cut processing time by half and possibly much more.

1 Introduction

Database Management Systems (DBMSes) in wide use today were designed for execution on a 'serial' processing unit. Even when multi-thread and multi-core capabilities are taken into account in the design, massive parallelism is typically not a significant consideration: The execution strategy, the fundamental internal operations used in executing queries, the representation of data in memory

---

Work carried out by all authors as members of the Heterogeneous Computing Group at Huawei Research, Israel. Authors appear in alphabetical order.

S. Blanas et al. (Eds.): ADMS 2016/IMDM 2016, LNCS 10195, pp. 57–78, 2017.
DOI: 10.1007/978-3-319-56111-0_4

— these are all incarnations of original designs with serial execution in mind, even if these days. Even when multiple threads are used, they mostly behaving like so many single-thread DBMSes, each processing a large chunk of the data, independently.

As the use of GPUs for computation more general than graphics processing is spreading, industry and academic have begun exploring its potential use in processing relational database queries. Initially, contributions such as [5] focused on efficient implementation of primitive query-processing-related computational operations: These relatively self-contained pieces of code are what the CPU actually spends time on; and replacing them with carefully-optimized kernels running on the GPU does accelerate them. However, this does not immediately translate to impressive acceleration in processing *entire* queries.

This fact has motivated two avenues of research. One of them, not explored here, focuses on integrated CPU-GPU processors, such as AMD's APUs. These remove the bandwidth limitations of the PCIe bus, a key reason for the underwhelming performance of GPU DBMSs; [14] is a recent contribution in this vein, with references to additional work. A second approach is processing *queries as a whole* rather than only their constituent operations. Most experimental work in this avenue (ours included) involves *grafts* onto an existing *host DBMS*. A graft overrides parts of the normal compilation process and modifies existing code to create interfaces and hooks for new and replacement functionality *of complete sub-sections* of the query plan. Instead of merely replacing the code for execution of *individual* query plan operations, they alter and substitute *large sections* of the entire plan. Thus the generated plans are significantly different, and so is the execution mechanism, which is sometimes replaced altogether. Prominent recent examples of such frameworks include Red Fox [21] and GPU-DB [23] (also cf. [4]). However, despite the progress made so far, these efforts have not produced systems with query processing speed on par with the more performant free-software DBMSes, such as MonetDB [10,11] (which are themselves bested by some closed-source DBMSes, such as Actian Vector [24] and HyPerDB [7]).

We perceived previous work as being overly attached to existing DBMS' massive-parallelism-unfriendly execution planning — in other words, it seems that most often *they are still having a GPU "do a CPU's job"*.

To gain a performance benefit from using a GPU, we decided that instead of optimizing its execution of the tasks it is given by the traditional SQL optimizer, we should instead focus our effort on creating new GPU-friendly tasks and feeding them conveniently-represented data on which they could shine. Very roughly, such computational work is characterized by:

- Less code path divergence;
- More work by related threads on small, localized data;
- Well-coalesced memory accesses;
- Avoidance and circumvention of data dependencies, or at least the 'flattening out' of dependency relation into a shallow forest;
- a focus on throughput rather than on latency;

Some constituent operations in CPU-targeted execution plans cannot be implemented as-is in this fashion; but often their semantics can be tweaked, or their input or output formats altered, so that they admit a GPU-parallelism-friendly implementation (as is well-evidenced by the recent study of approaches for optimizing LIKE pattern matching on string columns [16]). Although many operations do not allow for such an adaptation, or do not benefit from it as significantly as others — we need to remind ourselves of our objective: It is the *plan* whose execution we wish to speed up, not the individual operations that are just a means to that end. Often including a less-then-optimal operation in an optimal GPU query plan will still lead to an overall improvement for the entire plan. In most cases, however, we can, in fact, avoid computational operations which the GPU does not favor, choosing alternate (sub)plans for that part of the query's execution. This approach underpins the query processing framework we developed as a proof-of-concept, and as the rest of this article demonstrates, it provides a significant improvement over other state-of-the-art in processing systems for *full* TPC-H queries.

2   The Processing Framework

With numerous query processing frameworks utilizing GPUs already in existence, Breß, Heimel et al. devised a classification scheme for these in [4, Sect. 4.3]. Before describing our framework, here is how it fits into this scheme (Table 1):

Table 1. Breß-et-al.-style classification

Storage: location	In-memory only
Storage: model	Column store
JIT compilation	None (but with IR transforms)
Processing: [x] at-a-time	Operator (not tuple or block)
Device support	Single-device and multi-device
Transactions	Not supported (read-only)
Hardware portability	CPUs & (CUDA) GPUs

Implemented Breß-et-alia-listed optimizations: GPU-aware query optimizer; Efficient data placement strategy; Overlap of data transfer and processing (partial); Pinned host memory.

2.1   From Query to Execution Run

The processing framework adopts the common approach of grafting onto an existing DBMS; our choice was the analytics-oriented column store MonetDB. Figure 1 summarizes which components of MonetDB are replaced or modified

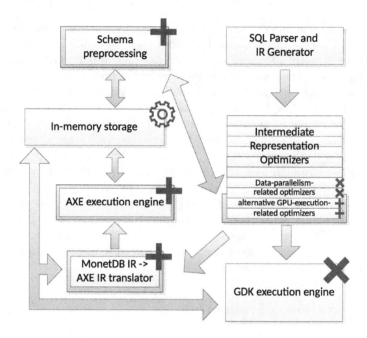

Fig. 1. The processing framework as a graft onto MonetDB

and which additions the graft introduces. It is helpful to the diagram keep in mind as the processing of incoming queries is described further below and in Sect. 3.

As a new (analytic) query arrives, the host DBMS parses it, considers its relational algebra, and generates an initial execution plan using its internal representation — for MonetDB, the single-assignment language MAL [19]. We interrupt the usual sequence of optimizers which MonetDB applies, replacing some of the final optimizers with a mock optimizer, whose task is to convert the sequence of MAL instructions into an alternative intermediate representation. Specifically, MonetDB's data-parallelism-inducing transformations are not applied; our execution engine will later transform the plan to utilize multiple CPU cores and/or GPU devices instead. Finally, instead of invoking MonetDB's execution engine/MAL program interpreter (named GDK), our own execution engine is invoked, ignoring the MAL sequence itself.

Our execution engine takes the following input: A (directed acyclic) graph, the 'execution' of which should obtain the query results; access to a library of GPU optimized computational primitive implementations (as these are not inherent to the engine); access to a library of similar implementations for CPUs; locations of buffers in the system's main memory (for schema columns and auxiliary data; see Subsect. 2.3); and a set of analytic-query-related transformation rules it may apply to its execution graph. When the execution engine completes its work, results are present in main memory and are passed back to MonetDB as though produced by its own native execution of the query.

2.2   The Execution Engine

Our query processing framework had at its core an execution engine called *AXE* (Adaptive Execution Engine) developed by the Heterogeneous Computing group of Huawei's Shannon Lab; this engine was designed independently of its specific use in this work — as the group's areas of interest are not limited to analytic DB query processing. It was designed to accommodate multiple types of computational devices and applications. It is built on the abstraction of a DAG of computational *operations*. Operations are drawn from a pool of hand-optimized domain-specific libraries. A run of the execution engine involves the concurrent and sequential execution of multiple operations. Some of these operations are massively parallel (e.g. binary vector operations) and others are run in task parallel fashion (e.g. host to device data transfers). AXE operations operate on *buffers* — an abstraction of regions of memory, which may be instantiated on the memory space of different devices, copied between memory spaces, pre-allocated, resized and set as inputs or outputs for operations both on and off the device. The AXE engine's IR (intermediate representation) is a DAG-like execution plan, describing the dependencies, operations and buffers needed for execution, along with additional information to help guide transformations by the engine. An internal queuing and scheduling mechanism allows for asynchronous execution of operations, dependency enforcement, synchronization and task level parallelism. Fine-grained, regularized (often synchronous) parallelism — typical of GPU code — is encapsulated into the implementations of the *operations* themselves, so that the engine is not GPU-specific. AXE also supports data parallelism, by cloning subgraphs at the IR level, splitting inputs among the subgraphs, and finally joining the results computed by each of these partition subgraphs. In order to accommodate the variegated of SQL semantics, a variety of partitioning and joining schemes are used (e.g. duplicate all, bit-or). Which scheme to use is providing by annotations over the inputs/outputs of individual operations, or reverts to a standard default.

Execution plan transformations occur at two distinct stages in the compilation/execution process. To see why this is so, consider the following: The *higher strata* of transformations, those within the DBMS interpreter itself, are *oblivious of the hardware* on which the plan will eventually execute, e.g. which computational devices, device capabilities, communication buses, memory space sizes, etc. The *lower stratum* of transformations, those taking place within our execution engine, is oblivious to the original application which provided the engine with the plan. It holds no information regarding databases, queries, relational tables, foreign-key relations and so on. This separation of concerns between the domain-specific (higher-strata, within DBMS) and hardware-specific (lower-strata, within AXE) is a useful technique, allowing for effective execution optimization catering to different applications (some more on this in Sect. 3). Of course, the separation is somewhat artificial, as hardware-related choices impact the benefit of domain-specific choices w.r.t. the plan; we therefore compensate with hints, statistics and suggested partitioning and transformation options, passed down to the runtime engine in addition to the actual plan, compensate address this fact partially. This aspect of the design merits a separate discussion which is beyond the scope of this paper.

2.3 Schema Preprocessing

When the modified host DBMS passes the execution engine a plan to execute, this execution will not be applied merely to the DB columns themselves, as-is. Instead, the execution engine receives references to the results of some offline preprocessing of the schema. In a row-oriented DBMS such preprocessed data might be multiple indices into different tables; and MonetDB has its "imprints" structure [15]. Preprocessing can theoretically be quite extensive (and time-consuming); in some work on GPU acceleration, authors go as far as pre-joining tables or materializing full denormalizations. Also, the more auxiliary information one maintains, the less one can scale a DBMS while remaining entirely in-memory; but such economy of resources is beyond the scope of this work (especially since we do not use compression; see Sect. 6).

For our work with the TPC-H benchmark, our preprocessing adhered strictly to its rules and restrictions, i.e. we limited it to single columns of data, never involving information regarding multiple columns. Of course, the different choices of preprocessed data made available to a query processor muddy the waters to some extent when measuring and comparing performance, and this is especially true for comparisons with processing frameworks not bound by TPC-H restrictions (such as GPU-DB [23] or the recent results in [14]).

The data derived from each column and used in this work falls into one the following categories:

scalars: Data of the column's own type (e.g. minimum, maximum, median, mode), integral statistics (e.g. support size) and binary predicates (e.g. sorted/unsorted)

same-dimension auxiliary columns: Such as a sorted copy of a column, or a breakdown of date/time columns into their constituent subfields

support-dimension auxiliary columns: Essentially a small auxiliary table with one row per distinct value in the original column, containing the histogram, as well as minimum and maximum positions of incidence, for each value (i.e. a reverse-index for the column).

The host DBMS, MonetDB, is not made aware of this preprocessed data — nor does our framework use MonetDB's Imprints or any other such auxiliary data.

3 Making Execution Plans More Amenable to (GPU) Parallelism

Setting aside the specifics of our framework design, and how it differs from the host DBMS's, this paper's title begs the following question: Why is query plan optimization *particularly critical* for GPU execution performance?

The general importance of query optimization to processing performance is well-recognized [17, Chap. 7] and widely studied; Join order, nested query reformulation, intelligent estimation of intermediary result cardinality and so on. Our framework does not actually brave this important task: It does not try to second-guess most of the host DBMSes decisions; while this would probably be useful as well, the focus of this work is more lower-level. Namely, our optimizing transformations regard.

Implementation special-casing for generally-challenging computations using statistics & predicates obtained by preprocessing the schema (or in some rare cases at query runtime).

Representation format change including mostly two aspects of how data is represented: dense vs. sparse representations of subsets/subsequences (see Subsect. 3.1), and sortedness constraints (whether plan operations are required to produce sorted output, and whether they require their inputs to be sorted).

Missing implementation circumvention: Replacement of operations without GPU implementations by multi-node subgraphs with equivalent output.

Fusion of certain particularly-suitable consecutive operations. This is not the comprehensive fusion of multiple operations using compilation infrastructure used in HyPer [12] or Spark 2.0 Catalyst [1]; instead, we apply more complex fusion, implemented a-priori in CUDA code, which a compiler could *not* automatically derive.

Fission: Some plan operations have inherently multi-staged implementations (at least on a GPU); others can be semantically decomposed (e.g. in a reversal of the fusion described above). This can be reflected in the plan, allowing constituent parts or phases to be involved with other operations in the further application of transformation rules.

Cleanup when duplicate/inverse operations are left in the plan following other transformations, or when an operation's outputs are unused, etc.

These transformations are applied greedily — that is, no change is made to the plan unless it is certain to be positively beneficial (to the plan as a whole, individual operations may not be optimal). Having examined the various kinds of query plans that MonetDB generates, we formulated a number of transformation rules — limited to small subgraphs — which are likely to speed up execution. For each of these we formulated constraints on columns, intermediary buffers and operations involved, under which this likelihood of benefit becomes a certainty. These constraints are expressible in terms of the statistics and predicates we obtain regarding the data as part of the schema preprocessing described in

Subsect. 2.3. Of course, we strove to formulate rules with the weakest possible applicability constraints, to maximize variety and usefulness over multiple queries. Rules are applied repeatedly until a fixed point is reached, with the exception of an initial analytic phase. Thus our optimization of an execution plan is *rule-based*, and mostly *heuristic*.

It should also be noted our current set of rules is not very extensive. Even for the queries for which we present results, one could well conceive of additional rules applicable as-is (see the end of Subsect. 3.3 below), or additional auxiliary data (Bloom filters, Imprints, etc.) and new rules able to utilize it. Although we probably missed many opportunities for further optimization, this paucity of rules prevented us from facing the problem of inopportune choice of rule application order leading our framework away from better optimization routes.

The rest of this section is an elaboration on two of the aspects mentioned above, followed by a detailed example of how all aspects combine in the optimization for a single specific query.

3.1 Optimization Aspect: Subset/Sequence Representation

Consider the result of some predicate applied to a DB column. In MonetDB (v11.15.11) this result is sparse — a column of matching record indices — rather than a dense bit vector. Computing the former, a (serial) CPU core repeatedly appends matching indices to the output; but this does not parallelize very well, since the final location to write to for any individual element satisfying the predicate requires information regarding previous matches. *Some* parallelization is still possible here: For example, one may compute a prefix-sum of the number of elements passing the filter — and well-optimized prefix sum implementations on GPUs are available [9, 18] — but this is still much slower than element-wise bit-setting.

From a complexity-theoretical perspective, a sparse representation is certainly the appropriate choice: Further computation is linear, based on the length of the result, not of the original data. But in practice, we count bits: A record index is likely 4 or 8 bytes; and memory is typically read in units of a cache line (64 B on Intel Haswell, 32 B/128 B on nVIDIA Kepler & Maxwell). So only for *very* selective predicates does the benefit-in-principle actually manifest. A sequential-CPU-oriented DB might prefer the sparse representation earlier: It has fewer elements to perform writes for, i.e. less sequential work (ignoring caching at least); and presumably this is the case for MonetDB. A DBMS oriented for massive regular parallelism will opt for the dense representation in most cases.

Most existing GPU acceleration frameworks seem to resign themselves to respecting the DBMS' data-structure choices, and will compute this sparse result as best they can; after all, the plan uses this array of indices later on. But you can ask the question — does the plan really have to use it? As will be illustrated in Subsect. 3.3 below, this use is itself conditioned on this choice, which can be undone or overruled. When doing so, one often ends up avoiding some reordering of data, a costly effort in itself, and expanding the opportunities for using more parallel-efficient computational primitives. Last but not least, dense subset representation often lends itself to avoiding the need to produce sorted intermediary results (again, see below).

3.2 Optimization Aspect: Join Special-Casing

A general-case single-column inner Join in a (MonetDB-like) column-store takes as inputs two columns (the LHS and the RHS; assume they hold integral values). The result of the Join are two columns, LHS_{out} and RHS_{out}, whose length is the number of matching pairs; the tuple $(LHS_{out}[i], RHS_{out}[i])$ is the ith match found by the Join, so i may range from 0 to $|LHS \times RHS| - 1$ theoretically (and the output is sorted lexicographically).

Our framework observes the following noteworthy features for each column with respect to a Join operation (phrased in terms of the LHS below):

- Is this a column coming directly from the schema, or is it an intermediate result following other operations?
- Are the column values sorted? If so, do they appear consecutively with no gaps (i.e. $LHS[i + 1] = LHS[i] + 1$)?
- What are the minimum and maximum column values?
- What are the minimum and maximum multiplicities of individual values within the column?
- Is the other input column known to contain all values in this one?
- Is every value in the column known to have at least one match on the other side?
- Is the Join output only used to filter the input column?

After applying our preprocessing, whenever a query comes in we have most of this information readily available, without computing anything — using scalar values and predicates regarding individual columns, and the schema structure. Some of these statistics may not be available — minimum and maximum values, multiplicities for non-schema columns — and in some cases (see below) we may take the time to compute them. Now, here are several cases of Joins for which we had special Join implementations (each corresponding to combinations of the above criteria):

FK to dense PK: LHS: All values match. RHS: Dense.
Self-join of filtered schema column: LHS: All values match. RHS: Subset of a schema column, sorted, known max. multiplicity.
FK to small-support PK: LHS: All values match. RHS: max. multiplicity 1; LHS values are in the range $[v_{min}, v_{min}]$; there's sufficient memory for a bit vector of length $v_{max} - v_{min} + 1$.
RHS-Unique Join: LHS: No assumptions. RHS: max multiplicity 1.

For each of these special cases we have a corresponding transformation rule; and these rules are applied, when applicable, in the above order of priority, to all Join operations encountered in the execution plan. Some of these rules are replacements of the single Join operation DAG node with the appropriate special-case-Join node — for which we've written hand-optimized special-case implementations. In other rules, the Join is replaced with a small subgraph of non-Join computations (e.g. using original values instead of hash keys).

3.3   A Query Example: Optimizing TPC-H Q4 Execution

Typically, no single transformation rule mentioned above is sufficient to fundamentally change how a query is processed; it's rather a combination of rules which allows for more fundamental changes. We illustrate how the rules combine using the sequence of transformations our framework applies for TPC-H Q4. We consider the main part of the original plan, but for brevity, dropping the part retrieving a string column at the end.[1]

Figure 2 represents our initial derivation of a plan from the one obtained from MonetDB. Without going into detail, this involves removing some redundant/irrelevant MAL statements from MonetDB's own plan, and more importantly: Splitting up these operations into constituent parts, to the extent we have kernels for them — particularly when sparse/dense format changes are involved. Now, this can be considered a non-greedy transformation — as fusing these operations back causes a slowdown — which our subsequent repeated transformation process would not apply. However, this slowdown is usually marginal: It's a write an intermediary buffer to global memory by the first constituent operation, and a read of that buffer by the second. This opens up the possibility of some proper optimization (see below); and if any such non-trivial optimization can be applied, it will most likely compensate for the extra I/O. The diagram is a dataflow DAG, with source nodes being schema columns or constant values, and all other nodes being computational operations. The full plan for TPC-H Q4 has two sink nodes — for the order counts and priority string columns— but the part of the plan generating the latter has been removed to focus the example on the former. Also removed — for brevity and legibility — are the details of which edge targets which parameter of its destination operation. Table 2 describes the semantics of the operations used on the plan and its transformed versions.

Considering the operations appearing in the initial plan, in Fig. 2, one notices they produce mostly sorted sparse-representations (sorted indices into columns) intermediary columns; and that many of the operations require inputs of this kind. Our optimizer performs the following transformations; note that for some of these transformations there are requirements not represented in the diagrams, most frequently "no other outgoing edges" when removing operations:

1. **Subsequence semi-join special-casing:** Initially it seems we cannot get rid of the DenseToSparse operations. Consider, however, the use of the ORDERS table in the plan: The table is 'first' used is to Gather data for the Foreign

---

[1] Q4 was chosen for this example for being a query with a short plan with few operations, but involving more than one table.

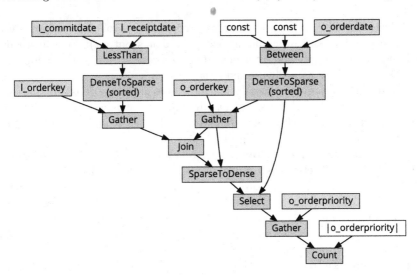

Fig. 2. The initial execution plan for Q4 (string output column clipped)

Table 2. TPC-H Q4 execution plan operation semantics

Operation	Column inputs	Output description
Select	data D bit vector F	Values in D whose corresponding bit in F is set
Gather	data D indices I	$ouput[i] = D[I[i]]$
Scatter Disjunction	data D indices I zero-initialized T	$T[I[i]] = D[i]$
DenseToSparse	bit vector D	The indices of all bits set in D
DenseToSparse	indices I	A bit vector with bit i set iff $i \in I$
LessThan, BitwiseAnd	L, R (of same type)	Elementwise binary operations
Between	input X	A bit vector with bit i set iff $c_1 \leq X[i] < c_2$
Join	L, R (of same type)	all pairs (i, j) such that $L[i] = R[j]$, in the form of columns of corresponding i's and j's
Count	indices I	A histogram of I, where the bins are $0 \ldots m$ for a known maximum value m

Key – Primary Key Join. The combination of DenseToSparse and Gather admits an optimization in itself (see below); but, there is a far more beneficial transformation possible here: The supposedly-general-case Join is actually made in the context of a Semi-join, a filtering of the ORDERS table. This can be inferred locally (seeing how the o_orderdate DenseToSparse output is used both in the Join and immediately with the Join's output); Now, instead of Join'ing, we can apply the filter on a dense representation in the value space of {1|o}_orderkey as a BitwiseAnd (Fig. 3).

2. **Cleanup I:** The previous transformation leaves us with a dense-to-sparse-to-dense conversion sequence; we can't eliminate it entirely, since the intermediate sparse result is still in use, but we may bypass it and thus discard one of its constituent operations (Fig. 4).

3. **Pushing DenseToSparse down:** The remaining use of the sparse ORDERS filter results is in Selecting from the semi-join results, which themselves are in the form of a dense subsequence representation due to transformation 1. The DenseToSparse can therefore be "pushed down" past the Select, which becomes a bitwise AND to preserve its semantics (Fig. 5).

4. **Cleanup II:** We now have an artifact due to previous transformations: redundant BitwiseAnd operations; we remove one of them (Fig. 6).

5. **Fusing DenseToSparse and Gather:** We note that the action of Select can be described as converting a bit vector input into a sparse representation, then replacing the indices with actual data using a Gather; and that if the DenseToSparse has sorted output, so will the Select. In the other direction, these two operations can be fused together into a Select (Fig. 7); we now do so for both our DenseToSparse's.

6. **Fusing Select and SparseToDense:** These two operations may be fused into a ScatterDisjunction (Fig. 8), similarly to transformation 5. This transformation has an attractive side-effect: We are now rid of the sortedness constraints for one of the filters, as its sorted (sparse) results are no longer used anywhere.

7. **Dropping last sortedness constraint:** The output of the remaining Select operation (of the created earlier by fusions), is only used by a Count operation. While Count might benefit from its input being sorted — it certainly doesn't require sortedness (and in this specific case the benefit would be marginal). Thus we have pushed the sortedness requirement further enough down the plan DAG to a point where it can be simply discarded (Fig. 9).

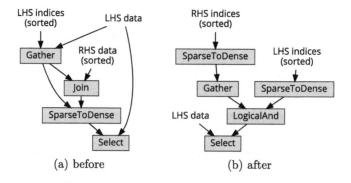

(a) before   (b) after

Fig. 3. TPC-H Q4 Transformation 1

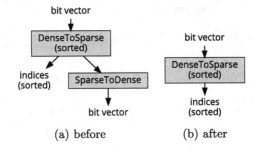

Fig. 4. TPC-H Q4 Transformation 2

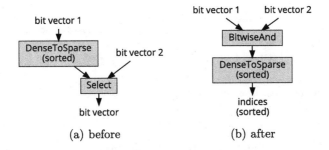

Fig. 5. TPC-H Q4 Transformation 3

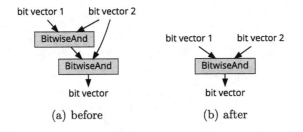

Fig. 6. TPC-H Q4 Transformation 4

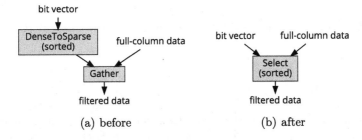

Fig. 7. TPC-H Q4 Transformation 5 (applied twice)

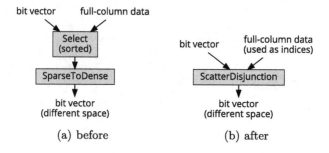

Fig. 8. TPC-H Q4 Transformation 6

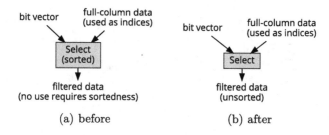

Fig. 9. TPC-H Q4 Transformation 7

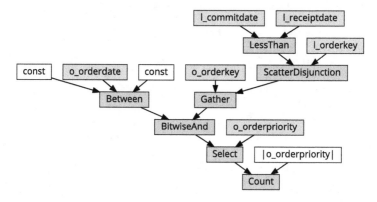

Fig. 10. Final execution plan for Q4 (string output column clipped) (Color figure online)

The end result is the pleasing, relatively parallelism-friendly execution plan in Fig. 10; the kernels corresponding to each of the green nodes would now gets scheduled to execute on the GPU. However, on closer inspection we note that even further optimization of the plan is possible: ScatterDisjunction can be avoided in favor of Gathering after applying a fixed offset to the indices, and

Select can be avoided altogether in favor of a predicated Count; this would make the plan embarrassingly parallel except for the final aggregation — so much so that it might theoretically be compiled into a single GPU kernel. However, these additional optimizations were not supported by our framework when the experimental results (Sect. 4) were obtained.

4   Experimental Results

4.1   Test Platform, Protocol and Procedures

Results were all obtained using a 2-socket machine, with 2 Intel Xeon E5-2690 CPUs (8-core each) clocked 2.9 GHz. Each socket had its won independent PCIe 3 bus, through which it was connected to a GeForce GTX 780 Ti card (MSI TwinFrozer, clocked at 875 MHz). The machine ran Kubuntu GNU/Linux 14.04, CUDA 7.0 RC and nVIDIA driver v346.29. The reference DBMS was an unaltered version of MonetDB [11] v11.15.11 (by now not the latest version), using 32 threads.

We tested using queries from the TPC-H benchmark [20]: Q1, Q4, Q9 and Q21 (ranging from simple to complex). This limitation is the result of a constrained amount of time and effort to put into this proof-of-concept — which is not a full-fledged query processor. We did not send random queries to the host DBMS repeatedly over a prolonged period of time (as in the actual TPC-H procedure); rather, we tested individual queries separately on the cold DBMS, immediately after it was loaded. Timing figures are the mean over 3 runs, in milliseconds. The database Scale Factor (SF) is 1 unless otherwise stated.

4.2   TPC-H Query Processing Time Comparison

A 'bottom line' of our results appears in Table 3: Execution time for the final query plan for all of our benchmarked queries. A result for CPU execution of Q21 is missing as it requires a yet-unimplemented feature of our subgraph partitioning feature; and without it, performance is dismal (as our multi-threaded execution depends on subgraph partition).

Table 3. Final plan execution times (SF 1 including I/O)

TPC-H query	Q1	Q4	Q9	Q21
MonetDB	159.4 ms	54.0 ms	125.9 ms	217.5 ms
MonetDB/AXE CPU	41.9 ms	24.5 ms	31.1 ms	
MonetDB/AXE GPU	25.8 ms	18.4 ms	21.5 ms	44.0 ms

The speedup over MonetDB execution ranges from 2.9 to 6.8; in a more apples-to-apples comparison — the same modified plan on a CPU rather than a GPU — the speedup factor ranges from 1.3 to 1.6. This too should be taken with a large grain of salt, since the comparison is between two CPUs "against" just one GPU. The more important figure is the GPU plan execution time itself.

The results charted in Table 3 do not include the time spent by MonetDB or our framework on parsing the query and preparing the plan; Fig. 11 adds this information, as part of a breakdown of the overall query processing time into (mostly-consecutive) phases.

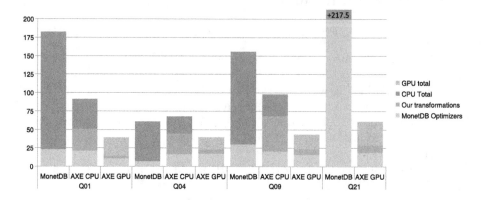

Fig. 11. Processing time breakdown (SF 1); clipped at 250 ms

One obvious problem is the large amounts of time spent before query execution even begins. This is particularly bad in our CPU-only configuration, which is unfortunately inefficient in transforming the plan (it performs a 32-way partitioning of the execution graph, in an unoptimized fashion; and this takes more time than all other transformations combined). MonetDB also seems to suffer from a similar phenomenon when adapting a complex execution plan such as Q21 to accommodate many threads. Such deficiencies can be mostly be done away with by straightforward optimization of our code (as opposed to optimizing the execution plan); we simply lacked the time to do so before our work needed to be wrapped up for publication.

Another issue noticeable in the chart is the 'GPU idle overhead', comprising an initial period before the GPU receives any data, and a final period after it has sent back all of its results. Some of this time is taken up by subgraph partition splitters and joiners; some is due to implementation artifacts which can probably be optimized away; and some of if it are some final operations on a tiny amount of data, which are not scheduled to run on the GPU (but possibly could have).

4.3   GPU Activity Breakdown

Let us dig into the GPUs' activity with Fig. 12, which breaks the GPU time down into the activities of I/O (over PCI/e) and Compute.

This illustrates very clearly what is the "bane" of discrete GPU; Most of the time is spent on nothing but I/O over the PCIe bus. This point is discussed

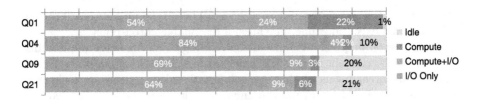

Fig. 12. GPU time breakdown (single-GPU, SF 1)

in Sect. 6 below. An interesting question is how much would this disappear in a multi-query situation, where contention over the GPU's and PCIe bus would be high.

Note that Fig. 12 shows some of the GPU time as entirely idle; this is an artifact of our implementation, due to over-conservative stream synchronization, and can be reduced to a negligible level with some programming effort, but no degradation of performance elsewhere.

Going another level deeper, let us consider the breakdown the GPU's Compute activity, presented in Fig. 13. A query execution run involves a few dozens of technically distinct kernels, but for clarity of presentation we place them in several groups (e.g. elementwise arithmetic of all data types), and limit ourselves

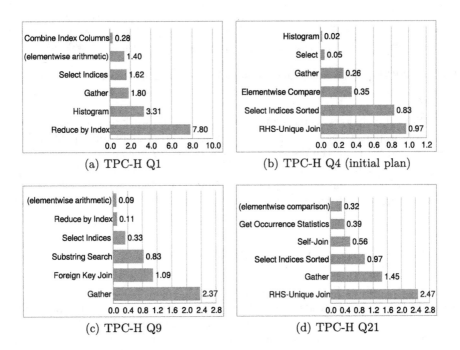

Fig. 13. Top time-consuming operations (msec)

to the top six time consumers for each query. These take up between 92% and 98.8% of kernel execution time, making 6 a reasonable cutoff point.

Space constraints preclude a discussion relating these time consumption distributions to the relevant queries. It is the authors' belief that, in general, such query-specific breakdowns of time by computational operation are lacking in many papers on DBMS performance enhancements, especially those involving GPUs — while they are an important guide for the researcher or engineer regarding what merits further optimization (or rather, circumvention).

4.4   Effects of Increasing Database Size

We tested our frameworks with scale factors 1–8 (1 GB–8 GB total size); these are not so high by today's standards, but our framework lacks a GPU memory management mechanism, and our GPU's available memory was just 3 GB. Fortunately, the sample points of SF 1,2,4,8 already allow some visualization of trends as the DB scales, in Fig. 14.

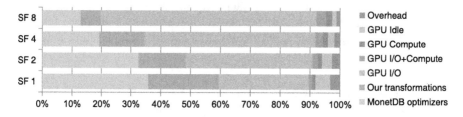

Fig. 14. TPC-H Q4 processing time breakdown with increasing DB size, GPU execution

Besides the obvious decrease in weight of the initial work on the plan relative execution proper, we note a further increase in the fraction of time spent on I/O only, i.e. the "bane of the discrete GPU" from Fig. 12 becomes even more pronounced. On the other hand, we note an improvement in Compute-I/O overlap, as deeper computation nodes in the execution DAG tend to scale sub-linearly in their duration with DB size. Note we have taken TPC-H Q4 as the example, but the trends are similar in the other three queries.

5   Comparison with Other Work

Unfortunately, most frameworks using GPUs for query processing presented so far are not pairwise-comparable in performance: For some, no benchmark results are presented; others focus on transactions rather than analytics; some use hardware for which comparison is difficult; and some alter the TPC-H schema significantly (e.g. by denormalization). Most work surveyed in [4] falls into one of those categories (and there's *GPU-DB* [23], which uses a different benchmark — SSB rather than TPC-H). The *design* of these various frameworks is interesting to compare with, however, as some of them exhibit desirable features missing in this work (and vice-versa); unfortunately, space constraints preclude this.

A GPU-featuring processing framework which is close-to comparable is the MonetDB-based *Ocelot* [6]: It was benchmarked with a "hot cache", i.e. much of the data already in GPU memory [6, Sect. 5.3]; with an older GPU (GeForce GTX 460); and with a focus on portable implementation rather than maximum performance. Still, the Ocelot on-GPU time of TPC-H queries 1, 4 and 21 is 200, 30 and 300 ms respectively (for SF1), compared to our 16.8, 4.7 and 9.6 ms. We believe this factor of 7-30x in execution speed is mostly the result of Ocelot adhering closely to MonetDB's CPU-oriented execution plan on the GPU as well.

The few remaining frameworks, which *are* possible to compare against, were executed on hosts DBMSs that were rather slow to begin with. The interesting example in this category is the *Red Fox* framework [21]: Its Breß-et-al classification is similar to ours; it has a similar IR–Compilation–Second-IR chain design, and its motivation also goes beyond the execution of SQL query plans (see [21, Sect. 4.3]; again, we skip a more in-depth comparison of design features). Red Fox is grafted onto LogicBlox [8] as its host DBMS; comparing [21, Table 3] with Table 3, we note that MonetDB is 5.3-14.7x faster than the unmodified Log-icBlox[2]. This seems to be a foil for Red Fox: Despite its solid speedup over its reference (7x average), it still only gets close to MonetDB speed, and is 5-12x slower than our framework on the four queries. One can also get a rough notion of how the execution plans differ by comparing the breakdown of execution time by computational operation: [21, Fig. 10] compared to Fig. 13 above.

Another example is Galactica [22]: Based on PostgreSQL, it also does not speed up execution to Monet-level speed, and is an order-of-magnitude slower than our framework (compare [22, Sect. 3.1.3] with Table 3 above).

Finally, a GPU-utilizing query processor named GPL (for "GPU Pipelining") has been described in the very-recently published [13] by Johns et alia. They take up the challenge of execution in chunks (a.k.a. tiles, or tablets), a concept first explored with Viriginian [2]. This reduces the size of materialized intermediary results and the overhead of communicating them via global memory. GPL also utilizes pipelining support in OpenCL 2.x, a theoretically promising approach. The paper does not report results for any TPC-H query with which we had tested, except Q9, and it does not make absolute results available for execution on a discrete GPU — making a proper, explicit comparison difficult. Still, the performance comparison it makes vis-a-vis Ocelot [13, Figs. 21 and 22] shows a speedup of up to 2.5x, and typically under 1.5x. It thus seems to be the case that this new query processor is still significantly slower than the one presented in this work (and typically slower on an nVIDIA K40 than MonetDB on a typical dual-socket Xeon system).

---

[2] LogicBlox figures normalized by 0.85 to account for HW differences.

6   Discussion and Further Performance Enhancement

Our framework does not process queries quickly; and it is certainly not a good measure of the potential for processing performance with a GPU. This much is evident merely from observing how most of our execution time is spent idly waiting for I/O over PCIe. Thus, instead of resolving the shortcoming of discrete GPUs our work has merely masked it with performance improvements elsewhere. This is an unintended and somewhat ironic outcome: During the initial phases of our work, the picture was the exact opposite: 80%–90% of the time was being spent on GPU Compute. As we were laboring on providing the GPU with a better-parallelizable plan and data that is more easily accessible in parallel (as well as improving some of naive kernel implementations), total Compute time decreased further and further, eventually losing its dominance — so that squeezing it even more no would no longer yield much benefit. This phenomenon was discussed in [23], with the metaphor of a changing "balance of Yin and Yang".

Having put much effort into suppressing the "Yang" (improving GPU Compute time), three actions now come to mind for curbing the effects of the "Yin" (PCIe transfer):

I/O-Compute overlap via mapped memory: GPUs offer the feature of host-device-mapped memory, which triggers PCIe transactions on memory reads. Using these can allow computation on the GPU to begin immediately, with data transferred on on-demand; this approach is taken in [23] (although it does not present an I/O-Compute breakdown). It does have several drawbacks, however (less cache-friendly; PCIe transaction overhead; potential underuse of the bus).

I/O-Compute overlap via 'chunk-at-a-time' execution: Several DBMSes process data at the resolution of a column/table chunk rather than an operator-at-a-time on entire columns. In the CPU world this is a key feature of Actian Vector [24] (although more for the reason of fitting data in the CPU's cache). With regard to GPU-utilizing query processing frameworks, Virginian [3,4] has employed it, but a more in-depth exploration of its merit and a case for its significance is the recent [13]. Considering our own results, even rough chunks of size, say, 1MB-4MB should already cut most of the initial idle period of the GPU waiting for data to arrive with nothing to work on. Chunk-at-a-time execution would also enable the use of chunk-level meta-data, potentially allowing a query processor to filter-out entire chunks rather than sending them to the GPU.

A refined variation of this approach is GPU pipelining, as in [13] (see Sect. 5). While not yet available in CUDA, it could theoretically allow for avoiding not only the initial idle time, but also much of the overhead inherent in manipulating chunks.

Data compression: In most real-world scenarios column data has many regularities and correlations, lower effective domain etc. — making it very amenable to compression; and this is true even for the somewhat artificial example of the TPC-H. Also, it just so happens we have a mostly-idle ALU-rich computational device to use for decompression on the receiving end. While the other two methods are limited in benefit by the amount of Compute Time (100% overlap), compression is limited the information inherent in the data and the GPU's ability to decompress effectively. Of course, such computation will itself contend with actual query operation application, so a different balance will need to be struck.

A fourth option we could have listed is using *bit weaving*, transferring columns one bit at a time; but we are skeptical of the utility in this approach, among other reasons because most of its potential benefit is subsumed by compressing the data.

Another important challenge in evaluating GPU-accelerated query processors is the scaling of benchmark schema. With only 1 GB of data overall, some queries take as little as 3 ms or less of actual computation time — with results potentially skewed by some minor inefficiency here or there. A larger scale also forces the more realistic setting of inability to hold all data in GPU memory, being limited on discrete GPUs compared to main system memory. For our framework, implementation of either *memory management* would obviously allow scaling beyond the equivalent of scale factor 10 for TPC-H queries, with no significant cost — even with 'operator-at-a-time' execution. The 'chunk-at-a-time' approach, mentioned above, automatically enables scaling to handle much larger benchmark data.

References

1. Armbrust, M., Xin, R.S., Lian, C., Huai, Y., Liu, D., Bradley, J.K., Meng, X., Kaftan, T., Franklin, M.J., Ghodsi, A., Zaharia, M.: Spark SQL: relational data processing in spark. In: Proceedings of the SIGMOD, SIGMOD 2015, pp. 1383–1394. ACM (2015)
2. Bakkum, P., Chakradhar, S.: Efficient data management for GPU databases. NEC Laboratories America, Princeton, NJ, Technical report (2012)
3. Bakkum, P., Chakradhar, S.: Efficient data management for GPU databases. NEC Laboratories America, Princeton, NJ, Technical report [2]
4. Breß, S., Heimel, M., Siegmund, N., Bellatreche, L., Saake, G.: GPU-accelerated database systems: survey and open challenges. In: Proceedings of BigDataScience. ACM/IEEE (2014)
5. He, B., Lu, M., Yang, K., Fang, R., Govindaraju, N.K., Luo, Q., Sander, P.V.: Relational query coprocessing on graphics processors. Trans. DB Sys. **34**(4), 21:1–21:39 (2009)
6. Heimel, M., Saecker, M., Pirk, H., Manegold, S., Markl, V.: Hardware-oblivious parallelism for in-memory column-stores. In: Proceedings of VLDB, vol. 9, pp. 709–720 (2013)
7. Kemper, A., Neumann, T., Garching, D.: HyPer: A hybrid OLTP&OLAP main memory database system based on virtual memory snapshots. In: Proceedings of ICDE (2011)
8. http://www.logicblox.com/
9. Luitjens, J.: Faster parallel reductions on Kepler (2014). http://devblogs.nvidia.com/parallelforall/faster-parallel-reductions-kepler/

10. Manegold, S., Kersten, M., Boncz, P.: Database architecture evolution: mammals flourished long before dinosaurs became extinct. Proc. VLDB **2**(2), 1648–1653 (2009)
11. MonetDB webpage. http://www.monetdb.org
12. Neumann, T.: Efficiently compiling efficient query plans for modern hardware. Proc. VLDB **4**(9), 539–550 (2011)
13. Paul, J., He, J., He, B.: GPL: A GPU-based pipelined query processing engine. In: Proceedings of SIGMOD. ACM (2016)
14. Power, J., Li, Y., Hill, M.D., Patel, J.M., Wood, D.A.: Toward GPUs being mainstream in analytic processing: an initial argument using simple scan-aggregate queries. In: Proceedings of DaMoN, p. 11. ACM (2015)
15. Sidirourgos, L., Kersten, M.: Column imprints: a secondary index structure. In: Proceedings of SIGMOD, pp. 893–904. ACM (2013)
16. Sitaridi, E.A., Ross, K.A.: GPU-accelerated string matching for database applications. J. VLDB, 1–22 (2015)
17. Stonebraker, M., Hellerstein, J., Bailis, P.: Readings in Database Systems (The Red Book), 5th edn (2015). http://www.redbook.io/
18. The CUB library. http://nvlabs.github.io/cub/
19. https://www.monetdb.org/Documentation/Manuals/MonetDB/MALreference
20. The TPC Council: TPC Benchmark H (rev 2.17.1) (2014). http://www.tpc.org/tpch
21. Wu, H., Diamos, G., Sheard, T., Aref, M., Baxter, S., Garland, M., Yalamanchili, S.: Red fox: an execution environment for relational query processing on GPUs. In: Proceedings of CGO, p. 44. ACM (2014)
22. Yong, K.K., Karuppiah, E.K., See, S.: Galactica: A GPU parallelized database accelerator. In: Proceedings of BigDataScience. ACM/IEEE (2014)
23. Yuan, Y., Lee, R., Zhang, X.: The Yin and Yang of processing data warehousing queries on GPU devices. Proc. VLDB **6**(10), 817–828 (2013)
24. Zukowski, M., Boncz, P.: Vectorwise: beyond column stores. IEEE Data Eng. Bull. **35**(1), 21–27 (2012)

To Copy or Not to Copy: Making In-Memory Databases Fast on Modern NICs

Aniraj Kesavan[✉], Robert Ricci, and Ryan Stutsman

University of Utah School of Computing, Salt Lake City, USA
{aniraj,ricci,stutsman}@cs.utah.edu

Abstract. When databases resided primarily on disks, the problem of data layout was focused on structures that enabled efficient reads and writes from that medium, as well the as effective use of main memory as a cache. With in-memory databases, this part of the I/O problem is largely gone, but that does not mean that I/O considerations can be completely ignored. We argue for the importance of considering the "other" side of the I/O equation—network communication with clients—when designing in-memory databases.

Modern NICs include a number of optimizations intended to improve I/O performance, including kernel bypass, zero-copy and scatter-gather DMA. Applied carefully, these features can reduce the involvement of the CPU in network transfers and can save memory bandwidth. However, our experiments show that some optimizations do not always provide a benefit in a database context, and using them can be tricky, as they affect strategies for processing updates and managing data lifetimes. In this paper, we explore the application of zero-copy NIC DMA to in-memory databases, and we explore how the NIC can influence and explicitly leverage data layout and concurrency control. We apply these results to the Bw-Tree structure by proposing a client-assisted design for transmitting large range scan results. Overall, the approach boosts throughput by 1.7× and reduces CPU overhead by 75% compared to simple zero-copy DMA.

1 Introduction

For decades, the performance characteristics of storage devices have dominated thinking in database design and implementation. From data layout to concurrency control, to recovery, to threading model, disks touch every aspect of database design. In-memory databases effectively eliminate disk I/O as a concern, and these systems now execute millions of operations per second, sometimes with near-microsecond latencies. It is tempting to believe that database I/O is solved; however, another device now dictates performance: the network interface (NIC).

As the primary I/O device in modern databases, NICs' performance characteristics should now be taken into consideration from the start in database designs. However, modern network cards have grown incredibly complex, partly

© Springer International Publishing AG 2017
S. Blanas et al. (Eds.): ADMS 2016/IMDM 2016, LNCS 10195, pp. 79–94, 2017.
DOI: 10.1007/978-3-319-56111-0_5

in response to demands for high throughput and low latency. Their complexity makes understanding them difficult, and it makes designing software to take advantage of them even harder. To design for NICs effectively, database engineers must understand their characteristics.

Database designers encounter a number of trade-offs when trying to use the NIC effectively. For example, when can the NIC efficiently transmit data directly from database records via direct memory access (DMA)? Should records be pre-materialized in a way that makes transmission efficient? Or can the NIC efficiently assemble scattered data on-the-fly? Does concurrent access to data records by the NIC complicate memory management? To answer these questions, and to understand how NICs can impact database design, we profiled a modern kernel-bypass capable NIC with remote direct memory access (RDMA) with specific attention to large transfers and query responses. This paper details our findings and makes several concrete suggestions on how NICs might influence data layout and concurrency control.

Specifically, we have found three factors that make it especially challenging to design NIC-friendly database engines:

- *Zero-copy* DMA engines reduce server load for transferring large data blocks, but large, static blocks are uncommon for in-memory databases, where records can be small and update rates can be high.
- The performance gains from zero-copy DMA do not generalize to *finer-grained objects* for two reasons: (1) transmit descriptors grow linearly in the number of records; (2) NIC hardware limits descriptor length, limiting speed for small records. Despite this, we find that zero-copy can make sense for small objects under certain conditions, such as small "add-ons" to larger transmissions.
- Zero-copy introduces complications for *locking and object lifetime*, as objects must remain in memory and must be unchanged for the life of the DMA operation (which includes transmission time).

These factors make advanced DMA difficult to use effectively. In fact, we find that conventional *copy-out* that assembles responses in transmit buffers has some advantages over zero-copy transmission. Most surprisingly, explicit copy-out can outperform zero-copy in transmit throughput even for "heavy" responses like large range query results from secondary indexes. Explicit copy-out does use more CPU and memory bandwidth: our experiments show it adds a modest 5% to CPU load, but more significantly, consumes up to one-third of the server's total memory bandwidth. In-memory databases are often capacity bound [4], not CPU or memory bandwidth bound; this may make copy-out preferable for some workloads, especially since the relative cost is likely to decrease over time.

To provide a concrete illustration of these issues, we investigate in the context of the Bw-Tree, an index whose properties give it flexibility in how it interacts with the NIC. Ultimately, we find that zero-copy can be a benefit. However, for significant gains, data layout has to be adjusted to suit the NIC, and the costs of maintaining that layout must be considered against the NIC performance benefits. Our findings yield a preliminary design for efficient transmission of heavy range query results that improves throughput by 1.7× (from 3.4 GB/s to

5.7 GB/s) and reduces CPU overhead by 75% compared to fully scattered zero-copy by relaxing the structure of the results that clients receive. We start with an overview of related work in this space, then describe a modern kernel-bypass NIC and the Bw-Tree. We continue with a set of microbenchmarks and draw conclusions for data structure/networking layer co-design.

2   Motivation and Related Work

Our analysis is inspired by in-memory database work that focuses on lock-freedom and/or no-update-in-place [5,10–13]. The unique features of these structures make them well positioned to leverage the sophisticated userlevel DMA capabilities of modern networking hardware (we explore the reasons for this in Sect. 4). A major goal of our work is to help in tuning these structures for low-overhead, high-throughput network transmission.

Several efforts are now underway to use userlevel NIC access and/or RDMA as a fabric for high-performance distributed databases [6,7,17,19,20]. Our findings should also aid in their design, especially those that build on the abstraction of a network-attached atomic record store [11,15].

Small, fixed-size request/response cycles have been optimized by existing research [6,8,9,14,17], but the efficient transmission of larger responses like range query results or data migrations has been less well studied. Studies focused on large transmissions have so far been limited to relatively static block-oriented data. Our work focuses on optimizing transmission of large and complex query results, which differs from these two categories. Database queries do access and transmit many fine-grained records, but the transmissions can be comprised of many records sent together. This makes the transmissions large like block data, but the contents are much more dynamic. This is because the set of records returned varies, and because the records themselves may be rapidly updated.

A complementary study by Kalia, Kaminsky, and Andersen [9] provides an analysis of host interaction with Mellanox Infiniband network adapters, and they extract rules of thumb to help developers get the best performance from the hardware. The low-level nature of their analysis is especially suited for optimizing dispatch-heavy workloads with a high-volume of small request-response operations. Our focus is on operations that require heavy responses where the precise content of the response cannot be anticipated or is under heavy mutation.

3   User-Level NIC Access

NICs have been rapidly adding features in the past decade in response to the demands of data center, cloud, and HPC networking. Direct application access to the NIC, or *kernel bypass*, is now available from several commodity NIC vendors [1,2], along with a myriad of offload and packet steering features to reduce CPU and message dispatch overheads. Kernel bypass allows an application to send and receive data without OS involvement. This results in several efficiency

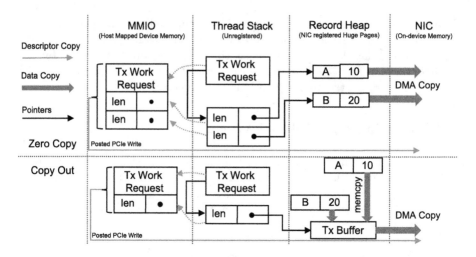

Fig. 1. Key structures involved in transmission for both zero-copy and copy-out. With zero-copy, transmit descriptors list several chunks of data for the NIC to DMA. With copy-out, all data to be transmitted is first explicitly copied into a transmit buffer by the host CPU; then, a transmit descriptor is posted that references just the transmit buffer rather than the original source data. (Color figure online)

gains. Latency is improved; in many cases kernel and syscall time is the dominant factor in round-trip time [17]. It can also improve throughput while reducing host load. One key feature is that the NIC can directly transmit application data rather than copying data from userspace to kernel buffers; this is called "zero copy". (Despite the colloquial zero-copy name, the NIC must still copy the data via DMA to on-device buffers and "copy" those bits onto the network cable.)

More interestingly, zero-copy isn't constrained to sending simple contiguous buffers. Because zero-copy already relies on the NIC's DMA capabilities, the application can provide a *gather list* to the NIC of chunks of data to be transmitted. The NIC assembles the chunks on-the-fly as it DMAs the data from host memory into NIC buffers. The rearrangement of the data happens "for free", since the NIC must perform DMA to get the data. This makes zero-copy especially promising for applications like databases where responses can be made up of near arbitrary arrangements of small or even variable size records.

Figure 1 details how the application interacts with a Mellanox ConnectX3, a modern 56 Gbps NIC that uses kernel bypass. Both zero-copy and the traditional copy-out approaches to transmission are shown. In both cases the same three key data structures are involved. The first important structure is the data to be transmitted, which lives in heap memory. For zero-copy, the memory where the records live must first be registered with the NIC. Registration informs the NIC of the virtual-to-physical mapping of the heap pages. This is required because the NIC must perform virtual-to-physical address translation since the OS is not involved during transmission and the application has no access to its own page tables. Registration is done at startup and is often done with physical memory backed by 1 GB hugepages to minimize on-NIC address translation costs.

The second key structure is the descriptor that a thread must construct to issue a transmission. With Mellanox NICs, a thread creates a work request and a gather list on its stack. The work request indicates that the requested operation is a transmission, and the gather list is a contiguous list of base-bound pairs that indicate what data should be transmitted by the NIC (and hence DMAed). For zero-copy, the gather list is as long as the number of chunks that the host would like to transmit, up to a small limit. The NICs we use support posting up to 32 chunks per transmit operation. Later, we find that this small limit bottlenecks NIC transmit performance when chunks are small and numerous (Sect. 5.1).

The key difference between zero-copy and copy-out is shown with the wide, red arrows in Fig. 1. Copy-out works much like conventional kernel-based networking stacks: chunks of data are first copied into a single transmit buffer in host memory. Then, a simple, single-entry descriptor is posted to the NIC that DMAs the transmit buffer to an on-device buffer for transmission. As a result, copy-out requires an extra and explicit copy of the data, which is made by the host CPU. Making the copy uses host CPU cycles, consumes memory bandwidth, and is pure overhead. Surprisingly, though, copy-out has advantages including better performance when records are small and scattered. In those cases, complex gather descriptors bottleneck the NIC, and using the host CPU to pre-assemble the responses can improve performance.

The final important structure is the control interface between the NIC and the host CPU. When the NIC is initially set up by the application, a region of the NIC's memory is mapped into the application's virtual address space. The NIC polls this region, and the host writes new descriptors to it from the thread's stack to issue operations. The region is mapped as write-combining; filling a cacheline in the region generates a cacheline-sized PCIe message to the NIC. The NIC receives it, and it issues DMA operations to begin collecting the data listed in the descriptor. The PCIe messages are posted writes, which means they are asynchronous from the CPU's perspective. Even though PCIe latencies are much higher than DRAM access, the CPU doesn't stall when posting descriptors, so the exchange is very low overhead.

4   Bw-Tree: Lock-Free Indexing

To show how these NIC features can be applied to in-memory database systems, we now examine a data structure that is well-positioned to take advantage of them. The Bw-Tree [13] is an atomic record store designed for extreme concurrency. It is an ordered index that supports basic record create, update, and delete (CRUD) operations in addition to search and range scans. It is fully lock-free and non-blocking, and is optimized for modern multicore workloads. It can store to flash, but is also intended for in-memory workloads; it serves as the ordered secondary index structure for in-memory SQL Server Hekaton [5] engine.

In many ways, the Bw-Tree is a conventional paged B-link tree, but it also has unique characteristics that interact with network-layer design choices.

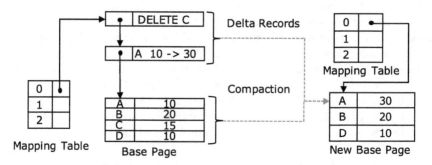

Fig. 2. The Bw-Tree avoids update-in-place by creating delta records "off to the side" that describe a logical modification to a page. Delta records are prefixed to a chain ultimately attached to a base page. When delta chains grow long they are compacted together with the base page to create a new base page.

Its lock-freedom, its elimination of update-in-place, and its lazily consolidation of updated records in virtual memory give it tremendous flexibility in how query results are transmitted by the NIC.

Records may be embedded within leaf pages, or the leaf pages may only contain pointers to data records. When used as a secondary index, typically leaf pages would contain pointers, since otherwise each record would have to be materialized twice and the copies would need to be kept consistent.

The key challenge in a lock-free structure is providing atomic reads, updates, inserts, and deletes without ever being able to quiesce ongoing operations (not even on portions of the tree). Bw-Tree solves this problem by eliminating update-in-place. All mutations are written to newly allocated memory, then the changes are installed with a single atomic compare-and-swap instruction that publishes the change. Figure 2 shows how this works. All references to pages are translated through a mapping table that maps page numbers to virtual addresses. This allows pages to be relocated in memory, and it allows the contents of a page to swapped with a single atomic compare-and-swap (CAS) operation.

One of the key innovations of the Bw-Tree is its use of *delta records*, which make updates inexpensive. Delta records allow the Bw-Tree to logically modify the contents of an existing page without blocking concurrent page readers, without atomicity issues, and without recopying the entire contents of the page for each update. Whenever a mutation is made to a page, a small record is allocated, and the logical operation is recorded within this delta record. The delta record contains a pointer to the page that it logically modifies. It is then atomically installed by performing a CAS operation on the mapping table that re-points the virtual address for a particular page number to the address of the delta record.

Some threads already reading the original page contents may not see the update, but all future operations on the Bw-Tree that access that page will see the delta record. As readers traverse the tree, they consider the base pages to be logically augmented by their delta records. Delta records can be chained together up to a configurable length. When the chain becomes too long, a new base page is formed that combines the original base page contents with the updates from the deltas. The new page is swapped-in the same way as other updates.

Read operations that run concurrent to update operations can observe superseded pages and delta records, so their garbage collection must be deferred. To solve this, each thread that accesses the tree and each unlinked object is associated with a current *epoch*. The global epoch is periodically incremented. Memory for an unlinked object can be recycled when no thread belongs to its epoch or any earlier epoch. The epoch mechanism gives operations consistent reads of the tree, even while concurrent updates are ongoing. However, there is a cost; if operations take a long time they remain active within their epoch and prevent reclamation of memory that has been unlinked from the data structure.

4.1   NIC Implications for Bw-Tree

Lock-freedom has major implications on the in-memory layout of the Bw-Tree. Most importantly, readers (such as the NIC DMA engine) can collect a consistent view of the tree without interference from writers, and holding that view consistent cannot stall concurrent readers or writers to the tree. This natural record stability fits with the zero-copy capabilities of modern NICs; because the NIC's DMA engine is oblivious to any locks in the database engine, structures requiring locking for updates would have to consider the NIC to have a non-preemtible read lock for the entire memory region until the DMA completes. Instead of copying records "out" of the data structure for transmission, records can be accessed directly by the NIC. Eliminating the explicit copy of the records into transmit buffers can save database server CPU and memory bandwidth.

Page consolidation can also benefit the NIC and improve performance. Records in the Bw-Tree are opportunistically packed into contiguous pages in virtual memory, but the view of a page is often augmented with (potentially many) small delta records that are scattered throughout memory. A database might save CPU and memory bandwidth by more aggressively deferring or even eliminating consolidation of records into contiguous regions of memory or pages. We show in Sect. 5.4 that highly discontinuous data can slow transmission throughput but that aggressive consolidation is inefficient; delta records can dramatically reduce consolidation overheads while keeping records sufficiently contiguous to make the NIC more efficient.

Overall, we seek to answer these key questions:

- When should records be transmitted directly from a Bw-Tree? Are there cases where explicitly copying records into a transmit buffer is preferable to gather DMA operations?
- How aggressive should a Bw-Tree be in consolidating records to benefit individual clients and to minimize database server load?
- How does zero-copy impact state reclamation in the Bw-Tree? Might long transmit times hinder performance by delaying garbage collection of stale records?

5   Experimental Results

To explore how different designs trade-off database server efficiency and performance, we built a simple model of an in-memory database system that concentrates on data transfer rather than full query processing. In all experiments, one node acts as a server and transmits results to 15 client nodes. Our experiments were run on the Apt [18] cluster of the CloudLab testbed: this testbed provides exclusive bare-metal access to a large number of machines with RDMA-capable Infiniband NICs. Details of the configuration are given in Table 1. All of the experiments are publicly available online[1].

Table 1. Experimental cluster configuration. The cluster has 7 Mellanox SX6036G FDR switches arranged in two layers. The switching fabric is oversubscribed and provides about 16 Gbps of bisection bandwidth per node when congested.

CPU	Intel Xeon E5-2450 (2.1 GHz, 2.9 GHz Turbo) 8 cores, 2 hardware threads each
RAM	16 GB DDR3 at 1600 MHz
Network	Mellanox MX354A ConnectX-3 Infiniband HCA (56 Gbps Full Duplex) Connected via PCIExpress 3.0 × 8 (63 Gbps Full Duplex)
Software	CentOS 6.6, Linux 2.6.32, gcc 4.9.2, libibverbs 1.1.8, mlx4 1.0.6

Experiments transmit from a large region of memory backed by 4 KB pages that contains all of the records. The region is also registered with the NIC, which has to do virtual-to-physical address translation to DMA records for transmission. In some cases, using 1 GB hugepages reduces translation look aside buffer (TLB) misses. The NIC can benefit from hugepages as well, since large page tables can result in additional DMA operations to host memory during address translation [6,9]. For our experiments, the reach of the NIC's virtual-to-physical mapping is sufficient, and hugepages have no impact on the results.

5.1   Zero-Copy Performance

The first key question is understanding how database record layout affects the performance of the transmission of query results. The transmission of large result sets presents a number of complex choices that affect database layout and design as well as NIC parameters. Range query results can be transmitted in small batches or large batches and either via copy-out or zero-copy.

To understand these trade-offs, we measure the aggregate transmission throughput of a server to its 15 clients under several configurations. In each experiment, the record size, s, is either 1024 B or 128 B. Given a set of records that must be transmitted, they are then grouped for transmission. For zero-copy,

---

[1] https://github.com/utah-scs/ibv-bench

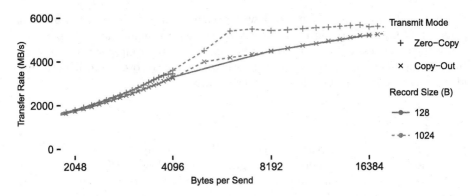

Fig. 3. Transmission throughput when using conventional copy-out into transmit buffers and when the NIC directly copies records via DMA (zero-copy). The line for 128-byte zero-copy stops at 4 K, as this is the maximum size of a send with 32 records of this size.

an n entry DMA gather descriptor is created to transmit those records where ns bytes are transmitted per NIC transmit operation. For copy-out, each of the n records is copied into a single transmit buffer that is associated with a transmit descriptor that only points to the single transmit buffer. Each transmission still sends exactly ns bytes, but copy-out first requires ns bytes to be copied into the transmit buffer. Intuitively, larger groups of records (larger sends) result in less host-to-NIC interaction, which reduces host load and can increase throughput; the benefits depend on the specific configuration and are explored below.

Figure 3 shows how each of these configurations impact transmission throughput. For larger 1024 B records, using the NIC's DMA engine for zero-copy shows clear benefits (aside from CPU and memory bandwidth savings, which we explore in Sect. 5.2). The database server is able to saturate the network with zero-copy so long as it can post 6 or more records per transmit operation to the NIC (that is, if it sends 6 KB or larger messages at a time).

The figure also shows that using copy-out with 1024 B records, the NIC can also saturate the network, but records must be packed into buffers of 16 KB or more. This is significant, since it determines the transmission throughput of the database when range queries only return a few results. In this case, the DMA engine could provide a throughput boost of up to 29% over copy-out, but the benefit is specific to that scenario. If range scans return even just 16 records per query, the throughput benefits of zero-copy are almost eliminated.

Next, we consider 128 B records. The decreased access latency of in-memory databases makes them well-suited to smaller, finer-grained records than were previously common. One expectation is that this will drive databases toward more aggressively normalized layouts with small records. This seems to be increasingly the case as records of a few hundreds bytes or less are now typical [3,16].

Figure 3 shows that for small 128 B records, the NIC DMA engine provides little throughput benefit. Our NIC is limited to gather lists of 32 entries, which is insufficient to saturate the network with such a small record size. Transmission peaks at 3.5 GB/s. Copying 128 B records on-the-fly can significantly outperform zero-copy transmission when there are enough results to group per transmission. In fact, copy-out can saturate the network with small records, and it performs identically to copy-out with larger 1024 B records.

5.2 Zero-Copy Savings

In addition to improved performance, a goal of zero-copy DMA is to mitigate server-side CPU and memory load. Figure 4 breaks down CPU time for each of the scenarios in Fig. 3: small and large records both with and without zero-copy. Most of the server CPU time is spent idle waiting for the NIC to complete transmissions. The results show that zero-copy always reduces the CPU load of the server, and, as expected, the effect is larger for larger records. With 1024 B records, the `memcpy` step of copy-out uses 6.8% of the total CPU cycles of the socket at peak transmission speed.

Zero-copy eliminates copy overhead, but it adds overhead to create larger transmit descriptors. Each gather entry adds 16 B to the descriptor that is posted to the NIC. These entries are considerable in size compared to small records, and they are copied twice. The gather list is first staged on the thread's stack and passed to the userlevel NIC driver. Next, the driver makes a posted PCIe write by copying the descriptor (including the gather entry) into a memory-mapped device buffer. For large records, constructing the list uses between 1 and 4% of total CPU time, so zero-copy saves about 3 to 6% of CPU time over copy-out.

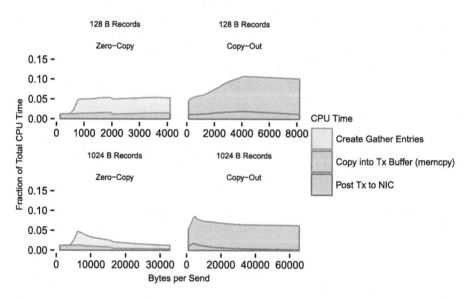

Fig. 4. Breakdown of server CPU time for transmission of small 128 B records and 1024 B records using copies into transmit buffers (Copy-Out) and zero-copy DMA.

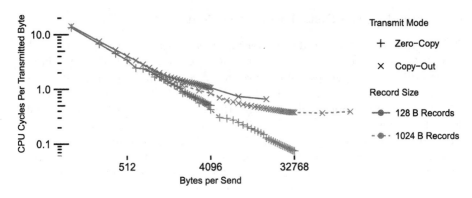

Fig. 5. Cycles per transmitted byte for large and small records with zero-copy and copy-out. Note the log-scale axes.

The memory bandwidth savings for zero-copy are more substantial. Figure 3 shows that copy-out transmit performance nearly matches zero-copy (5.6 GB/s versus 5.8 GB/s). Copy-out introduces exactly one extra copy of the data, and memcpy reads each cache line once and writes it once. So, copy-out increases memory bandwidth consumption by 2× the transmit rate of the NIC or 11.2 GB/s in the worst case. This accounts for about 32% of the available memory bandwidth for the machine that we used. Whether using zero-copy or copy-out, the NIC must copy data from main memory, across the PCIe bus, to its own buffers, which uses another 6 GB/s of memory bandwidth.

For smaller 128 B records, the CPU and memory bandwidth savings are nearly the same as for larger records. In this case, copy-out uses up to 10.8% of the CPU cycles on the socket, and zero-copy uses 5.5%. Eliminating the extra memcpy halves CPU overhead for transmission; a savings of about 5% of the total socket's CPU cycles. Just as before, the memory bandwidth savings is twice the transmission rate or 11.2 GB/s. Overall, this makes copy-out reasonable for small records scattered throughout memory, especially since zero-copy cannot saturate the network in these cases (Sect. 5.1).

The results break down where the CPU and memory bandwidth savings come from, but not all configurations result in the same transmit performance. For example, Fig. 3 shows that when transmitting 128 B records, copy-out gets up to 53% better throughput than zero-copy. As a result, minimizing CPU overhead can come at the expense of transmit performance. The real efficiency of the server in transmission is shown in Fig. 5. The figure shows how many cycles of work the CPU does to transmit a byte in each of the configurations, which reveals two key things. First, it shows that, though the absolute savings in total CPU cycles is small for zero-copy, it does reduce CPU overhead due to transmission by up to 76%. Second, the improvement is a modest 12% for small records, since copy-out can transmit in larger, more efficient batches.

5.3   Extending the Delta Format to Clients

The experiments so far consider delivering a clean, ordered set of records to the client. That is, the server collects and transmits the precise set of records in the correct order, either via copy-out or zero-copy. Another option is to transmit base pages along with their deltas and have clients merge the results. This approach is attractive because it organically fits with the design of the Bw-Tree and it suits the DMA engine of the NIC well. The NIC can transmit the large contiguous base pages (16 KB, for example) with little CPU overhead. It also eliminates copy-out for small records, but avoids the transmission throughput ceiling longer gather lists suffer (Sect. 5.1). Merging records on the client side is cheap; the server can even append them to the response in a sort order that matches the record order in the base page for efficient $O(n)$ iteration over the records that requires no copies or sorting.

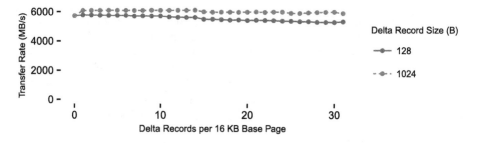

Fig. 6. Zero-copy transmit performance when a single 16 KB base page is transmitted at along with a varying number of delta records. Results are shown for delta records of both 128 B and 1024 B.

Figure 6 shows the benefits of this approach. In this experiment, each transmission consists of a single 16 KB base page while the number and size of the delta records attached to each transmission is varied. The NIC benefits from the large base page, and it manages to keep the network saturated. CPU overhead ranges from less than 1% when there are a few delta records up to about 2% when there are more. Compared to zero-copy of scattered small records this approach also yields a 1.7× throughput advantage; Fig. 3 shows that throughput peaks at 3.4 GB/s when records are scattered, while the delta format achieves 5.7 GB/s. The main cost to this approach is the cost of consolidating delta records into new base pages when chains grow long; we consider this overhead in more detail in the next section.

5.4   Tuning Page Consolidation

Bw-Tree and many indexing structures are paged in order to amortize storage access latency, and paging can have similar benefits for network transmission as well. However, the userlevel access of modern NICs makes interacting with them much lower-latency than storage devices. This raises the question of whether paging is still beneficial for in-memory structures. That is, is the cost of preemptively consolidating updates into pages worth the cost, or is it better to transmit fine-grained scattered records via zero-copy or copy-out?

The results of our earlier experiments help answer this question. If copy-out is used to gain faster transmission of small records, then the answer is simple. Even if every update created a complete copy of the full base page, the extra copies would still be worthwhile so long as more pages are read per second than updated. This true for most update/lookup workloads, and read-only range queries make this an even better trade-off.

However, consolidation must be more conservative when using zero-copy to yield savings, since zero-copy can collect scattered records with less overhead than copy-out. Yet, there is good reason to be optimistic. Delta records reduce the cost of updates for paged structures. If each base page is limited to d delta records before consolidation, the number of consolidations is $\frac{1}{d}$. This means that allowing short delta chains dramatically reduces consolidation costs, while longer chains offer decreasing returns. This fits with the NIC's preference for short gather lists; allowing delta chains of length 4 would reduce consolidation by 75% while maintaining transmit throughput that meets or exceeds on-the-fly copy-out. The large 16 KB base pages also improve transmit throughput slightly, which improves efficiency.

For small records, transmitting compacted base pages that have a few deltas gives a total CPU savings of about 8%. For the same CPU cost, a server can perform about 5.2 GB/s of page compaction or about 340,000 compactions per second for 16 KB pages. Even in the worst case scenario where all updates are focused on a single page, delta chains of length 4 would tolerate 1.3 million updates per second with CPU overhead lower than copy-out. So, delta records can give the efficiency of zero-copy with the performance of copy-out.

5.5   Impact on Garbage Collection

Using zero-copy tightly couples the higher-level database engine's record allocation and deallocation, since records submitted must remain stable until transmission completes. Fortunately, existing mechanisms in systems that avoid update-in-place accommodate this well, like Bw-Tree's epoch mechanism described in Sect. 4. Normally, the Bw-Tree copies-out returned records. While an operation and its copy-out are ongoing, memory that contains records that have been unlinked or superseded cannot be reclaimed. Zero-copy effectively defers the copy until the actual time of transmission. As a result, transmissions completions must notify the higher level database of transmission completion to allow reclamation. This delay results in more latent garbage and hurts the effective memory utilization of the system.

In practice, this effect will be small for two reasons. First, zero-copy adds a transmission, which completes within a few microseconds; however, it also saves a `memcpy` which accounts for 1 to 2 μs for a 16 KB transmission. Second, the amount of resulting data held solely for transmission should generally be more than compensated for by eliminating the need for explicit transmit buffers. With copy-out, the size of the transmit buffer pool is necessarily larger than the amount of data under active transmission, and internal fragmentation in the transmit buffers makes this worse.

5.6 Inlining Data into Transmit Descriptors

Mellanox NICs allow some data to be *inlined* inside the control message sent to the NIC over PCIe. Our NICs allow up to 912 B to be included inside the descriptor that is posted to the NIC control ring buffer. Inlining can improve messaging latency by eliminating the delay for the NIC to DMA the message data from host DRAM, which can only happen after the NIC receives the descriptor. Inlining benefits small request/response exchanges, but it does not help for larger transmissions. This is because even though there is an extra delay before the NIC receives the actual record data, that delay can be overlapped with the DMA and transmission of other responses. Other researchers have shown that sending data to the NIC via MMIO also wastes PCIe bandwidth [9]. All experiments in this paper have inlining disabled. Enabling inlining gives almost identical throughput and overhead to copy-out, except it only works for transmissions of 912 B or less.

6 Conclusions

Our findings show that understanding NIC performance has significant consequences for modern in-memory databases, and that careful co-design of data layout, concurrency control, networking impacts both performance and efficiency. Summarizing the key findings of our experiments:

- The sophisticated DMA capabilities of modern NIC's can be used to transmit directly from database records without any intermediate copying.
- For workloads with small records of a few hundred bytes or less where no significant computation is done server-side, using conventional copy-out transmission will yield better overall throughput even when the result sets are large.
- Zero-copy yields only a few percent total CPU savings, but may reduce server memory bandwidth load by one-third.
- Increasing core counts mean zero-copy CPU savings will become less significant over time, as per-server network speeds are likely remain in the 100s of gigabits per second for some time.
- The memory bandwidth savings are likely to be more important, but memory bandwidth is still growing faster than network bandwidth.
- Zero-copy is highly efficient when records can be transmitted from large contiguous blocks.

Revisiting the key questions posed by the Bw-Tree's unique structure, we apply our findings.

▶ **When should records be transmitted directly from a Bw-Tree? Are there cases where explicitly copying records into a transmit buffer is preferable to gather DMA operations?**

Gather list length limitations means that copy-out yields better throughput than zero-copy for small, scattered records. For example, this makes copy-out preferable when the tree is a secondary index that only holds pointers to records. Zero-copy always results in less server-side load, so zero-copy is preferable if the server also hosts computationally heavy operations. However, the load reduction is small and may be offset by increased delays at the clients.

▶ **How aggressive should a Bw-Tree be in consolidating records to benefit individual clients and to minimize database server load?**

If clients can receive and apply delta records themselves, then using zero-copy to directly transmit base pages and their deltas results in the best throughput and the lowest CPU load. Section 5.4 shows that short delta chains of up to length 4 will sustain millions of updates per second to a database with lower CPU load than either copy-out or zero-copy for transmission.

▶ **How does zero-copy impact state reclamation in the Bw-Tree? Might long transmit times hinder performance by delaying garbage collection of stale records?**

Transmission delays garbage collection of unlinked records, but the amount of accumulated state will be less than the amount that traditional transmit buffers would consume. This effect is compounded by the number of ongoing client operations, so Bw-Tree's ability to leverage zero-copy could improve fan-out to large numbers of clients.

Overall, our client-assisted design for bulk returning small records with the Bw-Tree reduces server-side CPU overhead by 75% and increases throughput by 1.7× compared to zero-copy DMA. With care, modern NICs can saturate the network with low overhead while returning 10s of billions of records per second, even with difficult workloads returning dynamic sets of fine-grained records.

We are applying these techniques to a high-bandwidth, low-impact data migration mechanism for RAMCloud that works to evacuate data away from hot servers with minimal disruption to its already overloaded CPU. Looking forward, we also plan to apply these findings to build a network-attached high-performance access method using techniques similar to the Bw-Tree.

Acknowledgments. This material is based upon work supported by the National Science Foundation under Grant No. CNS-1338155.

References

1. DPDK documentation. http://dpdk.org/doc/guides-16.04/
2. Mellanox ConnectX-4 product brief. http://www.mellanox.com/related-docs/prod_adapter_cards/PB_ConnectX-4_VPI_Card.pdf. Accessed 04 Aug 2016
3. Atikoglu, B., Xu, Y., Frachtenberg, E., Jiang, S., Paleczny, M.: Workload analysis of a large-scale key-value store. In: Proceedings of the 12th ACM SIGMETRICS/PERFORMANCE Joint International Conference on Measurement and Modeling of Computer Systems, SIGMETRICS 2012. ACM, New York (2012)

4. Bronson, N.: Personal Communication (2016)
5. Diaconu, C., Freedman, C., Ismert, E., Larson, P., Mittal, P., Stonecipher, R., Verma, N., Zwilling, M.: Hekaton: SQL server's memory-optimized OLTP engine. In: SIGMOD (2013)
6. Dragojević, A., Narayanan, D., Castro, M., Hodson, O.: FaRM: fast remote memory. In: USENIX NSDI, Seattle, WA, April 2014. USENIX Association (2014)
7. Dragojević, A., Narayanan, D., Nightingale, E.B., Renzelmann, M., Shamis, A., Badam, A., Castro, M.: No compromises: distributed transactions with consistency, availability, and performance. In: SOSP (2015)
8. Kalia, A., Kaminsky, M., Andersen, D.G.: Using RDMA efficiently for key-value services. In: Proceedings of the 2014 ACM SIGCOMM Conference, SIGCOMM 2014. ACM, New York (2014)
9. Kalia, A., Kaminsky, M., Andersen, D.G.: Design guidelines for high performance RDMA systems. In: 2016 USENIX Annual Technical Conference (USENIX ATC 2016), Denver, CO, June 2016. USENIX Association (2016)
10. Kejriwal, A., Gopalan, A., Gupta, A., Jia, Z., Yang, S., Ousterhout, J.: SLIK: scalable low-latency indexes for a key-value store. In: USENIX Annual Technical Conference, Denver, CO, June 2016
11. Levandoski, J., Lomet, D., Sengupta, S., Stutsman, R., Wang, R.: High performance transactions in Deuteronomy. In: Proceeding of CIDR (2015)
12. Levandoski, J., Lomet, D., Sengupta, S., Stutsman, R., Wang, R.: Multi-version range concurrency control in Deuteronomy. In: Proceeding VLDB Endowment (2016)
13. Levandoski, J.J., Lomet, D.B., Sengupta, S., Bw-Tree, T.: A B-tree for new hardware platforms. In: International Conference on Data Engineering (ICDE). IEEE (2013)
14. Lim, H., Han, D., Andersen, D.G., Kaminsky, M.: MICA: a holistic approach to fast in-memory key-value storage. In: 11th USENIX Symposium on Networked Systems Design and Implementation (NSDI 2014), Seattle, WA, April 2014
15. Loesing, S., Pilman, M., Etter, T., Kossmann, D.: On the design and scalability of distributed shared-data databases. In: Proceedings of the 2015 ACM SIGMOD International Conference on Management of Data, SIGMOD 2015. ACM, New York (2015)
16. Nishtala, R., Fugal, H., Grimm, S., Kwiatkowski, M., Lee, H., Li, H.C., McElroy, R., Paleczny, M., Peek, D., Saab, P., Stafford, D., Tung, T., Venkataramani, V.: Scaling memcache at Facebook. In: Symposium on Networked Systems Design and Implementation (NSDI). USENIX, Lombard (2013)
17. Ousterhout, J., Gopalan, A., Gupta, A., Kejriwal, A., Lee, C., Montazeri, B., Ongaro, D., Park, S.J., Qin, H., Rosenblum, M., Rumble, S., Stutsman, R., Yang, S.: The RAMCloud storage system. ACM Trans. Comput. Syst. 33(3), 7:1–7:55 (2015)
18. Ricci, R., Wong, G., Stoller, L., Webb, K., Duerig, J., Downie, K., Hibler, M.: Apt: a platform for repeatable research in computer science. ACM SIGOPS Operating Syst. Rev. 49(1), 100–107 (2015). http://dl.acm.org/citation.cfm?id=2723885
19. Rödiger, W., Mühlbauer, T., Kemper, A., Neumann, T.: High-speed query processing over high-speed networks. In: Proceeding VLDB Endowment, December 2015
20. Wei, X., Shi, J., Chen, Y., Chen, R., Chen, H.: Fast in-memory transaction processing using RDMA and HTM. In: Proceedings of SOSP, SOSP 2015. ACM, New York (2015)

DBMS Data Loading:
An Analysis on Modern Hardware

Adam Dziedzic[1], Manos Karpathiotakis[2(✉)], Ioannis Alagiannis[2],
Raja Appuswamy[2], and Anastasia Ailamaki[2,3]

[1] University of Chicago, Chicago, USA
ady@uchicago.edu
[2] Ecole Polytechnique Fédérale de Lausanne (EPFL), Lausanne, Switzerland
{manos.karpathiotakis,ioannis.alagiannis,raja.appuswamy,
anastasia.ailamaki}@epfl.ch
[3] RAW Labs SA, Lausanne, Switzerland

Abstract. Data loading has traditionally been considered a "one-time
deal" – an offline process out of the critical path of query execution. The
architecture of DBMS is aligned with this assumption. Nevertheless, the
rate in which data is produced and gathered nowadays has nullified the
"one-off" assumption, and has turned data loading into a major bottleneck of the data analysis pipeline.

This paper analyzes the behavior of modern DBMS in order to quantify their ability to fully exploit multicore processors and modern storage hardware during data loading. We examine multiple state-of-the-art
DBMS, a variety of hardware configurations, and a combination of synthetic and real-world datasets to identify bottlenecks in the data loading
process and to provide guidelines on how to accelerate data loading.
Our findings show that modern DBMS are unable to saturate the available hardware resources. We therefore identify opportunities to accelerate
data loading.

1 Introduction

Applications both from the scientific and business worlds accumulate data at
an increasingly rapid pace. Natural science experiments produce unprecedented
amounts of data. Similarly, companies aggressively collect data to optimize business strategy. The recent advances in cost-effective storage hardware enable storing the produced data, but the ability to organize and process this data has been
unable to keep pace with data growth.

Extracting value out of gathered data has traditionally required loading it
into an operational database. For example, in data warehouse scenarios, ETL
involves **E**xtracting data from outside sources, **T**ransforming it to fit operational
needs, and then **L**oading it into the target database [16,23]. The demand for
reduced data-to-query time requires data loading to be a fast operation [27].

A. Dziedzic—Work done while the author was at EPFL.

S. Blanas et al. (Eds.): ADMS 2016/IMDM 2016, LNCS 10195, pp. 95–117, 2017.
DOI: 10.1007/978-3-319-56111-0_6

The demand for high availability requires minimizing, if not eliminating, batch loading windows during which Database Management Systems (DBMS) can be taken offline. Finally, the ever-increasing growth of data requires data loading to be a scalable operation that can exploit hardware parallelism to load massive amounts of data in very short amounts of time [16,23]. Unfortunately, traditional DBMS are built around the assumption that data loading is a "one-time deal"; data loading is considered an offline process out of the critical path, with the user defining a schema and loading the majority of the data in one go before submitting any queries. When this architectural design assumption is combined with the explosive data growth, the result is the emergence of data loading as a major bottleneck in the data analysis pipeline of state-of-the-art DBMS.

While much research over the past few years has focused on innovative techniques to avoid or accelerate data loading [8,13,21,24], there has been no systematic study till date that quantifies the ability of modern DBMS to exploit multicore processors and modern storage hardware in order to parallelize data loading. The importance of such quantification has been recognized by the Big Data community, and has led the "BigData Top100" benchmark to consider the time spent to load data into the system as part of the benchmark metric [11]. Still, although there is a wide variety of benchmarks [5–7] which use diverse queries to evaluate the query processing capabilities of DBMS, a similar analysis of the (bulk) data loading capabilities of DBMS is missing.

This paper presents a detailed data loading analysis with the following goals: (1) analyze how parallel data loading scales for various DBMS, (2) identify bottlenecks, and (3) provide development guidelines to enable the design of efficient data loading pipelines, and administration guidelines to accelerate the time-consuming loading process. The analysis considers three dimensions: software, hardware, and application workloads. Along the software dimension, we investigate architectural aspects (row stores vs column stores) of four state-of-the-art DBMS, implementation aspects (the threading model used for parallel loading), and runtime aspects (degree of parallelism, presence and absence of logging/-constraints). Along the hardware dimension, we evaluate the impact of storage configurations with different I/O capabilities (HDD, SATA SSD, hardware RAID controller with SCSI disks, and DRAM). Finally, along the workload dimension, we consider data from popular benchmarks and real-world datasets with diverse data types, field cardinality, and number of columns. The results of the analysis show that:

- Bulk loading performance is directly connected to the characteristics of the dataset to be loaded: Each evaluated DBMS is stressed differently by the involved datatypes, the number of columns, the underlying storage, etc.
- Both single-threaded and parallel bulk loading leave CPU and/or storage underutilized. Improving CPU utilization requires optimizing the input I/O path to reduce random I/O and the output I/O path to reduce pauses caused by data flushes. Such optimizations bring a 2–10x loading time reduction for all tested DBMS.

- Despite data loading being 100% CPU bound in the absence of any I/O overhead, the speedup achieved by increasing DoP is sub-linear. Parsing, tokenizing, datatype conversion, and tuple construction dominate CPU utilization and need to be optimized further to achieve further reduction in loading time.
- In the presence of constraints, different DBMS exhibit varying degrees of scalability. We also list cases in which the conventional drop indexes-load data-rebuild indexes rule-of-thumb which is applicable to single-threaded index building and constraint verification is inappropriate under parallel loading.
- Under high DoP, constraints can create unwarranted latch contention in the logging and locking subsystems of a DBMS. Such overheads are a side-effect of reusing the traditional query execution code base for bulk data loading and can be eliminated by making data loading a first-class citizen in DBMS design.

2 Setup and Methodology

We now describe the experimental setup, the workloads employed to study and analyze the behavior of the different DBMS during data loading, and the applied methodology.

2.1 Experimental Setup

Hardware: The experiments are conducted using a Dell PowerEdge R720 server equipped with a dual socket Intel(R) Xeon(R) CPU E5-2640 (8 cores, 2 threads per core resulting in 32 hardware contexts) clocked at 2.00 GHz, 64 KB L1 cache per core, 256 KB L2 cache per core, 20 MB L3 cache shared, and 64 GB RAM (1600 MHz DIMMs).

The server is equipped with different data storage devices, including (i) individual SATA hard disk drives (HDD), (ii) a hardware RAID-0 array with SAS HDD (DAS), and (iii) a hardware RAID-0 array with SAS solid state drives (SSD). Table 1 summarizes the available storage devices and their characteristics.

OS: We run all the experiments using Red Hat Enterprise Linux 6.6 (Santiago - 64 bit) with kernel version 2.6.32.

Analyzed Systems: The analysis studies four systems: a commercial row-store (DBMS-A), an open-source row-store (PostgreSQL [2]), a commercial column-store (DBMS-B), and an open-source column-store (MonetDB [1]). To preserve

Table 1. Storage devices and characteristics.

Name	Capacity	Configuration	Read Speed	Write Speed	RPM
HDD	1.8 TB	4 x HDD (RAID-0)	170 MB/s	160 MB/s	7.5 k
DAS	13 TB	24 x HDD (RAID-0)	1100 MB/s	330 MB/s	7.5 k
SSD	550 GB	3 x SSD (RAID-0)	565 MB/s	268 MB/s	n/a

anonymity due to legal restrictions, the names of the commercial database systems are not disclosed. PostgreSQL (version 9.3.2) and MonetDB (version 11.19.9) are built using gcc 4.4.7 with -O2 and -O3 optimizations enabled respectively.

2.2 Datasets

The experiments include datasets with different characteristics: both industry-standard and scientific datasets, as well as custom micro-benchmarks. All datasets are stored in textual, comma-separated values (CSV) files.

Industrial Benchmarks. We use the TPC-H decision support benchmark [7], which is designed for evaluating data warehouses, and the transaction processing benchmark TPC-C [5], which models an online transaction processing database.

Scientific Datasets. To examine more complex and diverse cases compared to the synthetic benchmarks, we also include in the experiments a subset of the SDSS [3] dataset and a real-life dataset provided by Symantec [4].

SDSS contains data collected by telescopes that scan parts of the sky; it includes detailed images and spectra of sky objects along with properties about stars and galaxies. SDSS is a challenging dataset because (i) it includes many floating point numbers that require precision and (ii) most of its tables contain more than 300 attributes.

The Symantec spam dataset consists of a collection of spam e-mails collected through the worldwide-distributed spam traps of Symantec. Each tuple contains a set of features describing characteristics of the spam e-mails, such as the e-mail subject and body, the language, the sender's IP address, the country from which the spam e-mail was sent, and attachments sent with the e-mail. NULL values are common in the Symantec dataset because each e-mail entry may contain different types of features. In addition, the width of each tuple varies based on the collected features (from a few bytes to a few KB). The Symantec spam dataset also contains wide variable length attributes (e.g., e-mail subject) that considerably stress systems which use compression for strings.

2.3 Experimental Methodology

The goal of the experiments is to provide insight on "where time goes" during loading in modern DBMS – not to declare a specific DBMS as the fastest option in terms of bulk loading performance. The experiments thus explore a number of different configurations (software and hardware) and datasets, and highlight how different parameters and setups affect loading performance.

All DBMS we use in this analysis support loading data either by using a bulk loading COPY command or by using a series of INSERT statements. We found bulk loading using COPY to be much faster than using INSERT statements for all DBMS. Therefore, all experimental results reported in this paper were obtained by using the COPY command.

In addition to bulk loading, DBMS-A, MonetDB, and DBMS-B also offer built-in support for parallel loading. PostgreSQL, in constrast, does not support parallel loading. We work around this limitation by building an external parallel loader which we describe in Sect. 3.

Tuning. All tested systems are tuned following guidelines proposed by the DBMS vendors to speed up loading. For MonetDB, we also provide the number of tuples in the dataset as a hint to the parallel loader as we found that loading does not scale without providing this hint. To ensure fair comparison between the systems, we map datatypes used in benchmarks to DBMS-specific datatypes such that the resulting datatype size remains the same across all DBMS. Thus, the difference in loaded database size across DBMS is due to architectural differences, like the use of data compression.

Profiling. We collect statistics about CPU, RAM, and disk I/O utilization of the OS and the DBMS. We use `sar` to measure the CPU and RAM utilization, and `iostat` to measure disk utilization statistics. In addition, we use `iosnoop` to record disk access patterns and the Intel VTune Amplifier to profile the different systems and derive performance breakdown graphs.

3 Experimental Evaluation

We conduct several experiments to evaluate the bulk loading performance of the tested systems. We start with a baseline comparison of single-threaded data loading using a variety of datasets. We then consider how data loading scales as we increase the degree of parallelism. Following this, we analyze I/O and CPU utilization characteristics of each DBMS to identify where time is spent during data loading and investigate the effect of scaling the storage subsystem. Finally, we examine how each system handles the challenge of enforcing constraints during data loading.

3.1 Baseline: Single-Threaded Data Loading

This experiment investigates the behavior of PostgreSQL, MonetDB, DBMS-A and DBMS-B as their inputs increase progressively from 1 GB to 100 GB. Each variation of the experiment uses as input (a) TPC-H, (b) TPC-C, (c) SDSS, or (iv) Symantec dataset. The experiment emulates a typical enterprise scenario where the database is stored on a high-performance RAID array and the input data to be loaded into the database is accessed over a slow medium. We thus read the input from HDD, a slow data source, and store the database on DAS, a high-performance RAID array.

Figure 1(a-d) plots the data loading time for each system under the four benchmarks. As can be seen, the data loading time increases linearly with the dataset size (except when we load the SDSS dataset in DBMS-Aand the Symantec dataset in DBMS-B). DBMS-A outperforms the rest of the systems in the majority of the cases; when considering 100 GB database instances, DBMS-A is

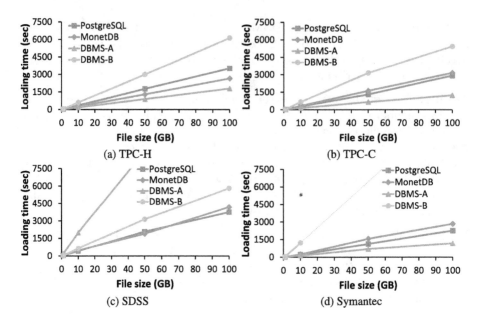

Fig. 1. Data loading time increases linearly with the dataset size (single-threaded loading, raw input from HDD, database on DAS).

1.5× faster for TPC-H, 2.3× faster for TPC-C, and 1.91× faster for Symantec compared to the second fastest system in each case. DBMS-A, however, shows the worst performance for the SDSS dataset (5× slower than the fastest system). The reason is that SDSS contains numerous floating-point fields, which are meant to be used in scientific processing. DBMS-A offers a compact datatype for such use cases, which facilitates computations at query time but is expensive to instantiate at loading time, thus stressing the storage engine of DBMS-A. Among the other systems, PostgreSQL exhibits robust performance, having the second fastest loading time in most experiments.

PostgreSQL and DBMS-A outperform DBMS-B and MonetDB under the Symantec dataset because of the architectural differences between the two types of DBMS. PostgreSQL and DBMS-A are row stores that follow the N-ary storage model (NSM) in which data is organized as tuples (rows) and is stored sequentially in slotted pages. OLTP applications benefit from NSM storage because it is more straightforward to update multiple fields of a tuple when they are stored sequentially. Likewise, compression is used less frequently because it makes data updates more expensive. On the other hand, DBMS-B and MonetDB are column stores that follow the decomposition storage model (DSM) and organize data in standalone columns; since they typically serve scan-intensive OLAP workloads, they apply compression to reduce the cost of data scans.

Table 2 shows the ratio between the input data file and the final database size for the experiments of Fig. 1. Even though the tested systems read the same

Table 2. Input data file/Database size ratio for each dataset (10 GB instance). Column stores achieve a better ratio (less is better).

Name	TPC-H	TPC-C	SDSS	Symantec
DBMS-A	1.5	1.3	1.5	1.5
PostgreSQL	1.4	1.4	1.4	1.1
DBMS-B	0.27	0.82	0.18	0.25
MonetDB	1.1	1.4	1.0	0.92

amount of data, they end up writing notably different amounts of data. Clearly, DBMS-B and MonetDB have smaller storage footprint than PostgreSQL and DBMS-A. The row-stores require more space because they store auxiliary information in each tuple (e.g., a header) and do not use compression. This directly translates to improved performance during query execution for column stores due to fewer I/O requests.

The downside of compression, however, is the increase in data loading time due to the added processing required for compressing data. DBMS-B compresses all input data during loading. Thus, it has the worst overall loading time in almost all cases. MonetDB only compresses string values. Therefore, the compression cost is less noticeable for MonetDB than it is for DBMS-B. The string-heavy Symantec dataset stresses MonetDB, which compresses strings using dictionary encoding. This is why MonetDB exhibits the second worst loading time under Symantec. Despite this, its loading time is much lower than DBMS-B. The reason is that MonetDB creates a local dictionary for each data block it initializes, and flushes it along with the data block. Therefore, the local dictionaries have manageable sizes and reasonable maintenance cost. We believe that DBMS-B, in contrast, chooses an expensive, global compression scheme that incurs a significant penalty for compressing the high-cardinality, wide attributes in the Symantec dataset (e.g., e-mail body, domain name, etc.).

Summary. The time taken to load data into a DBMS depends on both the dataset being loaded and the architecture used by the DBMS. No single system is a clear winner in all scenarios. A common pattern across all experiments in the single-threaded case is that the evaluated systems are unable to saturate the 170 MB/s I/O bandwidth of the HDD – the slowest input device used in this study. The next section examines whether data parallelism accelerates data loading.

3.2   Parallel Data Loading

The following experiments examine how much benefit a DBMS achieves by performing data loading in a parallel fashion. As mentioned earlier, PostgreSQL lacks support for parallel bulk loading out-of-the-box. We thus develop

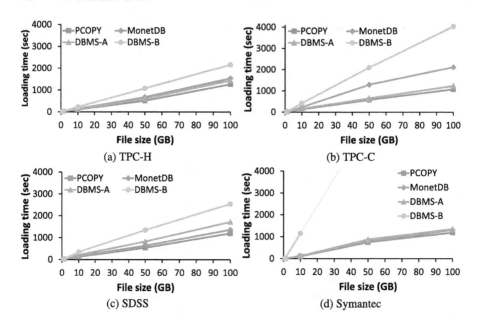

Fig. 2. Data loading time increases linearly with the dataset size (parallel loading, input on HDD, database on DAS).

an external loader that invokes multiple PostgreSQL COPY commands in parallel. To differentiate our external loader from native PostgreSQL, we will refer to it as PCOPY. PCOPY differs from other systems that support parallel loading as native feature in that it uses PostgreSQL as a testbed to show how parallelism can be introduced to an existing RDBMS without tweaking its internal components. PCOPY is a multithreaded application that takes as input the file to be loaded into the database, memory maps it, computes aligned logical partitions, and assigns each partition to a different thread. Each thread sets up a pipe and forks off a PostgreSQL client process that runs the COPY command configured to read from a redirected standard input. Then the thread loads the data belonging to its partition by writing out the memory mapped input file to the client process via the pipe.

Figure 2(a-d) plots the results for each dataset. We configure all systems to use 16 threads – the number of physical cores of the server. Comparing Figs. 1 and 2, we can see that parallel loading improves performance compared to single-threaded loading in the majority of cases. Similar to the single-threaded case, loading time increases almost linearly as the dataset size increases. DBMS-B shows the same behavior as in the single-threaded case for the Symantec dataset. On the other hand, parallel loading significantly improves the loading time of DBMS-A for SDSS; abundant parallelism masks the high conversion cost of floating-point values intended to be used in scientific computations.

The data loading code path of PostgreSQL proves to be more parallelizable for this experiment as PCOPY achieves the lowest loading time across the

different datasets. Compared to single-threaded PostgreSQL, PCOPY is 2.77×
faster for TPC-H, 2.71× faster for TPC-C, 3.13× faster for SDSS, and 1.9×
faster for Symantec (considering the 100 GB instances of the datasets). MonetDB benefits from parallel loading as well, being 1.72× faster for TPC-H,
1.49× faster for TPC-C, 3.07× faster for SDSS, and 2.16× faster for Symantec (100 GB instances). The parallel version of DBMS-A is 1.25× faster for
TPC-H and 10.78× faster for SDSS compared to the single-threaded version
(100 GB instances). On the other hand, DBMS-A fails to achieve a speed-up
for TPC-C and Symantec. Finally, DBMS-B is 2.84× faster for TPC-H, 1.34×
faster for TPC-C, and 2.28× faster for SDSS (100 GB instances) compared to its
single-threaded variation. Similar to the single-threaded case, DBMS-B requires
significantly more time to load the long string values of the Symantec dataset.
As a result, DBMS-B still processes the 10 GB dataset when the other systems
have already finished loading 100 GB.

Summary. Figure 2 again shows that there is no system that outperforms the
others across all the tested datasets. Generally, parallel loading improves data
loading performance in comparison to single-threaded loading in many cases.
However, scaling is far from ideal, as loading time does not reduce commen-
surately with the number of cores used. In fact, there are cases where a 16×
increase in the degree of parallelism fails to bring any improvement at all (e.g.,
DBMS-A for TPC-C and Symantec).

3.3   Data Loading: Where Does Time Go?

The next experiment looks into CPU and I/O resource usage patterns to identify
where time goes during the data loading process so that we understand the reason
behind lack of scalability under parallel data loading. This experiment presents
an alternative view of Fig. 2(a): It monitors the usage of system resources (CPU,
RAM, I/O reads and writes) when a 10 GB version of TPC-H is loaded using
the parallel loaders for various DBMS. As before, raw data is initially stored on
HDD and the database is stored on DAS. There are two patterns that can be
observed across all systems in Fig. 3:

First, both CPU utilization and write I/O bandwidth utilization exhibit alter-
nating peak and plateau cycles. This can be explained by breaking down the data
loading process into a sequence of steps which all systems follow. During data
loading, blocks of raw data are read sequentially from the input files until all
data has been read. Each block is parsed to identify the tuples that it contains.
Each tuple is tokenized to extract its attributes. Then, every attribute is con-
verted to a binary representation. This process of parsing, tokenization, and
deserialization causes peaks in the CPU utilization. Once the database-internal
representation of a tuple is created, the tuple becomes part of a batch of tuples
that are written by the DBMS and buffered by the OS. Periodically, these writes
are flushed out to the disk. This caching mechanism is responsible for the peaks
in write I/O utilization. During these peaks, the CPU utilization in all systems
except PCOPY drops dramatically. This is due to the buffer cache in DBMS

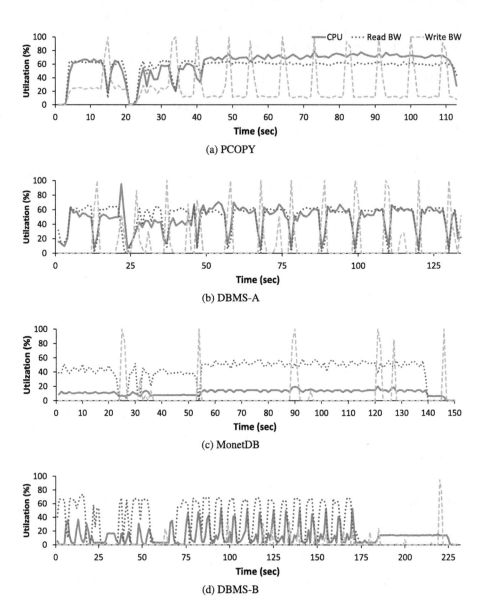

Fig. 3. Different CPU, Read/Write bandwidth utilization per system (Input TPC-H 10 GB, source on HDD, database on DAS).

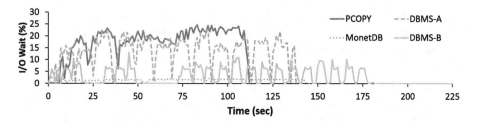

Fig. 4. I/O Wait per system (Input TPC-H 10 GB, source on HDD, database on DAS).

blocking on a write operation that triggers a flush, thereby stalling the loading process until the flush, and hence the issued I/O operation, complete.

The second pattern that can be observed across all systems is that CPU and I/O resources remain under-utilized. MonetDB exhibits the lowest CPU utilization among all systems. This is due to the fact that it uses one "producer" thread that reads, parses, and tokenizes raw data values, and then N "consumer" threads convert the raw values to a binary format. The parsing and tokenization steps, however, are CPU-intensive and cause a bottleneck on the single producer; CPU utilization is therefore low for MonetDB. The CPU usage for DBMS-B has bursts that are seemingly connected with the system's effort to compress input values, but is otherwise very low. DBMS-B spawns a very high number of threads with low scheduling priority; they get easily pre-empted due to their low priority and they fail to saturate the CPU. PCOPY and DBMS-A have higher CPU usage (61% and 47% on average, respectively) compared to MonetDB and DBMS-B, yet they also fail to fully exploit the CPU resources.

Figure 4 illustrates the percentage of time that each DBMS spends waiting for I/O requests to be resolved during each second of execution. Except MonetDB, all other systems spend a non-trivial portion of time waiting for I/O which explains the low CPU utilization. Still, read throughput utilization of various systems in Fig. 3 barely exceeds 60% even in the best case. This clearly indicates that all systems except MonetDB issue random read I/O requests during parallel data loading which causes high I/O delays and an underutilization of CPU resources.

Summary. Contrary to single-threaded loading, which is CPU bound, parallel data loading is I/O bound. Except MonetDB, parallel data loaders used by all systems suffer from poor CPU utilization due to being bottlenecked on random I/O in the input data path. MonetDB, in contrast, suffers from poor CPU utilization due to being bottlenecked on the single producer thread that parses and tokenizes data.

3.4 Impact of Underlying Storage

The previous experiments showed that a typical DBMS setup under-utilizes both I/O bandwidth as well as the available CPUs because of the time it spends waiting for random I/O completion. This section studies the underutilization issue from both a software and a hardware perspective; it investigates (i) how the different read patterns of each tested DBMS affect read throughput, and (ii) how different storage sub-systems affect data loading speed.

I/O Read Patterns. This set of experiments uses as input an instance of the orders table from the TPC-H benchmark with size 1.7 GB and records the input I/O pattern of different systems during data loading. We extract the block addresses of the input file and the database file using *hdparm*, and we use *iosnoop* to identify threads/processes that read from/write to a disk. The input data file is logically divided on disk into 14 pieces (13 with size 128 MB and a smaller one with size 8 MB). To generate each graph, we take (i) the start and end times of the disk requests, (ii) the address of the disk from where the reading for the request starts and (iii) the size of the operation in bytes. Then, we draw a line from the point specified by (start time, start address) to the (end time, start address + # of read bytes). There are two kinds of plots: The first one depicts the whole file address space, while the other zooms in the first contiguous LBAs (Logical Block Addresses), further on called chunk. Different colors in the graphs represent distinct processes/threads.

Figures 5, 6, 7, and 8 plot the read patterns for PCOPY, MonetDB, DBMS-A, and DBMS-B respectively. All systems operate in parallel mode. MonetDB reads data from disk sequentially using one thread, while the other systems use multiple

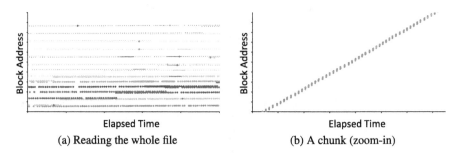

(a) Reading the whole file   (b) A chunk (zoom-in)

Fig. 5. Read pattern for PCOPY (parallel).

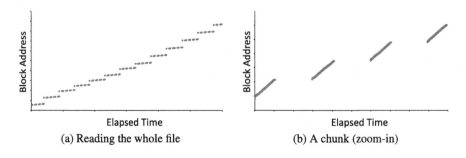

(a) Reading the whole file   (b) A chunk (zoom-in)

Fig. 6. Read pattern for MonetDB (both single-threaded and parallel).

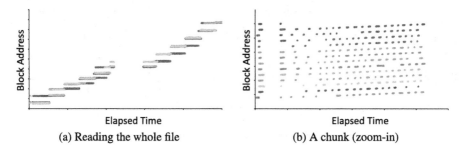

(a) Reading the whole file   **(b) A chunk (zoom-in)**

Fig. 7. Read pattern for DBMS-A (parallel).

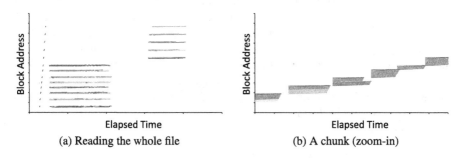

(a) Reading the whole file   **(b) A chunk (zoom-in)**

Fig. 8. Read pattern for DBMS-B (parallel).

concurrent readers (plotted with different colors in the graphs). Figure 6(a) depicts the 13 pieces read serially which mirror the 13 main contiguous address spaces of the input file. By looking closer into Fig. 6(b) we observe that MonetDB reads big contiguous chunks. In total, the plots depict four different read patterns:

– PCOPY exploits 16 threads to read different parts of the file simultaneously. Then, each thread reads consecutive blocks of the assigned part of the file (Fig. 5(b)).
– MonetDB uses a single "producer" thread to read data and provide each data block to a "consumer" (Fig. 6).
– DBMS-A accesses a part of the file and processes it using multiple threads. Each thread is assigned its own contiguous area within the accessed chunk (Fig. 7(b)).
– DBMS-B first samples the whole file with one process, and then it accesses a big chunk of the file (roughly 1 GB) in one go. Similar to DBMS-A, each thread is assigned a contiguous portion of a chunk. Contrary to DBMS-A, which reads one part of the file at a time (1 out of the 13 chunks), DBMS-B accesses a wider address space in the same period of time (8 out of the 13 chunks). However, they behave alike on the lower level where each thread reads a contiguous sequence of blocks.

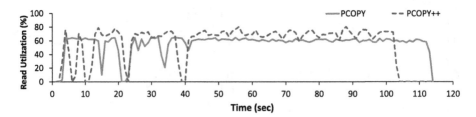

Fig. 9. Using a serial reader improves the read throughput of PCOPY.

Analyzing each system further reveals that MonetDB uses a sequential read pattern, whereas the rest of the systems use parallel readers that read small data chunks from different seeks to the disk and cause random I/O. To gauge which of the two approaches is more beneficial for a system, we implement PCOPY++, which is a variation of PCOPY that uses a single serial reader. As depicted in Fig. 9, PCOPY++ achieves higher read throughput because it uses a serial data access pattern, which minimizes the costly disk seeks and is also disk-prefetcher-friendly. As a result, PCOPY++ reduced loading time by an additional 5% in our experiments.

Effect of Different Storage Devices. While sequential accesses are certainly useful for slow HDD-based data sources, it might be beneficial to use multiple readers on data sources that can sustain large random IOPS, like SSD. Thus, another way to eliminate the random I/O bottleneck is to use faster input and output storage media.

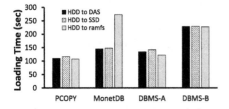

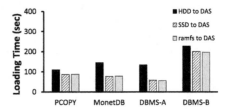

Fig. 10. Loading 10 GB TPC-H: Varying data destination storage with slow data source storage (HDD).

Fig. 11. Loading 10 GB TPC-H: Varying data source storage with DAS data destination storage.

To examine the impact of the underlying data storage on parallel loading, we run an experiment where we use as input a 10 GB instance of TPC-H and vary the data source and destination storage devices. Figure 10 plots the loading time when the slow HDD is the data source storage media, as in previous experiments, while varying the destination storage used for storing the database. Varying the database storage has little to no impact on most systems despite the fact that

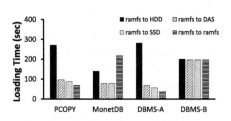

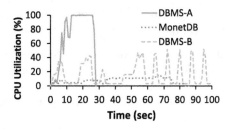

Fig. 12. Varying data destination storage with fast data source storage (ramfs).

Fig. 13. CPU Utilization for ramfs-based source and destination.

ramfs is an order of magnitude faster than DAS. This again shows that all systems are bottlenecked on the source media. The random I/O requests that the DBMS trigger when loading data in parallel force the HDD to perform many seeks, and therefore the HDD is unable to serve data fast enough.

For MonetDB, the loading time increases when the database resides on ramfs. To clarify this trend, we analyze the performance of MonetDB using VTune. We notice that most of the CPU time is spent in the *internal_fallocate* function. MonetDB by default uses the *posix_fallocate* function, which instructs the kernel to reserve a space on disk for writes. ramfs, however, lacks support for the *posix_fallocate* function and as a result the *glibc* library has to re-create its semantics – a factor that slows down the loading process[1].

Figure 11 plots the loading time when we vary the data source storage while using DAS as the data destination storage. Using a faster data source storage accelerates loading for all the systems. Nevertheless, the difference between the configurations that use SSD- and ramfs-based source storage is marginal, which implies that the write performance of DAS eventually becomes a bottleneck for very fast input devices.

To further look into the write bottleneck, Fig. 12 plots the loading time when we vary the data destination storage while using ramfs – the fastest option – as the data source storage. The observed behavior varies across systems: DBMS-B has little benefit from ramfs because of its thread overprovisioning; the numerous low-priority threads it spawns get pre-empted often. For PCOPY and DBMS-A, using ramfs as the data destination storage achieves the best overall performance. Loading time reduces by 1.75× for DBMS-A and 1.4× for PCOPY when ramfs is used as the destination storage compared to DAS. This clearly shows that DAS, despite being equipped with a battery-backed cache for buffering writes, is still a bottleneck to data loading due to the negative impact that dirty data flushing has on the data loading pipeline.

Figure 13 shows the CPU utilization for the DBMS that support parallel loading when source and destination are ramfs. Only DBMS-A reaches 100%

---

[1] We reported this behavior to the MonetDB developers, and it is fixed in the current release.

CPU utilization, with its performance eventually becoming bound by the CPU-intensive data parsing and conversion tasks.

Summary. The experiments demonstrate the effect of the interaction between the DBMS and the underlying storage subsystem, both from a software and a hardware perspective. Our analysis showed that the way in which DBMS issue read requests and the degree of parallelism they employ has an effect on the read throughput achieved.

Writes are also challenging for parallel loading because multiple writers might increase I/O contention due to concurrent writes. In fact, slow writes can have a bigger impact on the data loading performance than slow reads, as slow flushing of dirty data stall the data loading pipeline. Thus, it is important to use storage media that perform bulk writes quickly (using write caches or otherwise) to limit the impact of this problem.

Finally, for the fastest combinations of data source and destination storage, which also allow a high degree of IOPS, there are DBMS that become CPU-bound. However, on measuring the storage bandwidth they use in that case (250 MB/s), we found that they will still be unable to fully utilize modern storage devices, like PCIe SSD, indicating that the data loading code path needs to be optimized further to reduce loading time.

3.5   Hitting the CPU Wall

Data loading is a CPU-intensive task – a fact that becomes apparent after using the fastest data source and destination storage combination. This section presents a CPU breakdown analysis using VTune for the two open-source systems (PostgreSQL and MonetDB). For this experiment, we use as input a custom dataset of 10 GB which contains 10 columns with integer values and we examine the CPU overhead of loading this data file. Figure 14 shows the results; we group together the tasks corresponding to the same functionality for both systems based on the high-level steps described above.

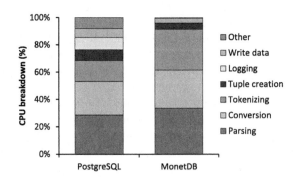

Fig. 14. CPU breakdowns for PostgreSQL and MonetDB during data loading of integers. Most of the time is spent on parsing, tokenizing, conversion and tuple creation.

Even though PostgreSQL is a row-store and MonetDB is a column-store, both databases go through similar steps to perform data loading. Both systems spend the majority of their processing time to perform the parsing, tokenizing, and data type conversion steps (69% for PostgreSQL and 91% for MonetDB). Overall, data loading is CPU-intensive; however, parsing and tokenizing data from a file and generating tuples can be decomposed into tasks of smaller size. These tasks do not require any communication (i.e., there are no dependencies between them), thus they are ideal candidates for parallel execution. Modern DBMS are based on this property to provide parallel loading. The CPU cost for parsing and tokenizing can also be further reduced if the general-purpose file readers used by the DBMS for bulk loading are replaced by custom, file-specific readers that exploit information regarding the database schema [21] (e.g., number of attributes per tuple, datatype of each attribute). Finally, PostgreSQL spends 8% of the time creating tuples and 9% of the time for logging related tasks. On the other hand, MonetDB spends 5% of the loading time on the same steps.

3.6   Data Loading in the Presence of Constraints

Enforcing integrity constraints adds overheads to the data loading process. An established rule of thumb claims that populating the database and verifying constraints should be separated and run as two independent phases. Following this adage, database administrators typically drop all preexisting primary and foreign key constraints, load data, and add constraints back again to minimize the total data loading time. This section investigates the performance and scalability implications of primary-key (PK) and foreign-key (FK) constraint verification, and tests conventional knowledge.

Primary Key Constraints. Figure 15 shows the total time taken to load the TPC-H SF-10 dataset in the single-threaded case when (a) no constraints are enabled, (b) primary key constraints are added before loading the data (*"Unified"* loading and verification), (c) primary key constraints are added after loading the data (*"Post"*-verification). All the experiments use an HDD as the input source and DAS to store the database. We omit results for DBMS-B because it lacks support for constraint verification, and for MonetDB because its *Unified* variation enforces a subset of the constraints that this section benchmarks[2]. We consider PK constraints as specified in the TPC-H schema.

Figure 15 shows that for both DBMS-A and PostgreSQL, enabling constraints before loading data is 1.16× to 1.82× slower than adding constraints after loading. The traditional rule of thumb therefore holds for single-threaded data loading. A natural question that arises is whether parallel loading techniques challenge this rule of thumb.

DBMS-A supports explicit parallelization of both data loading and constraint verification phases. Thus, DBMS-A can parallelize the *Unified* approach by loading data in parallel into a database which has PK constraints enabled, and

---

[2] https://www.monetdb.org/Documentation/SQLreference/TableIdentityColumn.

parallelize the *Post* approach by performing parallel data loading without enabling constraints and then triggering parallel PK constraint verification. PostgreSQL is unable to independently parallelize constraint verification. Thus, the *Post* approach for PostgreSQL performs parallel data loading (using PCOPY) and single-threaded constraint verification.

Figure 16 shows the total time taken to load the database using 16 physical cores. Comparing Figs. 15 and 16, the following observations can be made:

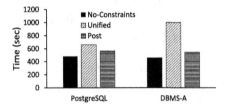
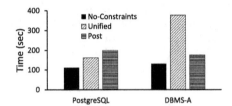

Fig. 15. Single-threaded loading in the presence of PK constraints.

Fig. 16. Parallel loading in the presence of PK constraints.

- Parallel loading reduces the execution time of both *Unified* and *Post* approaches for both DBMS (4.08× under PCOPY, 2.64× under DBMS-A).
- The conventional rule of thumb is no longer applicable to both DBMS shown in Fig. 16: While *Post* provides a 2.14× reduction in loading time over *Unified* under DBMS-A, the trend reverses under PostgreSQL as *Unified* outperforms *Post* by 19%. The reason is that the *Post* configuration for PostgreSQL performs single-threaded constraint verification while *Unified* parallelizes loading and constraint verification together as a unit.
- Despite outperforming *Post*, *Unified* is still 1.45× slower than the *No-Constraints* case for PostgreSQL. Similarly, *Post* is 1.34× slower than *No-Constraints* for DBMS-A. The PostgreSQL slowdown is due to a cross interaction between write-ahead logging and parallel index creation; Fig. 17 shows the execution time of *No-Constraints* and *Unified* over PostgreSQL when logging is enabled/disabled. DBMS-A lacks support for an explicit logging deactivation, therefore it is not presented. Logging has minimal impact in the absence of constraints, but it plays a major role in increasing execution time for *Unified*. In the presence of a PK constraint, PostgreSQL builds an index on the corresponding attribute. As multiple threads load data into the database, the index is updated in parallel, and these updates are logged. Profiling revealed that this causes severe contention in the log manager as multiple threads compete on latches.

Foreign Key Constraints. Figure 18 shows the time taken to load the TPC-H dataset in the single-threaded case when both PK and FK constraints are enabled. Comparing Figs. 15 and 18, it is clear that FK constraints have a substantially larger impact on loading time compared to PK constraints. *Unified* is

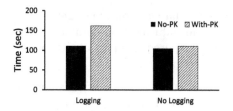

Fig. 17. Effect of logging in PostgreSQL.

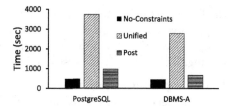

Fig. 18. Single-threaded loading in the presence of FK constraints.

7.8× and 6.1× slower under PostgreSQL and DBMS-A when the systems perform FK checks as well, compared to 1.38× and 2.1× when they only perform PK checks.

Figure 19 shows the time it takes to enforce FK constraints in parallel. Unlike the PK case, each approach tested benefits differently from additional parallelism. While the *Unified* approach benefits from a 4× reduction in loading compared to the single-threaded case for PostgreSQL, it fails to benefit at all for DBMS-A. However, the *Post* approach benefits from parallelism under both systems; DBMS-A and PostgreSQL achieve a 3.45× and 1.82× reduction in loading time respectively. In addition, similarly to the PK case, disabling logging has significant impact on loading time: *Unified (No Log)* is 1.73× faster than the logging approach.

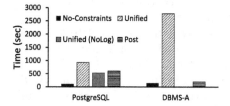

Fig. 19. Parallel loading in the presence of FK constraints.

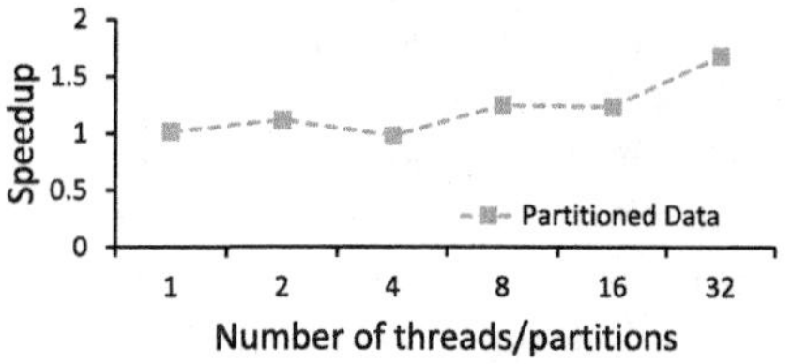

Fig. 20. Re-organizing input to facilitate FK validation.

The conventional rule of enforcing constraints after data has been loaded is again only applicable under specific scenarios: Under DBMS-A, *Post* is indeed the only approach to scale and thus, the rule of thumb holds. Under PostgreSQL, *Post* lags behind *Unified (NoLog)* by 1.12×.

In total, adding constraint verification to the loading process increases time by 1.43× under DBMS-A and 5.1× under PostgreSQL for the parallel case. We profiled PostgreSQL with logging disabled to identify the root cause of performance drop; latching was the reason. PostgreSQL implements foreign keys as triggers, therefore each record insertion into a table fires a trigger which performs a select query on the foreign table to verify that the insertion does not violate the FK constraint. Such selections acquire a Key-Share lock on the target record to preserve consistency. As multiple threads load data into the database, they compete over the latch (spin lock) that must be acquired as a part of Key-Share locking. This contention causes performance deterioration.

Reducing Contention. One way to reduce contention is to modify the DBMS by implementing more scalable locks. An alternative that this study adopts is to avoid contention by re-organizing the input. Specifically, we partition the raw data of the "child" table so that any records having an FK relationship with the same "parent" record are grouped together within a partition. Therefore, two threads loading two different partitions will never contend over latches while acquiring Key-Share locks.

Figure 20 shows the speedup achieved when loading the TPC-H lineitem table using the *Unified* approach over partitioned input data, compared to the case when the input is not partitioned. In the partitioning case, we split lineitem in N chunks, one per thread, such that two records in different partitions will never refer to the same parent record in the supplier table. In cases of low contention (1–4 threads), speedup is marginal. When multiple threads are used to load the input data, the input partitioning strategy yields up to a 1.68× reduction in loading time.

Summary. The traditional rules of thumb for loading data with constraints have to be updated. This section showed that enforcing constraints during loading (i.e., the *Unified* approach) offers performance which is competitive to applying constraints after loading the data (the *Post* approach), and even outperforms it in almost all cases. Besides the performance benefits, the *Unified* approach enables a DBMS to be kept online while loading data, compared to the *Post* approach which requires the DBMS to be taken offline. Thus, administrators should be wary of these trade offs to optimize bulk loading.

In addition, it is time to refactor the loading pipeline in traditional DBMS. The loading pipeline is typically implemented over the same code base that handles single-record insertions and updates, therefore parallelizing loading externally using several client threads results in latch contention in several DBMS subsystems like the lock and log managers. Instead, DBMS should make bulk loading a first-class citizen and develop a code path customized for loading. With such changes, the loading time can be substantially reduced further even in the presence of constraints, all while the DBMS remains online during data loading.

4   Related Work

As the growth of collected information has turned data loading into a bottleneck for data analysis tasks, researchers from industry and academia have proposed ideas to improve the data loading performance and in some cases to enable data processing without any requirement for data loading. This section briefly reviews this body of related work.

Bulk loading. Numerous approaches examine ways to accelerate data loading. Starting from general-purpose approaches, the authors of [10] introduce the idea of partitioning the input data and exploiting parallelism to load the data partitions faster. Instant loading [24] presents a scalable bulk loader for main-memory systems, designed to parallelize the loading phase of HyPer [22] by utilizing vectorization primitives to load CSV datasets as they arrive from the network. It applies task- and data- parallelization on every stage of the data loading phase to fully leverage the performance of modern multi-core CPUs and reduce the time required for parsing and conversion. Disk-based database systems can also benefit from such vectorized algorithms to reduce the CPU processing cost. Sridhar et al. [26] present the load/extract implementation of dbX, a high performance shared-nothing database system that can be deployed on commodity hardware systems and the cloud. To optimize the loading performance the authors apply a number of techniques: (i) asynchronous parallel I/O (*aio*) for read and write operations, (ii) forcing every new load to begin at a page boundary and using private buffers to create database pages to eliminate lock costs, (iii) using a minimal WAL log, and (iv) forcing worker threads to check constraints on column values.

Other related works offer specialized, domain-specific solutions: The authors of [9,28] consider the problem of bulk loading an object-oriented DBMS, and focus on issues such as inter-object dependencies. Bulk loading for specialized indexing structures is also an active research area [14,25]. Finally, the authors of [12] put together a parallel bulk loading pipeline for a specific repository of astronomical data.

Querying external data. Motivated by the blocking nature of data loading, vendor lock-in concerns, and the proliferation of different data formats, numerous works advocate launching queries directly over raw data. Multiple DBMS allow SQL queries over data files without loading them a priori. Such approaches, such as the External tables of Oracle and the CSV Engine of MySQL, tightly integrate data file accesses with query execution. The integration happens by "linking" a data file with a given schema and by utilizing a scan operator with the ability to access data files and create the internal structures (e.g., tuples) required from the query engine. Still, external tables lack support for advanced database features such as DML operations, indexes or statistics.

Speculative loading [13] proposes an adaptive loading mechanism to load data into the database when there are available system resources (e.g., disk I/O throughput). Speculative loading proposes a new database physical operator (SCANRAW) that piggybacks on external tables. Adaptive loading [15] was presented as an alternative to full a priori loading. The main idea is that any data loading operations happen adaptively and incrementally during query processing and driven by the actual query needs. NoDB [8] adopts this idea and extends it by introducing novel data structures to index data files, hence making raw files first-class citizens in the DBMS and tightly integrating adaptive loads, caching, and indexing. RAW and Proteus [19–21] further reduce raw data access costs by generating custom data access paths at runtime via code generation.

Data vaults [17] aim at a symbiosis between loaded data and data stored in external repositories. Data vaults are developed in the context of MonetDB and focus on providing DBMS functionality over scientific file formats, emphasizing on array-based data. The concept of just-in-time access to data of interest is further extended in [18] to efficiently handle semantic chunks: large collections of data files that share common characteristics and are co-located by exploiting metadata that describe the actual data (e.g., timestamps in the file names).

5   Conclusion

Data loading is an upfront investment that DBMS have to undertake in order to be able to support efficient query execution. Given the amount of data gathered by applications today, it is important to minimize the overhead of data loading to prevent it from becoming a bottleneck in the data analytics pipeline.

This study evaluates the data loading performance of four popular DBMS along several dimensions with the goal of understanding the role that various software and hardware dimensions play in reducing the data loading time of several application workloads. Our analysis shows that data loading can be parallelized effecively, even in the presence of constraints, to achieve a 10× reduction in loading time without changing the DBMS source code. However, in order to achieve such improvement, administrators need to be cognizant of the fact that conventional wisdom that applies to single-threaded data loading might no longer hold in for parallel loading under some circumstances.

Despite such improvement, we still find that most of the systems are not able to fully utilize the available CPU resources or saturate available storage bandwidth. This suggests there is still room for improving the data loading pipeline. Our analysis reveals that moving forward, DBMS designers should refactor the data loading pipeline by using a dedicated code base for bulk loading to avoid latch contention in various subsystems. While some systems do use such techniques when the database can be taken offline, we believe that it is necessary to apply the same principles to load data while keeping the database online in order to eliminate DBMS down time.

Acknowledgments. This work is partially funded by the EU FP7 Programme (ERC-2013-CoG) under grant agreement number 617508 (ViDa), and the EU FP7 Programme (FP7 Collaborative project) under grant agreement number 317858 (BigFoot).

References

1. MonetDB. http://www.monetdb.org/
2. PostgreSQL. https://www.postgresql.org/
3. SkyServer project. http://skyserver.sdss.org
4. Symantec Enterprise. https://www.symantec.com/
5. TPC-C Benchmark: Standard Specification. http://www.tpc.org/tpcc/
6. TPC-DS Benchmark: Standard Specification. http://www.tpc.org/tpcds/

7. TPC-H Benchmark: Standard Specification. http://www.tpc.org/tpch/
8. Alagiannis, I., Borovica, R., Branco, M., Idreos, S., Ailamaki, A.: NoDB: efficient query execution on raw data files. In: SIGMOD (2012)
9. Amer-Yahia, S., Cluet, S.: A declarative approach to optimize bulk loading into databases. ACM Trans. Database Syst. **29**(2), 233–281 (2004)
10. Barclay, T., Barnes, R., Gray, J., Sundaresan, P.: Loading databases using dataflow parallelism. SIGMOD Record **23**(4), 72–83 (1994)
11. Baru, C., Bhandarkar, M., Nambiar, R., Poess, M., Rabl, T.: Benchmarking big data systems and the bigdata top100 list. Big Data **1**(1), 60–64 (2013)
12. Cai, Y.D., Aydt, R.A., Brunner, R.: Optimized data loading for a multi-terabyte sky survey repository. In: SC2005, p. 42 (2005)
13. Cheng, Y., Rusu, F.: Parallel in-situ data processing with speculative loading. In: SIGMOD (2014)
14. den Bercken, J.V., Seeger, B.: An evaluation of generic bulk loading techniques. In: VLDB, pp. 461–470 (2001)
15. Idreos, S., Alagiannis, I., Johnson, R., Ailamaki, A.: Here are my data files. Here are my queries. Where are my results? In: CIDR (2011)
16. Imhoff, C., Galemmo, N., Geiger, J.: Mastering Data Warehouse Design, 2nd edn. Wiley Publishing Inc., Indianapolis (2003)
17. Ivanova, M., Kersten, M.L., Manegold, S.: Data vaults: a symbiosis between database technology and scientific file repositories. In: Proceedings of International Conference on Scientific and Statistical Database Management, June 2012
18. Kargin, Y., Kersten, M.L., Manegold, S., Pirk, H.: The DBMS - your big data sommelier. In: ICDE (2015)
19. Karpathiotakis, M., Alagiannis, I., Ailamaki, A.: Fast queries over heterogeneous data through engine customization. PVLDB **9**(12), 972–983 (2016)
20. Karpathiotakis, M., Alagiannis, I., Heinis, T., Branco, M., Ailamaki, A.: Just-in-time data virtualization: lightweight data management with ViDa. In: CIDR (2015)
21. Karpathiotakis, M., Branco, M., Alagiannis, I., Ailamaki, A.: Adaptive query processing on RAW data. PVLDB **7**(12), 1119–1130 (2014)
22. Kemper, A., Neumann, T.: HyPer: a hybrid OLTP&OLAP main memory database system based on virtual memory snapshots. In: ICDE (2011)
23. Kimball, R., Ross, M.: The Data Warehouse Toolkit: The Complete Guide to Dimensional Modeling, 2nd edn. Wiley, New York (2002)
24. Mühlbauer, T., Rödiger, W., Seilbeck, R., Reiser, A., Kemper, A., Neumann, T.: Instant loading for main memory databases. Proc. VLDB Endow. **6**(14), 1702–1713 (2013)
25. Papadopoulos, A., Manolopoulos, Y.: Parallel bulk-loading of spatial data. Parallel Comput. **29**(10), 1419–1444 (2003)
26. Sridhar, K.T., Sakkeer, M.A.: Optimizing database load and extract for big data era. In: Bhowmick, S.S., Dyreson, C.E., Jensen, C.S., Lee, M.L., Muliantara, A., Thalheim, B. (eds.) DASFAA 2014. LNCS, vol. 8422, pp. 503–512. Springer, Cham (2014). doi:10.1007/978-3-319-05813-9_34
27. Vassiliadis, P., Simitsis, A.: Near real time ETL. In: Kozielski, S., Wrembel, R. (eds.) New Trends in Data Warehousing and Data Analysis. Annals of Information Systems, vol. 3, pp. 1–31. Springer, London (2009)
28. Wiener, J.L., Naughton, J.F.: OODB bulk loading revisited: the partitioned-list approach. In: VLDB, pp. 30–41 (1995)

Locality-Adaptive Parallel Hash Joins Using Hardware Transactional Memory

Anil Shanbhag$^{(\boxtimes)}$, Holger Pirk, and Sam Madden

MIT CSAIL, Cambridge, USA
{anil,holger,madden}@csail.mit.edu

Abstract. Previous work [1] has claimed that the best performing implementation of in-memory hash joins is based on (radix-)partitioning of the build-side input. Indeed, despite the overhead of partitioning, the benefits from increased cache-locality and synchronization free parallelism in the build-phase outweigh the costs when the input data is randomly ordered. However, many datasets already exhibit significant spatial locality (i.e., non-randomness) due to the way data items enter the database: through periodic ETL or trickle loaded in the form of transactions. In such cases, the first benefit of partitioning — increased locality — is largely irrelevant. In this paper, we demonstrate how hardware transactional memory (HTM) can render the other benefit, freedom from synchronization, irrelevant as well.

Specifically, using careful analysis and engineering, we develop an adaptive hash join implementation that outperforms parallel radix-partitioned hash joins as well as sort-merge joins on data with high spatial locality. In addition, we show how, through lightweight (less than 1% overhead) runtime monitoring of the transaction abort rate, our implementation can detect inputs with low spatial locality and dynamically fall back to radix-partitioning of the build-side input. The result is a hash join implementation that is more than 3 times faster than the state-of-the-art on high-locality data and never more than 1% slower.

1 Introduction

As the clock rate of processor cores has stagnated, parallelization has become the primary means to saturate the increasing memory bandwidth of modern computers. Fortunately, in the field of data management, many problems have efficient data-parallel solutions. In particular analytical queries can often saturate the bandwidth using horizontal partitioning of the input and parallelized computation by different cores on each partition, followed by merging of results.

This approach works particularly well, when the result is small and the merge trivial, as in operations such as grouped aggregation with few groups.

When the result is large, as, e.g., in the case of hash joins the balance shifts: the overhead of partitioning and/or merging may well become the most expensive step. One way to avoid this overhead is to update the hash table in-place. Doing so requires the use of locks or atomic instructions during inserts, which, unfortunately, also introduces significant overhead. Which of these two approaches is

© Springer International Publishing AG 2017
S. Blanas et al. (Eds.): ADMS 2016/IMDM 2016, LNCS 10195, pp. 118–133, 2017.
DOI: 10.1007/978-3-319-56111-0_7

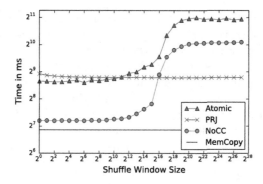

Fig. 1. Sharing vs. partitioning in hash-building

better is not immediately evident and depends on spatial locality in the underlying data.

Such locality may stem from many real-world effects such as, (a) periodic bulk
updates (common in data warehouses) which create locality in date attributes or
an attribute that is correlated with the load order (e.g., physical location), (b)
trickle loading through transactions in OLTP systems which also creates locality
in date columns, (c) automatically assigned IDs which are often monotonically
increasing counters or (d) the occurence of temporarily hot items (e.g., star wars
action figures before movie releases). In fact, spatial locality, is one of the most
commonly exploited aspects of code and data in computer architecture design.

To illustrate the relative costs of these two approaches depending on the
degree of spatial locality, we compared a state-of-the-art, hand-optimized radix-
based hash-building phase [1] to an implementation using a shared hash table
with linear probing, that is protected using atomic instructions (both implementations use identity hashing). To isolate the effects of insert locality, the input
data keys are unique (from 1 to 2^{27}) but (knuth-)shuffled within a sliding window
(the authors of [1] study the case of fully shuffled data, i.e., window size equal to
input data size). By varying the size of the window, we can study the sensitivity to locality in the input data. Figure 1 shows that for small shuffle windows,
the shared hash table approach using atomic instructions ("Atomic") performs
slightly better than the radix-based partitioning approach ("PRJ"). For larger
shuffle windows, we observe the typical effects of poor cache locality: a staircase
like pattern that exposes the sizes of the CPU's caches. The (radix-)partitioned
implementation is robust against poor locality because the partitioning creates
locality using a hardware-conscious implementation.

However, neither implementation performs close to the memory bandwidth,
which gives hope for an even faster implementation. To illustrate this, we implemented a third variant: insert values into the shared hash table without protecting the buckets ("NoCC"). Since the values are unique and there are no
collisions, this implementation yields the correct result in this case (although,
of course, this would not be true in general). The graph shows that this

implementation outperforms the others by more than a factor 3. NoCC comes very close to the time taken by `memcopy` to write the same amount of data. While this illustrates the overhead of the existing approaches, unfortunately, it is not easily generalizable to cases in which there are conflicts.

Fortunately, there is a third technique that can achieve correctness and performance close to the "NoCC" approach by exploiting the hardware transactional memory (HTM) features in modern (Intel) processors (and, hopefully, AMD soon). In this paper, we explore the potential of this (relatively new) technology for the purpose of parallel hash-joins. In particular:

- We extensively study the effect of locality and transaction size on the performance of HTM-protected parallel hash-building.
- We devise a hash-building technique that dynamically balances the per-transaction overhead and the abort rate that comes with larger transactions.
- We use the number of aborted transactions as an indicator of poor locality allowing us to adaptively fall back to the partitioning implementation [1] when appropriate.

This results in a hash join implementation that outperforms existing ones by about a factor 3 when spatial locality in the input is high and never performs significantly (i.e., more than 1%) worse than the state of the art.

We structured the rest of this paper as follows: in Sect. 2, we discuss primitives to ensure memory consistency. In Sect. 3, we present the current state of the art in parallel hash joins. In Sect. 4, we develop our approach to parallel hash joins by step-by-step analyzing and addressing the relevant bottlenecks. This section also contains our evaluation. We conclude in Sect. 5.

2 Synchronization Primitives

Building a hash table in parallel involves concurrent inserts into to the table. In this section, we briefly review the different means used to ensure correct results: transactional memory, atomic instructions and input partitioning.

2.1 Transactional Memory

The key idea of a transaction is that multiple operations can be combined into a unit that is executed atomically and in isolation from others. Multiple transactions can be executed concurrently as long as they affect different objects - otherwise one of the transactions fails. Transactional memory is the application of this concept to the reading and writing of a system's memory, thus providing an alternative to fine-grained locking which is more expensive and prone to deadlocks.

The concept of Transactional Memory existed for a long time [4]. Shavit and Touitou [12] are credited for the first Software Transactional Memory (STM) proposal. Due to entirely software controlled validation overhead, STM causes significant slowdown during execution and found little resonance in the database systems community. Only recently hardware vendors, such as Intel [14] and IBM [5] realized transactional memory support in hardware (HTM).

While IBM relies on dedicated HTM components, Intel extended the CPU's cache-coherence infrastructure, based on the well known MESI protocol [3], to enable HTM. In MESI, each cache line can be in one of the four states: modified, exclusive, shared or invalid. Different caches are kept in-sync by snooping each other's load and store requests. For example, when a core updates a cache line which is also present on other caches in shared state, the local state is updated to modified and other caches update their state for the cache line to invalid. The key idea used to implement HTM in Haswell is to use the L1 cache as a buffer for executing transactions. All the updates made by the transaction happen locally in the L1 cache and the changes are propagated to main memory only if the transaction successfully commits. Since the cache coherence protocol is an integral part of multicore CPUs and commits/aborts require no extra communication across cores, the transactional execution has very little overhead.

The downside of using HTM in Haswell is that the transaction size is limited to size of L1 cache. Even though this limitation imposes constraints on the type of transactions that can be executed, it has caught the attention of database researchers due to its low overhead. The HTM support has been used to implement database transactions in in-memory databases [7,13]. To the best of our knowledge, ours is the first work that explores using HTM for adaptive parallel hash-building in hash joins.

2.2 Atomic Instructions

Another means to provide mutual exclusion without using a lock is using atomic instructions. Atomic instructions allow the programmer to concurrently access and update variables of basic data types. Like HTM, atomic instructions rely on the MESI cache coherence protocol to provide atomicity and isolation. When a core wishes to read a variable, the corresponding cache line is loaded in shared mode. On a store request, the core sets the cache line to modified and the cache line gets invalidated on the other cores. A more expensive operation like compare-and-swap requires loading the cache line as exclusive before comparing and swapping.

Spinlocks are implemented using atomic instructions and require one atomic operation to set the lock variable and one store to update the variable. Since join columns are often integers or dictionary-encoded strings, atomic instructions can be used to directly update the hash table entries, making it much faster than using spinlocks in low-contention scenarios.

2.3 Partitioning

Consistency primitives are needed in the event of concurrent data access to the same address. An alternative approach is to partition the input such that no such conflicts arise. While partitioning itself can be expensive, there is no need for synchronization in the processing phase. In particular for the construction of hashes, this technique has been applied to great effect.

3   State-of-the-Art Hash-Building

One of the fundamental differences when comparing a database's hash-table requirements to those of generic hash-tables implementations stems from the bulk-processing nature of database query processing: where generic hash-tables have to guarantee consistent reads after every insert, database query processing usually only requires consistency at the end of the build process. For that reason, few databases incorporate off-the-shelf hash-table implementations.

Consequently, hash building has been extensively studied in the database literature in the context of hash joins. Two main lines of thought exist: the first argues that the best performance can be achieved by using a hardware-conscious (radix) partitioning to minimize cache misses during the build-phase [6]. The second approach holds that a hash-build implementation can be efficient by using a single shared hash table across threads and synchronizing using locks [2]. Through careful evaluation, Balkesen et al. [1] showed that the radix partitioning approach performs significantly better than the shared hash table approach for fully shuffled data. Since this approach is the current state-of-the-art (and also our prime competitor), we discuss it in more detail in the following.

3.1   Radix Partitioned Hash Joins

The main insight motivating radix partitioning based hash-building is that when the hash table is larger than the cache size, almost every insert into the hash table causes a cache miss. This can be avoided by pre-partitioning the data using an approximation of the hash-function and building a hash-table per partition, thus improving insert locality. Since the partitions are filled sequentially, the memory access locality in the partitioning phase is improved. Manegold et al. [9] noted that since each partition ends up residing on a different memory page, having a very high fanout ($=inputSize/L1Size$) results in excessive TLB thrashing. To circumvent this, the input data is partitioned in multiple passes (two is usually sufficient). Each pass has a fanout less than or equal to the number of TLB entries. Each pass looks at a different set of bits from the hashed value, hence the name *Radix Partitioning*.

In addition to its cache-friendliness, the radix partitioning approach is easily parallelized. The input relation is divided into horizontal partitions. In the first pass, each part is scanned independently to generate a histogram over the input data, so that the exact output size is known per thread per partition. A single contiguous output array is allocated. A synchronization barrier is used to indicate the end of first pass, at which point each thread computes the prefix-sum over the relevant histograms to find the exact offset of each partition it writes to. Finally, the threads execute a second pass over its partition of the data to write the tuples to the right place in the output array, without any synchronization.

We end up having two passes over data per radix partition pass. For our evaluation dataset, we require two radix partitioning passes i.e. four passes in total.

3.2 Using Atomics

To access the suitability of atomic instructions for parallel hash-building, we implemented a shared hash table using the built-in C++11 atomics. The implementation performs linear probing on insert and a single catch-all overflow bucket that is used after checking a configurable number of slots. Note that, while it is possible to implement a lock-free hash-table with bucket chaining, the build-time overhead (most importantly creating an intermediary copy of a bucket) is much higher than the catch-all scheme we implemented. The implementation is mostly straight forward with a single optimization: we first use an atomic read to ensure the slot is empty, following which a compare-and-swap is used to insert the tuple. The swap might fail if the slot has been filled by another thread since the read was performed. We found that the benefits of cheap checking to ensure a slot is free outweighs the cost for occasionally failing to insert.

3.3 Hash-Function Design

Naturally, the selection of an appropriate hash-function is crucial when designing a hash-table. The desirable property of uniform output distribution has to be balanced against locality preservation and computational efficiency. The design space ranges from cryptographic hash functions [11] that have near-perfect output through efficient hashes such as Murmur Hashing[1] to simple modulo hashing. Different in-memory database systems took different decisions to address this question: while HyPeR and Pivotal Gemfire/Apache Geode aim for skew-resilience using Murmur Hashing, MonetDB implements the locality-preserving and cheap modulo hashing. In this paper, we limit ourselves to modulo hashing. We leave the development of a hybrid hash-function (preserving cache-line locality while mitigating global skew) to future work.

4 Exploiting Locality Using HTM

The hypothesis we want to establish and substantiate in this section is that is possible to develop a single pass hash table implementation that, given enough locality in the input data, becomes (close-to) memory bandwidth bound. While the ultimate goal of our efforts is an adaptive hash-join, we construct it "bottom up": by analyzing the impact of the relevant hardware- and data-characteristics. We analyze the effects and costs of Virtual Memory (Sect. 4.2), Atomic Instructions (Sect. 4.3), HTM overhead (Sect. 4.4) and the impact of locality (Sect. 4.5). Only after establishing the importance of these factors, do we develop our final contribution (Sects. 4.6 to 4.8): a hash-join implementation that adapts to the

---

[1] https://sites.google.com/site/murmurhash.

degree of locality in the underlying data, using an HTM-based approach for high-locality and the state-of-the-art partition-based approach [1] for low-locality data.

The key ingredient of our approach is the use of Intel's Restricted Transactional Memory (RTM). Before diving into the experiments and implementation, however, let us briefly discuss our experimentation setup as well as the data-structure we use for the hash-table.

4.1 Setup

To ensure comparability with previous work, we adopted the same workload as previous work [1,2]: unique keys (32 bit) carrying a 32 bit payload with every tuple finding exactly one join-partner (Appendix B contains the results for non-unique keys including conflict handling). Note that, while there is currently some discussion about the prevalence of this specific case in practical applications, it constitutes a harder challenge than the case of larger payloads in which copy overhead dominates the costs. We also feel that, in particular in highly-optimized, column-oriented databases, small payloads are the rule, rather than the exception.

The parameter we are interested in is the locality of the input: where previous work applied a global (knuth-)shuffle to the input, we slide window through the array and shuffle one value in the window per slide step - the size of the window is the primary parameter of our experiments. This allows us to create data locality ranging from fully sorted (window size 1) to fully shuffled (window size equal to input size).

The structure of our hash-table is similar to that of bucket-chaining based hash table implementations [1,2]: insert conflicts are handled using buckets of size three that are chained in a linked list on overflow. Later in Sect. 4.6 we describe the full design with pseudocode. While bucket chaining is vulnerable to inputs with a *very* high number of conflicts, we found that performance for (non-unique) uniform random data is very similar to that of unique, shuffled data (see Appendix B)

The experiments were run on a single socket Intel E3-1270 v5 @ 3.60 GHz (Skylake with 4 Cores, 8 hardware threads) fully equipped with 64 GB DDR-4 RAM (2133 MHz bus clock) running Ubuntu Linux 15.10 (Kernel 4.2.0-30). The input sizes were 134 million tuples (2^{27}) on each side, fitting comfortably in main-memory. All experiments were compiled using gcc 5.2.1 using the "-O3-march=native" flags and we report the average of 5 runs.

An interesting aspect to study, would be the interplay of HTM and NUMA. Unfortunately, multi-socket CPUs that reliably[2] implement RTM only became available in early 2016 - too late to be included in this study. We did, however, find a number of relevant, hitherto undocumented, effects that we describe in the following.

---

[2] Earlier implementations suffered from a bug that caused Intel to deactivate the feature in a microcode update.

4.2   Interaction with Virtual Memory

The first effect we noticed when developing our approach is the fragility of Intel's transactional memory implementation with respect to the events that cause transactions to abort. The hazardous effects of, e.g., the size of the working set of the transaction or evictions due to associativity are well documented [14] and are of little importance to us. However, in our experiments, we noticed an effect that has substantial impact on our design: when accessing unmapped virtual memory, transactions fail with no chance of success upon retry but without indicating so using the respective status flags. This is due to the intricate interplay of restricted transactional memory and lazy physical page allocation. When allocating zeroed-out memory using `calloc`, the Linux Kernel does not eagerly allocate the memory and run a loop to initialize it. Instead, it maps all allocated pages to a single, read-only page that is statically initialized to zero. Any write to that page causes a page fault and subsequent copying of the read-only page (copy-on-write). If the write is protected by a transaction, however, the page fault immediately aborts the transaction without triggering the page fault. Consequently, the read-only page is never copied and a retry of the transaction will fail. This problem percolates to subsequent transactions on the page causing all transactions to fail.

This effect has been reported in the context of updates to tree-indices [8] and resolved by initializing pages using an atomic instruction before retrying a transaction. In the case of hash-building, an alternative is to eagerly pre-fault memory which avoids complex conflict handlers in the critical path. Unfortunately this prevents some optimizations that are often applied to the process of hash-building. Generously over-allocating the hash table is, e.g., an effective to means deal with the unknown domain of input values. This optimization is no longer feasible when the entire table has to be pre-faulted. We're considering the extension of our work to cases with unknown domains for future work.

4.3   Hardware Transactions vs. Atomics

To establish a baseline for the usefulness of hardware transactions, we started by comparing them to their most direct competitor: atomic instructions. Note that this comparison is not entirely apples to apples because Intel's restricted transactions are not guaranteed to succeed. However, we will show in the rest of this section that, given enough locality, restricted transactions virtually always succeed (fewer than one abort in 10,000 transactions) when protecting every insert with its own transaction (denominated TS = 1).

In Fig. 2, we compare the cost of the two techniques in the extreme cases: building a hash table using identity hashing on fully sorted or fully shuffled data. The figure illustrates that protecting an insert using a hardware transaction is, in fact, cheaper than using atomic instructions in both cases. This is to be expected because Compare-and-Swap (used in atomic insert) is a more expensive operation compared to an optimistic load and store. The reason for this lies in the fact that the CPU has to guarantee that the write was actually performed.

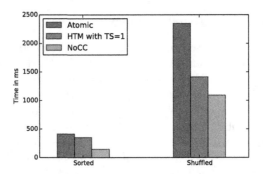

Fig. 2. Transactional memory vs. atomic instructions

For that, it has to MESI-invalidate the cache line in all other cores and (potentially) write it back to memory. This makes little difference in the sorted case (since virtually no cache-lines are shared) but is substantial in the shuffled case because cache-lines are frequently shared. However, using HTM is still significantly more expensive than processing without concurrency control: around 5 times in the sorted case and 20% on shuffled data. Consequently, we, turn our attention to means to reduce the per-transaction cost next.

4.4 Transaction Overhead

It is natural to expect some overhead for setting up a transaction. This overhead is, of course, relative to the cost for other operations. As established in Fig. 1 on page 2, locality in the input data, which translates into access locality for the hash-buckets, is arguably the determining factor for overall performance. Consequently, we assessed the overhead to protect hash-inserts by transactions for the two extreme input data distributions: sorted (optimal locality) and fully shuffled (least locality[3]), while varying the number of inserts per transaction. The per-transaction overhead can, thus, be amortized over multiple inserts. The results (Fig. 3a and b, respectively) show that, in the presence of locality, the overhead of setting up a transaction for every insert is almost $4x$[4] and becomes apparent in the steep drop left of the plateau in Fig. 3a. The picture changes when considering fully shuffled data: while the overhead is still significant, it is no longer the dominating cost factor (cache misses are).

However, larger transactions increase the chance of transaction aborts even if there are no actual conflicts at CPU word granularity: factors such as suboptimal cache associativity and context switching which lead to L1 cache evictions lead to aborts. This effect can even be observed in the sorted data case (Fig. 3a): the abort rate starts to increase notably at around 64 inserts per transaction.

---

[3] Note that fully shuffled unique data items have even worse locality than uniform randomly generated (non-unique) data items because there is zero probability for re-accessing a data item.

[4] The ratio is even higher for smaller datatypes.

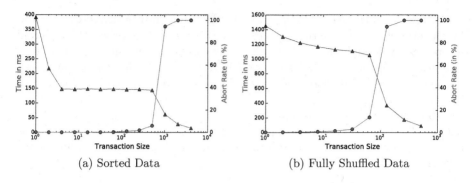

(a) Sorted Data   (b) Fully Shuffled Data

Fig. 3. Assessing per transaction overhead

When the active set size grows beyond the size of the L1 cache, all transactions abort - as expected.

For fully shuffled data (Fig. 3b), the abort rate increases much earlier as the inserts are spread out over many cache lines, which amplifies the active set size and increases the probability of false conflicts. This naturally raises the question of the impact of locality on performance and abort rate, which we study in the following.

4.5   Impact of Locality

To assess the impact of locality on the build performance and abort rate we applied the same shuffle that was used to create Fig. 1 to the input data and evaluated the HTM-based implementation. In addition to the shuffle window size, we varied the size of the transactions and measured build time (Fig. 4a) and abort rate (Fig. 4b). Figure 4a re-iterates the point that, given enough locality, larger transactions perform better. The point of the (inevitable) cost explosion, however, is only slightly influenced by the transaction size.

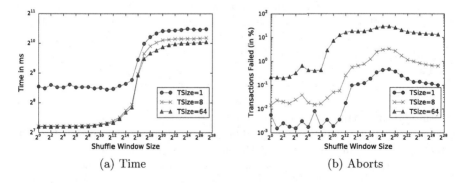

(a) Time   (b) Aborts

Fig. 4. Varied size and shuffle window

Figure 4b, on the other hand, shows that the abort rate is strongly influenced by the size of the transactions (as expected): transactions of size 1 rarely fail when locality is high (left side of the chart) while larger transactions have a significantly higher chance of failing. With less locality (right side of the chart), the abort rate for all transaction sizes increases up to around two orders of magnitude.

Note that these experiments did not include the retrying of transactions and would, thus, not guarantee that values to actually get inserted into the hash table. We will discuss an implementation without that shortcoming in the following.

4.6   Putting it Together

The last step to providing a full hash-build implementation is to develop a strategy to deal with aborted transactions. For that purpose, we simply record the input position range associated with the aborted transactions in a preallocated buffer while building the hash table. We also record the tuples that landed in full buckets in an overflow buffer. When the build-phase is complete, we perform a wrap-up phase that traverses the abort- and overflow-buffers, resolves the positions and inserts the values into the hash table. Note that the bucket chaining happens only in the wrap-up phase, we do not do bucket chaining in the transactions to keep their cache line footprint small. The pseudocode of the full implementation is given in Fig. 5.

We found that it is not worth parallelizing the wrapup phase due to its unique characteristics: for high-locality data, its cost are insignificant relative to the overall runtime because there are few failed transactions. For low-locality data, the cost of the wrap-up phase is dominated by cache- and TLB-thrashing, leaving even a single CPU core mostly idle.

With the wrap-up in place, the hash-build implementation is complete. As established, however, optimal performance hinges on the appropriate selection of the transaction size. To remove transaction size as a tuning parameter we adopt a simple adaptation strategy: we start with a transaction size of 16, monitor the abort rate and define a high- and a low-watermark. When the abort rate exceeds the high-watermark we half the transaction size, when it drops below the low-watermark we double it. We found 0.4% to be a good low and 2% a good high watermark and check every 16×1024 inserts.

Figure 6 shows the total runtime of the static transaction sizes as well as our adaptive approach (TSize-Adaptive). Note how the adaptive approach matches the performance of the best static case and occasionally outperforms them, selecting optimal parameters between the static values.

We experimented with varying number of threads and noticed that the performance does not improve after 3 threads, indicating that the application is memory-bound. While hyper-threading is expected to increase cache contention, we did not observe any significant difference in performance with 4 thread (one per core) and using all 8 threads. This is because the adaptive approach used in

```
struct Bucket:
  Tuple tuples[3]
  int count
  int nextBucketIndex

HashTable table
table.buckets = Bucket[ceil(numTuples/3)]

// Each thread gets an input range [start,end)
for (i = start; i<end; i += transactionSize):
  status = _xbegin()
  if status == _XBEGIN_STARTED:
    for (j = i; j < i + transactionSize; j++):
      slot = hash(tuple[j].key)
      for (k = slot; k < slot + probeLength; k++):
        if table.buckets[k] is not full:
          table.buckets[k].add(tuple); break
      if not inserted:
        overflow.add(tuple)
    xend()
  else: // Transaction Failed
    failedTransactionRanges.add(i)

// Wrap-Up
for (i in failedTransactionRanges)
  // Insert tuples[i] to tuples[i + transactionSize]
for (i in overflow)
  // Insert overflow[i]
```

Fig. 5. HTM-enabled hash-building

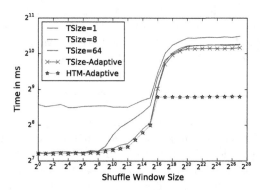

Fig. 6. Adaptive hash building (including wrap-up)

TSize-Adaptive adjusts the transaction size to keep the abort rates low and the application remains memory-bound.

4.7 Fallback for Fully Shuffled Data

When there is sufficient locality in the data, our adaptive approach performs best. However, for large shuffle windows, the radix-partitioned approach is still more efficient. Fortunately, as can be see in Fig. 4b, the large shuffle windows coincide with high transaction abort rates. We use this insight to develop a hybrid approach that falls back to the radix-partitioned approach when it detects poor locality. We implement this in a straight-forward manner: we use the first 16×1024 tuples of each thread for training and inspect the average abort rate at the end of the training phase[5]. If the abort rate exceeds a threshold (we found 4% to be appropriate in our experiments), we fall back to the radix-partitioning implementation. The training phase runs on a small subset of tuples and hence the overhead (about $4ms$ when using 8 threads) is negligible. Figure 6 shows how the adaptive approach with fallback (HTM-Adaptive) effectively adapts to the data distribution. While our approach does not currently deal with skewed data locality, the identical data structure format of the two approaches make the development of a fully adaptive strategy straight forward.

4.8 Probing

To assess the impact of the presented optimizations on the performance of a full join, we also evaluated performance including the probe phase (counting the number of matches). Note that parallelizing the probe itself is usually not difficult because it does not modify the hash table. However, probe performance is, just as build performance, affected by data access locality. Just like the build, the probe can, therefore benefit from a pre-partitioning step if the tuples are partitioned according to their hashes (or an approximation thereof). Since this effect is independent of the way the hash table is built, we only evaluated the probe using input data with perfect locality (i.e., sorted input data).

In Fig. 7, we present the final result of our efforts: an adaptive hash-join implementation using HTM abort rate as runtime feedback variable. The figure illustrates the performance of the full join: build and probe (labeled HTM-Adaptive). It shows that, while our implementation effectively falls back to partitioning the input if locality is low, it outperforms the partitioned approach by more than $3\times$ when locality is high.

For reference, we also included the results of a fully parallel sort-merge join and the Non-Partitioned Join implementation that was used for comparison by Balkesen et al. [1] (labeled "NPJ" in the figure).

The sort-phase of the sort-merge join is based on Timsort [10] which is designed to work well an almost-sorted data. We observe that, only for data

---

[5] We considered breaking it down by abort code but found no useful correlation (see Appendix A).

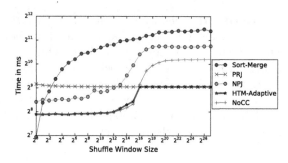

Fig. 7. Full hash join (build and probe)

that is perfectly sorted (shuffle window size equal to 1) does the sort-merge join outperform our adaptive implementation.

The Non-Partitioned Join was implemented (by Balkesen et al.) using per-bucket spinlocks. As apparent in Fig. 7, NPJ performs about 42% worse than HTM for sorted data but degrades in performance once randomness (and thus contention) increases. The reason is two-fold: firstly, the use of spinlocks instead of HTM leads to a 14% slowdown. Second, in NPJ, the locks are co-located with the tuples in the buckets which increases the memory footprint of the resulting table. The HTM approach does not use locks, hence is able to fit 3 tuples per 32 byte bucket compared to 2 tuples in the case of NPJ, which results in another 25% speed-up. Finally, and most apparently, the implementation is not adaptive which can be seen by the performance for inputs with low-locality.

5   Conclusion

Locality in input data is an important, yet often underutilized, factor when developing and selecting appropriate implementations of data management operators. We demonstrated how the state-of-the-art parallel hash join implementations fail to recognize and exploit locality of the input data. To mitigate that problem, we developed an adaptive hash join implementation that uses hardware transactional memory to protect inserts into a shared hash table. We recognized the number of inserts per transaction as the most important performance factor and adaptively tune this parameter at runtime. In addition, our implementation recognizes input data with poor locality and automatically falls back to the current state-of-the-art: parallel radix-partitioned hash joins. The result is a hash join implementation that is more than 3 times faster than the state-of-the-art on high-locality data and never more than 1% slower.

A   Transaction Abort Breakdown

When studying the pseudocode of our approach in Sect. 4.6, a reader may note that one might use the status code to determine the reason for aborted transactions and use this as runtime feedback. Figure 8 shows a breakdown of the reason for aborts observed with when running the *TSize-Adaptive* implementation (when varying the shuffle window size). Capacity aborts occur if transaction working set exceeds L1 cache size or if more than A cache lines of the same cache set are accessed, where A is the L1 cache associativity. Conflict abort happens if two transactions read/write sets overlap. The main reason we cannot use this information as runtime feedback is that most transaction aborts have return code set to 0, i.e., giving no information about the reason for abort ($RC = 0$ line) and degree of noise is high for the other return codes.

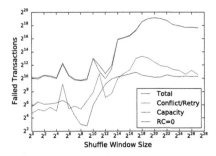

Fig. 8. Reason for transaction abort

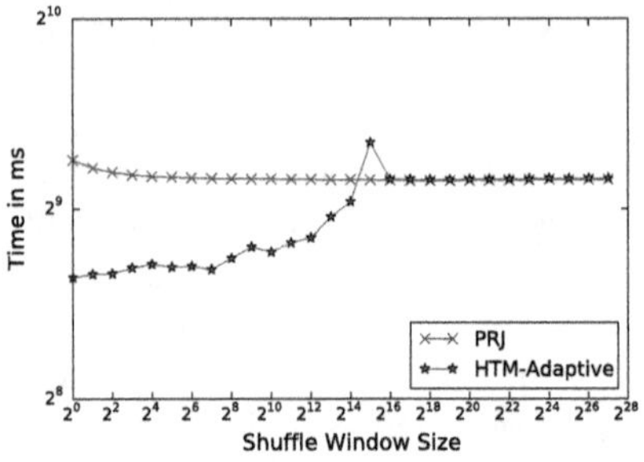

Fig. 9. Processing uniform random data

B   Non-unique Inputs

While we consider the problem of efficient conflict handling out of scope of this paper, we still consider it important to establish that the presented techniques do not prevent conflict handling. To illustrate this, consider Fig. 9 which corresponds to Fig. 7 run on uniform randomly generated integers in the domain 1 to n (the size of the input) which, naturally, includes duplicate values. As in Fig. 7, the experiment is to perform the full join but only counting the number of matches. As stated in Sect. 4, we use bucket-chaining to handle overflows of the buckets and re-inserting to handle aborted transaction. The figure shows a similar pattern to Fig. 7 but exposes a suboptimal configuration of the threshold for switching to the radix-partitioned implementation. This indicates that a conflict-aware fallback strategy may be worthwhile.

References

1. Balkesen, C., et al.: Main-memory hash joins on multi-core CPUs: tuning to the underlying hardware. In: ICDE (2013)
2. Blanas, S., Li, Y., Patel, J.M.: Design and evaluation of main memory hash join algorithms for multi-core CPUs. In: SIGMOD (2011)
3. Hennessy, J.L., Patterson, D.A.: Computer Architecture: A Quantitative Approach. Elsevier, Amsterdam (2011)
4. Herlihy, M., Moss, J.E.B.: Transactional memory: architectural support for lock-free data structures. ACM (1993)

5. Jacobi, C., Slegel, T., Greiner, D.: Transactional memory architecture and implementation for IBM system Z. In: MICRO (2012)
6. Kim, C., et al.: Sort vs. hash revisited: fast join implementation on modern multicore CPUs. In: VLDB (2009)
7. Leis, V., Kemper, A., Neumann, T.: Exploiting hardware transactional memory in main-memory databases. In: ICDE (2014)
8. Makreshanski, D., Levandoski, J., Stutsman, R.: To lock, swap, or elide: on the interplay of hardware transactional memory and lock-free indexing. Proc. VLDB Endow. 8(11), 1298–1309 (2015)
9. Manegold, S., Boncz, P., Kersten, M.: Optimizing main-memory join on modern hardware. In: TKDE (2002)
10. Peters, T.: Description of timsort. http://bugs.python.org/file4451/timsort.txt
11. Rogaway, P., Shrimpton, T.: Cryptographic hash-function basics: definitions, implications, and separations for preimage resistance, second-preimage resistance, and collision resistance. In: Roy, B., Meier, W. (eds.) FSE 2004. LNCS, vol. 3017, pp. 371–388. Springer, Heidelberg (2004). doi:10.1007/978-3-540-25937-4_24
12. Shavit, N., Touitou, D.: Software transactional memory. Distrib. Comput. 10, 99–116 (1997)
13. Tran, K.Q., Blanas, S., Naughton, J.F.: On transactional memory, spinlocks, and database transactions. In: ADMS (2010)
14. Yoo, R.M., et al.: Performance evaluation of Intel transactional synchronization extensions for high-performance computing. In: SC (2013)

SwingDB: An Embedded In-memory DBMS Enabling Instant Snapshot Sharing

Qingzhong Meng[1(✉)], Xuan Zhou[1], Shiping Chen[2], and Shan Wang[1]

[1] MOE Key Laboratory of DEKE,
Renmin University of China, Beijing 100872, China
mqz@ruc.edu.cn

[2] CSIRO Data61, PO Box 76, Epping, NSW 1017, Australia

Abstract. Data transmission between an in-memory DBMS and a data analytical program is usually slow, partially due to the inadequate IPC support of modern operating systems. In this paper, we present SWING, a novel inter-process data sharing mechanism of OS, which allows processes to share physical memory through an instant system call. Based on SWING, we develop an embedded in-memory DBMS called SwingDB, which enables data analytical applications to access databases in their own memory space, instead of resorting to traditional inter-process communication. Extensive experiments were conducted to demonstrate the advantage of such a DBMS-OS co-design.

1   Introduction

As the capacity of RAM keeps growing exponentially, it has become an important instrument for big data processing. In the emerging paradigm of in-memory computing, people prefer to store an entire database in RAM, and perform data processing completely on RAM. This can substantially speed up the processes of data manipulation and data analysis. However, most data analytical workflows are multi-stage. They usually involves a number of data processing programs and services that cooperate to generate results. In a typical case of data analysis, data is usually stored in a DBMS; when an analytical process starts, it first issues queries (e.g., in SQL) to the DBMS to retrieve required data; then, the data is passed to a data analytical program to perform data preparation and statistical analysis; finally, a data visualization program is used to present the analytical results to the end user. Sometimes, large volume of data needs to be transmitted across various programs and services. If data transmission is slow, as it always is, it will obliterate the performance advantage of in-memory computing.

To the best of our knowledge, the mechanisms of inter-program data exchange provided by today's operating systems can hardly meet the performance requirement of in-memory computing. The IPC Mechanisms of FIFO and Socket appear extremely slow, as they need to move data physically. While the shared memory mechanism does not move data, the programs using shared memory have to deal with space allocation and data synchronization on their own, which incurs extra cost. On the one hand, when multiple programs are tied to a single piece of

© Springer International Publishing AG 2017
S. Blanas et al. (Eds.): ADMS 2016/IMDM 2016, LNCS 10195, pp. 134–149, 2017.
DOI: 10.1007/978-3-319-56111-0_8

shared memory, they become tightly coupled, which may raise the cost of software development and maintenance. On the other hand, it is sometimes unsafe to allow applications to access the memory space of a DBMS – once an application is malfunctioning, it may impair the integrity of the data.

In this paper, we introduce a new copy-on-write solution to inter-process data sharing. It is fast and convenient. In contrast to shared memory, it enables loose coupling between data processing programs, so that it matches today's practice of software engineering. We call our approach *SWING*, which analogizes the transmission of data to how Tarzan swings from a tree to another. The memory allocated by the SWING mechanism is called *COW Memory*, which is a type of *virtual memory* with the following characteristics:

1. Two chunks of COW memory can be mapped to the same set of physical memory pages, to share data.
2. Modifications on different chunks of COW memory (that share physical memory pages) are isolated through copy-on-write.

When a process wants to share data to another process, it can place the data in a COW memory area and let the other process allocate another COW memory area that is mapped to the same physical memory space. After the allocation, both processes can see the same contents in their own COW memory areas. This approach allows us to avoid physical movement of data. Afterwards, the two processes can modify their own COW memory areas independently. A copy-on-write mechanism makes sure that their modification should be invisible to each other, so that no synchronization is required.

Based on SWING, we create a new in-memory DBMS called SwingDB. SwingDB works as an embedded DBMS, such that each application operates on a database in its own memory space, without incurring inter-process communication. Each database instance of SwingDB is completely placed in a COW memory area, so that independent applications can share the snapshots of their databases using the SWING mechanism. SwingDB is especially suitable to multi-stage in-memory data processing, in which several loosely coupled programs cooperate in performing data analysis.

We implemented the SWING mechanism in Linux[1], and then constructed our SwingDB system by re-engineering an open-source in-memory DBMS called SuperSonic. We conducted experiments to characterize the performance of SWING and SwingDB. We also compared SwingDB against traditional in-memory DBMS, to demonstrate its suitability in in-memory data analytics.

The rest of the paper is organized as follows. Section 2 introduces the related work. Section 3 presents the design and implementation of SWING. Section 4 introduces SwingDB and discusses its potential applications. Section 5 presents the results of our experimental evaluation. Section 6 concludes the paper and discusses our future research plans.

---

[1] Source code: http://swinglinux.github.io/swing/.

2   Related Work

In-memory Databases. Data movement is an expensive operation for data intensive applications, while it often occurs between a DBMS and a data analytical application. Especially when conducting large scale statistical analysis, we need to transmit large volumes of data from a DBMS to an analytical tool, such as R or SAS. In the context of in-memory computing, such data transmission is heavy and may kill the performance.

Folk wisdom believes that it is cheaper to move programs to data than to move data between programs. To this end, a number of database systems integrate components of data analysis and data mining [5], and expect applications to perform data analysis within the database systems. Some in-memory DBMS even combines the database server and the application server into one single system, to minimize the cost of data movement [7,15]. However, the tight coupling between database systems and data analytical tools is a double-edged sword – while it reduces the communication cost, it raises the cost of software engineering [4,8], which regards "separation of concerns" as an essential principle. In many cases, developers of a DBMS do not know what analytical algorithms applications will demand, while developers of applications have little knowledge about how a DBMS works. The design of SwingDB aims to minimize the cost of data exchange, while keeping the coupling between DBMS and data analytical programs as loose as possible.

The most relevant work to SwingDB is the in-memory DBMS named Hyper [9]. Hyper was designed to support OLTP and OLAP simultaneously. Hyper's main process is responsible for maintaining the integrity of a database and performing updates. When an analytical request arrives, the main process invokes the system call $fork()$ to initiate a child process. As the child process shares the memory space of the main process, it can immediately see a complete snapshot of the in-memory database and conduct data analysis independently on that snapshot. A copy-on-write mechanism is employed by the operating system to guard the isolation between the parent and child processes. To the best of our knowledge, SAP HANA [7,15] also utilizes $fork()$ to share data between the DBMS and the analytical applications. Although the $fork()$ approach successfully avoids the cost of data movement, it does not offer good usability. To perform data analysis, an application needs to pack its analytical program and ships it to the DBMS (e.g., in the form of dynamic link libraries). This makes the development of analytical applications complicated. On the other hand, it does not allow joint analytics over multiple database systems, as multiple parent processes cannot share the same child process. By comparison, SwingDB is more flexible and efficient than the $fork()$ approach.

There have been several recently proposed techniques which utilizes copy-on-write to realize concurrency control on in-memory data [2,11,14]. As their use cases are different from that of SWING, we regard them less relevant to our work.

Inter-process Communication. The most commonly used inter-process communication methods include named pipe (FIFO), socket and shared memory. When transmitting data, both FIFO and socket need to move data physically. In particular, they need to copy data from the source to a buffer, and then copy it from the buffer to the destination. Sometimes multiple layer buffers exist, such that data needs to be copied for multiple times [12]. Copying data physically is expensive in the context of in-memory computing.

Shared memory is so far regarded as the fastest IPC approach, as it does not move data physically. Normally, an operating system offers two modes to access shared memory. In the *shared* mode, a process' writes to the shared memory are completely visible to the others. In the *private* mode, a process' writes to the shared memory are only visible to itself – once it attempts to write to the shared memory, copy-on-write operations will be invoked to hide the write from the other processes.

Applying shared memory to data transmission between a DBMS and an analytical process, the DBMS can choose the shared mode, and the analytical process can choose the private mode. Although this setting seems safe, it is not as powerful as our SWING approach. First, the DBMS' writes on the shared memory are constantly visible to the analytical process. As a result, concurrency control is required, to prevent the DBMS from further updating the snapshot. In SWING, after the transmission of data, the DBMS' updates are no longer visible to the receiver. Thus, synchronization is not required. Second, the analytical process cannot further share the memory to other processes. Sometimes, an analytical workflow is multi-stage. For instance, in the early stage of data analysis, some intermediate results are generated and added to the data as annotation; then, the annotated data is passed to the subsequent stage for more advanced analysis. Such multi-stage data processing is difficult to realize on shared memory. In contrast, SWING allows recursive data sharing, which suits multi-stage data processing much better.

3   The SWING Mechanism

3.1   The Data Sharing Model

The data sharing model of SWING is illustrated in Fig. 1. Processes A and B are two applications. They both send copies of their data to Process C, which performs data integration and data preparation. After the work, Process C sends its copies of data, with its modification, to the Processes D and E, which are responsible for data analysis. Such a data transmission process can be repeated infinitely. After the data sharing, all processes can work on their own copies of data independently, such that their modification of the data is invisible from each other.

The same effect can be achieved by FIFO and socket. In contrast to those approaches, the SWING method does not replicate or move data physically. It just maps the physical memory space containing the data to the virtual memory space of the target processes. The actual replication is delayed to the time when

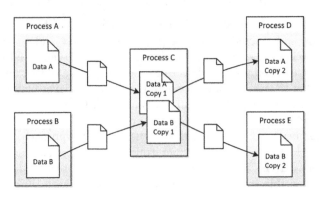

Fig. 1. Data sharing model of SWING

a process attempts to modify a block of the data – upon modification, a copy-on-write operation is invoked and a new version of the data block is created. In typical data processing scenarios, write operations are much less frequent than read operations. Therefore, the overhead of data replication can be minimized through SWING.

Using the SWING mechanism, the processes involved in data sharing are kept loosely coupled – they share only data and the code/library for interpreting data. They do not share any controlling code, such as the code to ensure data consistency. According to the principles of software engineering [3], data coupling is much more flexible than code coupling. If using shared memory, the processes have to share the code dealing with concurrency control.

Such a data sharing model cannot be realized by the $fork()$ approach either, as Process A and Process B cannot both be the parent of Process C.

3.2   The Interfaces

We implemented five system calls to realize the SWING mechanism. In SWING, the memory space used to transmit data is called COW (Copy-on-Write) memory.

1. *long createarea(long length)*. A process uses this system call to apply for a COW memory area. The input parameter *length* indicates the size of the COW memory. The return value (64 bits on an x86_64 platform) contains two parts of information. The lowest 12 bits are a *token*, a unique identifier in the whole system to identify the COW memory area. It works as a file descriptor of shared memory. The other 52 bits point to the start address of the COW memory. As the size of a memory page is normally 4 KB, the address of a COW memory area is aligned with 4 KB.
2. *long hook(int token)*. A process uses this system call to obtain a new COW memory area and maps it to the physical memory space of an existing COW memory area. Its input parameter is *token*, representing an existing

COW memory area. The returned value of *hook*() is the same as that of *createarea*(), which contains a token and an address. The returned *token* is different from the input *token*, as they represent different COW memory areas.

3. *void enablehook(int token)*. A process uses this system call to inform the operating system kernel that a COW memory area is ready to be mounted (by calling *hook*()). This system call is used to ensure data consistency. Before a process finishes modifying the data in its COW memory area, it may not wish other processes to hook the area and see a dirty version of the data. If a COW memory cannot be mounted, *hook*() returns −1.

4. *void disablehook(int token)*. A process uses this system call to inform the operating system kernel that a COW memory area cannot be hooked. It reverses the effect of *enablehook*(). When a COW memory area is just created, it is automatically disabled.

5. *void release(int token)*. A process uses this system call to release a COW memory area created by *createarea*() or *hook*(). After the call, the input *token* is released and available to represent a new COW memory area. When a process terminates, its COW memory areas will be automatically released.

3.3   The Implementation

In modern operating systems, when a process accesses a byte in its virtual memory space, the *virtual address* of the byte will first be translated to a *physical address*, through which the processor addresses the physical memory on the memory bus [1]. In a typical x86-64 architecture, a 4-level page table is used to perform the translation. Basically, a linear address space is divided into pages, normally 4 KB in size. Each virtual memory page of a process is mapped to a physical page in the physical memory, and the mapping is recorded in the page table of the process.

Page entries of different page tables can be mapped to the same physical page, such that multiple processes can share the same segment of physical memory. For instance, when *fork*() is invoked, Linux will replicate the entire page table of the parent process to that of the child process, so that their memory space are identical. After *fork*(), all the page entries of the page tables are marked as *read-only*. When a process attempts to write to a page marked as read-only, a page fault occurs; then the operating system will allocate a new physical memory page to the process, copy the contents of the original page to the new page and flags the new page as *writable*. Then, the write operation can be conducted on the new page. This is known as a typical copy-on-write process.

One possible way to implement SWING is to reuse the mechanism of *fork*(). Instead of replicating an entire page table as what *fork*() does, we can replicate only the fraction of the page table that corresponds to the COW memory area. However, partial replication of page table is still costly, especially when the COW memory area is big. In addition, as the replication procedure will block both the sending and receiving processes, it may prevent *hook*() from being frequently invoked. To avoid the cost of replication, SWING abandons the *fork*() approach

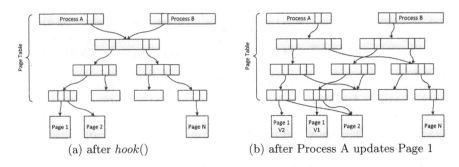

(a) after *hook*()   (b) after Process A updates Page 1

Fig. 2. Memory sharing on SWING

and allows different processes to share page tables or parts of page tables [13] as well. This is illustrated in Fig. 2(a). When *hook*() is invoked, the subtree of the page table of Process A that corresponds to the COW memory area is entirely shared to Process B. The whole procedure only requires an update on a single entry in the page table of Process B. Afterwards, both processes can see the same contents in their COW memory areas.

After the *hook*() operation, when a process attempts to update a page in the shared subtree, a copy-on-write process is invoked and the shared subtree is split into a double rooted tree. This is illustrated in Fig. 2(b). When Process A writes on Page 1, a new version of Page 1 is created to receive the write, and a new path to this version is instantiated and merged into the subtree. Afterwards, the subtree contains two roots, belonging to Processes A and B respectively. As updates continue to occur on other pages, the part of the subtree rooted at A and that rooted at B will become more and more detached. To ensure the correctness of the copy-on-write mechanism, we only need to mark the shared parts of the subtree as read-only and the parts exclusively belonging to one process as writable. When one of the processes quits or releases its COW memory, only the part of the subtree exclusively belonging to that process is removed.

In our SWING mechanism, the data sharing step (i.e., invocation of *hook*()) is extremely fast and almost nonblocking. Therefore, it can be invoked frequently. Although it incurs additional copy-on-write overhead during updates, this overhead is controllable.

4   SwingDB

SwingDB is an embedded in-memory DBMS dedicated for data analytical applications. It provides the basic functionality of a stand alone relational DBMS. In particular, it allows an application to include an entire database in its memory space, so as to avoid expensive inter-program communication. SwingDB achieves this by utilizing the SWING mechanism.

4.1   The Functionality of SwingDB

SwingDB works as an embedded DBMS – an application requiring data management functionality can have the entire SwingDB system in its program; each database instance of SwingDB resides entirely in the memory space of the application's process, so that data manipulation does not require any inter-process communication. Another application attempting to perform data analysis can retrieve a snapshot of the database and places it in its own memory space, so that it can access the database cheaply too. Moreover, the second application can further share its snapshot to a third application for more advanced data analysis. This process is illustrated in Fig. 3.

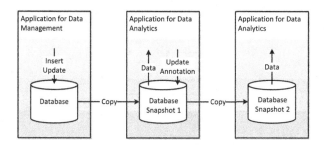

Fig. 3. SwingDB allows in-process data access

SwingDB assigns each snapshot of a database a unique name. An application can retrieve a database snapshot into its space simply through the following function call:

$$bool\ getsnapshot(string\ proposedname, string\ targetname)$$

Basically, this function retrieves a database snapshot named *targetname* into the memory space of the active process, and names the new snapshot as *proposedname*. Afterwards, the process can perform standard database operations on its own snapshot through SQL queries. Or it can directly address the data records in the snapshot through low-level interfaces, to perform advanced data analysis and data mining. As a result, each database snapshot of SwingDB resides in only one process and can be accessed only within that process. When an application no longer needs a database snapshot or regards a snapshot outdated, it can abandon the snapshot through the following function call:

$$bool\ discardsnapshot(string\ name)$$

The advantage of SwingDB lies in the efficiency of its snapshot sharing, which is almost costless. By utilizing the SWING mechanism, the snapshot sharing of SwingDB requires no physical data movement.

4.2   The Implementation of SwingDB

SwingDB stores each database instance or snapshot in a single COW memory area of SWING. When a database is created, a new COW memory area is allocated for the database. Initially, the COW memory area consumes no physical memory, though it takes 512 GB of virtual space. When more data is inserted into the database, more physical memory is allocated to the corresponding COW memory area. The memory space manager of SwingDB is responsible for managing the space allocation within the COW memory areas, as shown in Fig. 4. Based on such a design, the function *getsnapshot*() can be realised through the SWING function *hook*(), which is highly efficient.

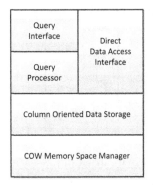

Fig. 4. The basic architecture of SwingDB

We built our SwingDB on top of Supersonic[2], an in-memory column store developed by google. We re-engineered the storage layer of Supersonic to move the entire storage space into COW memory of SWING. To enable snapshot sharing, we locate the meta data of a database in the first segment of its COW memory area, so that a database can be easily identified by a new process. The source code of SwingDB can be found in GitHub (see Footnote 1).

4.3   Application Scenarios

In a traditional setting of multi-stage data analysis, data is physically transmitted from program to program. Each program receives data from its previous programs, performs a certain type of data processing and sends its results, along with the original data, to the subsequent programs. Transmission of data can be conducted in several ways – each program can transmit data individually, or all programs can send and receive data to and from a mediated database. Such multi-stage data analysis is commonly used in modern scientific study [6,10,17].

---

[2] https://code.google.com/archive/p/supersonic/.

When performing in-memory data analysis, we store data entirely in RAM. In this context, we expect the whole process of data analysis can be finished in a few seconds, such that the data analytical application can become really interactive [18]. Such a speed cannot be achieved, if data has to be moved physically from program to program or between programs and a mediated database. SwingDB provides an efficient solution to multi-stage in-memory data analysis. Data is always stored in SwingDB, and the snapshots of the data are passed around by the programs. Each program retrieves the data snapshots from its previous programs, performs data processing within its own memory space and passes the resulting snapshots to its subsequent programs. No matter how complex the workflow is, no physical data movement is actually performed.

5   Performance Evaluation

We conducted experiments to study the performance characteristics of the SWING mechanism and SwingDB. The experiments were conducted on a HP Z820 workstation, equipped with two 2.60 GHz Intel Xeon processors E5-2670 and 64 GB DDR3 RAM. The operating system installed on the workstation was CentOS 7.1.

5.1   Overheads of SWING

Our first set of experiments was intended to measure the overhead of data transmission. We compared the SWING mechanism against FIFO (a.k.a. pipe) and shared memory. For FIFO, the overhead was measured by the execution time of the entire data transmission process. As to shared memory, we assume that the receiving process needs to block the sending process when reading the data. Its overhead is measured by the execution time of $mmap()$ and the time for locking and scanning the data. Fine grained concurrency control can be used to improve the concurrency of shared memory. However, due to the complexity of the implementation of a fine grained concurrency controller, we did not consider it in our experiments. For SWING, its overhead is measured by the executing time of $hook()$. In the experiments, we varied the amount of data from 1 GB to 8 GB. The measured overheads are shown in Fig. 5. As expected, SWING is way faster than FIFO and shared memory when transmitting data.

Our second set of experiments was intended to measure the overhead incurred by copy-on-write operations. In the experiments, we let Process A allocate a COW memory area of 8 GB and keep updating the data in the area; then, we let Process B *hook* the COW memory periodically. Thus, Process A's updates will incur copy-on-write operations. Our experiments were intended to quantify how much Process A is slowed down by copy-on-write.

In the first experiment, we let Process A perform sequential update. We varied the frequency of the invocations of $hook()$ and measured the variation of Process A's throughput. We compared the results against the case where no data sharing was performed. As shown in Fig. 6(a), copy-on-write operations do affect

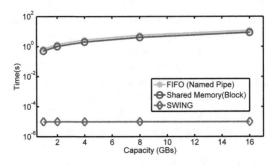

Fig. 5. Overhead of data transmission

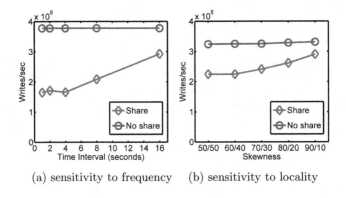

(a) sensitivity to frequency   (b) sensitivity to locality

Fig. 6. Overhead of copy on write

performance. The influence increases as we raise the frequency of data sharing. Nevertheless, the overhead is controllable. In the worst case, the performance of updating drops by around 50%. If we keep the frequency of data sharing to a moderate level (e.g. once per 20 s), the performance loss can be minimized.

In the second experiment, we fixed the frequency of *hook*() to once per 8 s and let Process A perform random updates. We varied the skewness of update distribution and measured the variation of Process A's throughput. This allows us to see how data locality affects the overhead of copy-on-write. As shown in Fig. 6(b) (on *x*-axis, 80/20 means that 80% of updates were performed on 20% of data), when the locality of updates increases, the penalty caused by copy-on-write drops. In most real world applications, data accesses normally show strong locality. Thus, the overhead of copy-on-write should not be outstanding most of the time.

5.2   Experiments on OLTP Workload

Our second set of experiments aimed to evaluate how the copy-on-write operations of SWING affects the performance of database update. As SwingDB does not specialize in OLTP, we used Redis, an OLTP oriented in-memory database.

We applied SWING to Redis, by moving the entire storage space of Redis to a single COW memory area. Then, we let a data analytical process to hook the COW memory of Redis periodically. After each *hook*() operation, the analytical process performs a sequential scan of the data. At the same time, we ran the YCSB Benchmark on Redis, to see how data sharing affects Redis' performance. We compared the COW mechanism against FIFO and shared memory. (When using shared memory, the analytical process needs to block Redis while reading the data, as Redis does not support fine grained access control.)

In the experiments, we set *recordcount* of YCSB to 900,000 for Workloads A, B, C, F and 500,000 for Workloads D,E. With such a data size, Redis' storage space can be accommodated in an 8 GB COW memory area. We set *operationcount* of YCSB to 10,000,000. As to the other parameters, we used the default values of YCSB. We varied the frequency of invocation of *hook*() from once per 10 s to once per 80 s. The performance of Redis is shown in Fig. 7. (Due to limited space, we only show the results on Workloads A, B, D, F.)

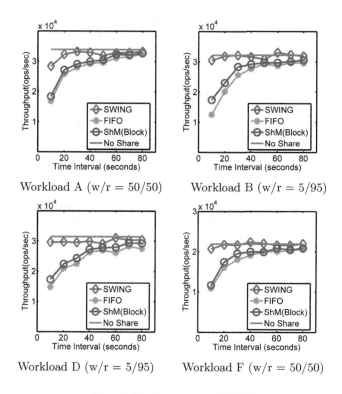

Workload A (w/r = 50/50)   Workload B (w/r = 5/95)

Workload D (w/r = 5/95)   Workload F (w/r = 50/50)

Fig. 7. Performance on YCSB

As we can see, SWING does not have significant influence on Redis's normal work. Even when the frequency of data sharing went up to once per 10 s, we still could not see any significant drop of Redis' performance. (The TPS of the original Redis is a bit more than 30 thousands. While some recent experimental in-memory systems [16] claim to achieve a million TPS, such throughput does not apply to Redis, which is a single threaded full-fledged system.) As updates in YCSB show strong locality, the performance penalty caused by copy-on-write seems quite limited. (Note that YCSB's data accesses follow the Zipfian distribution.) For update intensive workloads, such as Workloads A, the performance of Redis falls slightly when SWING is used. This indicates that copy-on-write can be an overhead for update intensive applications, though its influence is limited. In contrast to SWING, FIFO and shared memory did affect the performance of Redis significantly, especially when the frequency of data sharing is high.

5.3   Experiments on SwingDB

To evaluate the performance of SwingDB, we compared it against Vectorwise (Version 4.2.0), one of the most efficient in-memory DBMS specializing in OLAP. While it is difficult for SwingDB to beat Vectorwise in OLAP performance, SwingDB is way faster than Vectorwise in data transmission. We put both systems in a workflow of data analytics, consisting of a DBMS and a data analytical application. SwingDB and Vectorwise play the role of the DBMS, which is responsible for data management and query processing. The analytical application retrieves data from the DBMS through SQL queries, and performs advanced analytical study on the data. To work with Vectorwise, the application makes use of the APIs of Vectorwise to establish a connection with the database, issue queries and move the query results from Vectorwise to its own space. To work with SwingDB, the analytical application first retrieves the whole snapshot of the database into its own space, and then executes SQL queries and advanced analysis on the data. The main difference is that SwingDB does not require inter-process data movement.

In our experiments, we created a simple database composed of only one relational table and loaded 10 GB of data into the database. To retrieve data, we used a selection query with varying selectivity. When data is retrieved, the application conducts statistical analysis over the data, which mainly consists of calculation of standard deviation. The execution time of the whole analytical process was recorded and plotted in Fig. 8.

As we can see, when the size of query results is very small (i.e., selectivity as low as 1%), SwingDB does not necessarily perform as well as Vectorwise. In this case, query execution consumes the majority of the time, and SwingDB is not as optimized as Vectorwise in query processing. When the size of query results become larger (i.e., selectivity higher than 5%), SwingDB starts to outperform Vectorwise. In this case, the transmission of query results from Vectorwise to the application becomes more expensive than query execution. When large amount of data needs to be transmitted, the superiority of SwingDB becomes obvious. For instance, when the selectivity is as high as 100% and 2 GB of data needs to be transmitted, SwingDB is faster than Vectorwise by two orders of magnitude.

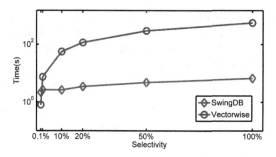

Fig. 8. Execution time of data analysis

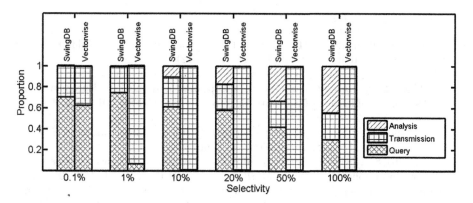

Fig. 9. Breakdown of the execution time

If we break down the execution time of data analysis, as shown in Fig. 9, we can see that the majority of the cost for Vectorwise was incurred by inter-process data transmission. In large scale data analysis, data transmission can be intensive. It may obliterate the performance advantage of in-memory databases. In contrast, SwingDB successfully avoids physical data movement by utilizing SWING. Therefore, it can be much more efficient in multi-stage data analysis than traditional in-memory DBMS.

6   Conclusion

In this paper, we introduced SWING, a new inter-process data sharing mechanism, and SwingDB, an embedded database system built on top of SWING. Different from traditional database systems, SwingDB is able to share database snapshots instantly among processes. This DBMS-OS co-design proves to be suitable for multi-stage data analytics, in which multiple loosely coupled systems or components cooperate to generate analytical results. (We believe that such multi-stage settings/cases will be increasingly common for future data analytics, as witnessed by today's scientific data management [6,17].) We conducted extensible performance evaluation on our systems. The results showed that SwingDB is highly efficient in snapshot sharing and its extra overhead caused by copy-on-write operations is moderate and controllable.

As our future work, we will continue to enrich the functionality of SwingDB as both a database system and a tool for advanced data analytics. We would also like to invite the communities of DB and OS to join our effort of making SWING a standard instrument in data processing platforms.

References

1. Intel® 64 and IA-32 architectures software developer's manual. Basic Architecture, vol. 1. Intel Corporation, August 2012
2. Aviram, A., Weng, S.-C., Hu, S., Ford, B.: Efficient system-enforced deterministic parallelism. Commun. ACM **55**(5), 111–119 (2012)
3. Beck, F., Diehl, S.: On the congruence of modularity and code coupling. In: Proceedings of the 19th ACM SIGSOFT Symposium and the 13th European Conference on Foundations of Software Engineering, ESEC/FSE 2011, pp. 354–364. ACM, New York (2011)
4. Castellano, G.V.: System object model (SOM) and Ada: an example of CORBA at work. In: ACM Sigada Ada Letters XVI, pp. 39–51 (1996)
5. Chaudhuri, S.: Review - integrating mining with relational database systems: alternatives and implications. In: ACM SIGMOD Digital Review, vol. 2 (2000)
6. Curcin, V., Ghanem, M.: Scientific workflow systems - can one size fit all? In: 2008 Cairo International Biomedical Engineering Conference, pp. 1–9, December 2008
7. Färber, F., Cha, S.K., Primsch, J., Bornhövd, C., Sigg, S., Lehner, W.: SAP HANA database: data management for modern business applications. ACM SIGMOD Rec. **40**(4), 45–51 (2012)
8. Garlan, D., Schmerl, B., Garlan, D., Schmerl, B.: Component-based software engineering in pervasive computing environments. In: Proceedings of the 4th ICSE Conference (2001)
9. Kemper, A., Neumann, T.: Hyper: a hybrid OLTP&OLAP main memory database system based on virtual memory snapshots. In: Proceedings of 27th ICDE, pp. 195–206. IEEE (2011)
10. Leipzig, J.: A review of bioinformatic pipeline frameworks. Brief. Bioinform. (2016). doi:10.1093/bib/bbw020
11. Liu, T., Curtsinger, C., Berger, E.D.: Dthreads: efficient deterministic multithreading. In: Proceedings of the Twenty-Third ACM Symposium on Operating Systems Principles, pp. 327–336. ACM (2011)
12. Majer, K.: Linux Kernel Internals, 2nd edn. Addison-Wesley, US (1998)
13. McCracken, D.: Sharing page tables in the Linux kernel. In: Linux Symposium, p. 315 (2003)
14. Merrifield, T., Eriksson, J.: Conversion: multi-version concurrency control for main memory segments. In: Proceedings of the 8th ACM European Conference on Computer Systems, pp. 127–139. ACM (2013)
15. Sikka, V., Färber, F., Goel, A.K., Lehner, W.: SAP HANA: the evolution from a modern main-memory data platform to an enterprise application platform. PVLDB **6**(11), 1184–1185 (2013)

16. Tu, S., Zheng, W., Kohler, E., Liskov, B., Madden, S.: Speedy transactions in multicore in-memory databases. In: Proceedings of the Twenty-Fourth ACM Symposium on Operating Systems Principles, pp. 18–32. ACM (2013)

17. Yu, J., Buyya, R.: A taxonomy of scientific workflow systems for grid computing. SIGMOD Rec. **34**(3), 44–49 (2005)

18. Zaharia, M., Chowdhury, M., Das, T., Dave, A., Ma, J., Mccauley, M., Franklin, M., Shenker, S., Stoica, I.: Fast and interactive analytics over hadoop data with spark. USENIX Login **37**(4), 45–51 (2012)

Runtime Fragility in Main Memory

Endre Palatinus[(✉)] and Jens Dittrich

Information Systems Group, Saarland University, Saarbrücken, Germany
palatinuse@gmail.com
http://infosys.cs.uni-saarland.de

Abstract. In this paper we investigate the following problem: Given a
database workload (tables and queries), which data layout (row, column
or a suitable PAX-layout) should we choose in order to get the best possible performance? We show that this is not an easy problem. We explore
careful combinations of various parameters that have an impact on the
performance including: (1) the schema, (2) the CPU architecture, (3) the
compiler, and (4) the optimization level. We include a CPU from each
of the past 4 generations of Intel CPUs.

In addition, we demonstrate the importance of taking variance into
account when deciding on the optimal storage layout. We observe considerable variance throughout our measurements which makes it difficult
to argue along means over different runs of an experiment. Therefore,
we compute confidence intervals for all measurements and exploit this
to detect outliers and define classes of methods that we are not allowed
to distinguish statistically. The variance of different performance measurements can be so significant that the optimal solution may not be the
best one in practice.

Our results also indicate that a carefully or ill-chosen compilation
setup can trigger a performance gain or loss of factor 1.1 to factor 25 in
even the simplest workloads: a table with four attributes and a simple
query reading those attributes. This latter observation is not caused by
variance in the measured runtimes, but due to using a different compiler
setup.

Besides the compilation setup, the data layout is another source of
query time fragility. Various size metrics of the memory subsystem are
round numbers in binary, or put more simply: powers of 2 in decimal. System engineers have followed this tradition over time. Surprisingly, there
exists a use-case in query processing where using powers of 2 is always
a suboptimal choice, leading to one more cause of fragile query times.
Using this finding, we will show how to improve tuple-reconstruction
costs by using a novel main-memory data-layout.

Keywords: Main-memory databases · Data layouts · Robust query
processing · Tuple reconstruction

1 Introduction

The two most common data layouts used in todays database management systems are row and column layout. These are only the two extremes when vertically

© Springer International Publishing AG 2017
S. Blanas et al. (Eds.): ADMS 2016/IMDM 2016, LNCS 10195, pp. 150–165, 2017.
DOI: 10.1007/978-3-319-56111-0_9

partitioning a table. In-between these extremes there exists a full spectrum of column-grouped layouts, which under certain settings can beat both of the afore-mentioned traditional layouts for legacy disk-based row-stores [7]. However, for main-memory systems column grouped layouts have not proved to be of much use for OLTP workloads [5], unless the schema is very wide [9].

Another axis of partitioning a table is horizontal partitioning, where the partitions are created along the tuples instead of along the attributes. This is usually based on the values of an attribute with low cardinality, e.g. geograph-ical regions, but this is not a strict requirement. Forming horizontal partitions can also be done by simply taking repeatedly k records from the table, which we will call chunks in the following. Within a horizontal partition we can have any vertically partitioned layout, including row and column as well. One notable example in disk-based database systems is the PAX-layout [1], where the hor-izontal partitions have a size that is the multiple of the hard disk's block size, and inside these partitions the tuples are laid out in column layout. Another notable example is MonetDB X/100 [2,12], which chooses the chunk size such that all column chunks needed by a query fit into the CPU cache.

We can apply a strategy similar to PAX in main memory as well, however, we have more freedom in choosing the size of the horizontal partitions. Therefore in main-memory we can simply form so-called chunks of the table by repeatedly taking k records from the table and laying them out in column layout *within* the chunk. We denote this layout by memPAXk. In this sense, row layout is the same as memPAX1, and column layout is equivalent to memPAXn, where n is larger or equal to the cardinality of the table. The chunks of these layouts are analogous to PAX pages [1], however, there are two important differences: (1) we can choose any chunk size (in bytes or tuples) that is a multiple of the tuple size, while for PAX we are restricted to multiples of the disk's block size, and (2) we neither store any helper data structures per chunk, nor use mini-pages as in the disk-based PAX-layout. The possible memPAX layouts of a table having 2 columns and 8 records, and using chunk sizes of powers of 2 are illustrated in Fig. 1. Here we can see the two extremes: row- and column layout, and memPAX layouts with a chunk size of 2- and 4 tuples.

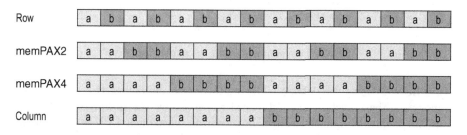

Fig. 1. memPAX layouts of a table having 2 columns and 8 records, considering powers of 2 chunk sizes.

2   The Six-Dimensional Parameter Space of Our Experiments

We are going to explore a six-dimensional parameter space of a fairly simple workload: a table with four attributes and two simple queries reading those attributes. The whole experiment is conducted on memory resident tables, and using hand-coded queries implemented in C++. We are going to refer to this workload as our micro-benchmark. In the following we specify the dimensions:

(1) The datatype used in the schema. Our dataset is a single memory-resident table with four integer columns, with a total size of 10 GB. Depending on the data type chosen (1-byte, 4-byte, or 8-byte integers denoted by `int1`, `int4`, and `int8`, respectively) we get the following scenarios (Table 1):

Table 1. The schemas used in our experiments

Label	Schema	Tuple count
char	(a int1, b int1, c int1, d int1)	$2560 * 1024^2$
int	(a int4, b int4, c int4, d int4)	$640 * 1024^2$
long	(a int8, b int8, c int8, d int8)	$320 * 1024^2$

(2) The presence of conditional statements in the query code. We use two queries requiring all tuples to be reconstructed for processing as shown in Fig. 2. Q1 performs a minimum-search on the sum of all attributes of a tuple, which being a conditional expression yields a branch in the implementation. We have tried out a branch-free implementation of the min[1] calculation as well, which, however, was consistently slower. Q2 on the other hand performs a branchless calculation: it sums up the product of the attribute values of each tuple. Since Q2 has no branches, the measured query times are not affected by branch-mispredictions.

```
Q1:  SELECT  MIN(a+b+c+d)  FROM T;
Q2:  SELECT  SUM(a*b*c*d)  FROM T;
```

Fig. 2. The queries used in the experiments

(3) The CPU architecture. The performance characteristics of a main-memory database system are influenced the most by the machine's CPU. As there are usually significant changes between the subsequent CPU architectures, we have chosen machines equipped with Intel CPUs of four subsequent architectures, all running Debian 7.8.0 with Linux kernel version 3.2.0-4-amd64 as shown in Table 2, with hyper-threading either disabled or not supported.

---

[1] min = min XOR ((temp XOR min) AND NEG(temp < min)).

Table 2. The machines used in our experiments

CPU	Architecture	RAM
Xeon 5150	Core	16 GB DDR2 @ 266 MHz
Xeon X5690	Westmere	192 GB DDR3 @ 1066 MHz
Xeon E5-2407	Sandy Bridge	48 GB DDR3 @ 1333 MHz
Xeon E7-4870 v2	Ivy Bridge	512 GB DDR3 @ 1600 MHz

(4) The compiler. In our experiments we have chosen the three most commonly used compilers[2]: clang (3.0-6.2), gcc (Debian 4.7.2-5), and icc (15.0.0). clang and gcc are both open-source, while icc is proprietary software. clang is actually a C-compiler front-end to the LLVM compiler infrastructure. It compiles C, Objective-C, and C++ code to the LLVM Intermediate Representation (IR), similar to other LLVM front-ends, which allows for a massive set of optimizations to be performed on the IR before translating it to machine code. GCC is short for GNU Compiler Collection, a compiler supporting among others the C/C++ language. It support almost all hardware platforms and operating systems, and it is the most popular C/C++ compiler, and also the default one in most Linux distros. Intel's C/C++ compiler can take advantage of Intel's insider knowledge on Intel CPUs. It is said to generate very efficient code especially for arithmetic operations.

(5) The optimization level. We intuitively expect to get higher performance from higher optimization levels, yet there is no guarantee from the compiler's side that this will also hold in practice. Thus, we have decided to evaluate all three standard optimization levels: -O1, -O2, and -O3.

(6) Compile time vs. runtime layouts. The tables in our dataset are physically stored in a one-dimensional array of integers, using a linearisation order conforming to one of the layouts described in Sect. 1. Any query fired against this dataset needs to take care of determining the (virtual) address of any attribute value, and possibly reconstructing tuples as well. To do this it is required to know the chunk size, which can either be specified prior to compiling a given query, i.e. at compile time, or only provided at runtime.

To allow for any compiler optimization to take place, we have been extensively using templates to create a separate executable for each element of the parameter space, i.e. we have an executable for every dataset, query, machine, compiler, O-level, and layout. In case of compile time chunk sizes we have created a separate executable for each chunk size, while for runtime memPAX layouts only a single generic one. The generic executable processes the query chunk by chunk, for which it needs the chunk size provided the latest at runtime. For smaller chunk

---

[2] More precisely their C++ front-ends: clang++, g++, and icpc.

sizes this approach has an inherent CPU-overhead caused by the short-living loops.

3 Methodology

3.1 Motivating Example

The most common way of measuring the performance of algorithms, systems, or components in the database community is to report the average runtime out of 3 or 5 runs. Let's look at an example: assume we measured runtimes of a query when executed against two different layouts. Layout A has an average runtime of 1.75 s and Layout B of 1.82 s. In this case we would clearly declare Layout A as superior to Layout B.

However, if we take a look at the runtimes of all 5 runs in Fig. 3, we can see that Layout A has a high variance (0.06), whereas the query time for Layout B is rather stable (its variance is 0.00075). Most system designers would probably prefer Layout B, due to its performance being more predictable. This example demonstrates that reporting the average runtime alone is not sufficient for comparing two solutions [6, Chap. 13]. Therefore at a minimum the variance or standard deviation of the sample should be provided along with the average to get a proper description of the sample.

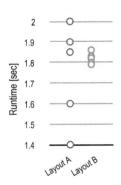

Fig. 3. Query times for two different layouts, each measured five times

We should keep in mind that when experimentally comparing multiple systems, we only get a *sample* of their performance metrics which can only be used to *estimate* the populations' performance metrics. Thus, there is always a level of uncertainty in our estimates, which renders the necessity of expressing this uncertainty in some way. One possible way to do this is to use confidence intervals, which express the following in natural language: "There is a 95% chance that the actual average runtime of System A is between 1.7 and 1.8 s."

3.2 Confidence Intervals

To create a confidence interval we first have to choose our confidence level, typically 90%, 95% or 99%, denoted by $1 - \alpha$, where α is called the significance level. We require the sample size n, the sample mean $\overline{x}$, sample standard deviation σ, and the significance level α. Then the confidence interval is defined as follows: $(\overline{x} - C \times \frac{\sigma}{\sqrt{n}}, \overline{x} + C \times \frac{\sigma}{\sqrt{n}})$, where C is the so-called confidence coefficient. The choice of the confidence coefficient is determined by the sample size [6, p. 206]. If we have a large sample ($n \geq 30$), we can use the $1 - \alpha/2$-quantile of the standard normal distribution for the confidence coefficient: $C = Z_{1-\alpha/2}$. However, in experiments we usually run only 5 measurements, thus we have a sample size of $n = 5$. Therefore, we should only use the $1 - \alpha/2$-quantile of the Student's t-distribution with $n - 1$ degrees of freedom: $C = t_{[1-\alpha/2,n-1]}$. The prerequisite is that the population needs to have a normal distribution, which is a fair assumption for our runtime measurements. For instance, the 95% confidence intervals for our example in Fig. 3 are: (0.23, 3.27) for Layout A, and (1.65, 1.99) for Layout B. This makes Layout B a safer choice, if predictability is of great importance for the system designer. (See [6, Chap. 13] for details.) When looking at the measured query times on Layout A in Fig. 3, we can see that the relatively wide confidence interval for Layout A is due to the large variance of the sample: the points are scattered out across the (1.4, 2.0) interval. However, a sample can have a large variance even if most measured values are "near" to each other, and only a few of them having a higher or lower value than the rest. These latter are called outliers.

3.3 Outlier Detection

An outlier is an element of a sample that does not "fit" into the sample in some way. It is hard to quantify the criteria for labelling an element as an outlier, and it also depends heavily on the use-case. Therefore, the most common technique used for detecting outliers is plotting the sample on a scatter plot, and visually inspecting the plot by a human. If we assume, that there is only one outlier in the sample, and it is either the minimum, or the maximum value, then we can use Grubbs' test [4] to automatically detect outliers. The only problem is that this method tends to identify outliers too often for samples with less than eight elements. To counter the error rate of the method we have included an additional condition for labelling an outlier: $\text{margin\_of\_error}/\bar{x} \geq 2.5\%$, where the margin of error is defined as the radius of the confidence interval.

3.4 Choosing the Best Solution When There Is No Single Best Solution

Choosing the best solution using the average runtime is easy, we simply take the one with the smallest one. We have also seen that this can be arbitrarily wrong, and that is why confidence intervals provide a better basis of comparison than the sample mean. However, comparing confidence intervals is not that straight-forward as comparing scalars. If two intervals are disjoint, they are easily comparable. If they are not disjoint, and the mean of one sample is inside the other sample's confidence interval, they are indistinguishable from each other with the same level of confidence, as that of the intervals. Finally, if they are not disjoint, but their means do not fall into the other sample's interval, an independent two-sample t-test (Welch's t-test [11]) can decide whether they are distinguishable, and if so, which one is better.

4 Micro Benchmark Results

In this section we investigate the connection between the query time and the elements of the parameter space. We will consider all dimensions mentioned in

Sect. 2, and show their effect on performance. We have executed all executables single-threaded, and have pinned the process to a given CPU core to avoid runtime variance cased by data- and thread shuffling. We have noticed that varying the chunk size of the memPAX layouts between 2^{16} and the biggest possible one does not make a significant difference in the query times, regardless of the query, machine, and compiler. Thus, we have excluded those results from our discussion.

4.1   Runtime Fragility

We start our discussion with runtime fragility, by which we denote the performance difference caused by using another layout, compiler, O-level, etc. Note the difference between query time variance and fragility: fragility is *not* caused by query time variance, but by using another parameter combination that simply yields a different runtime, potentially a factor better or worse.

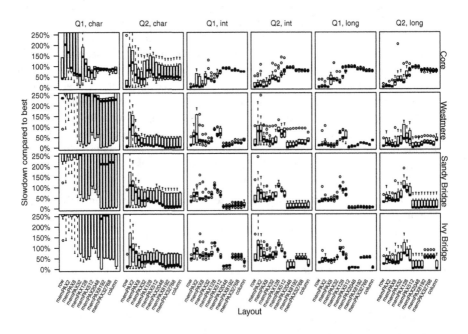

Fig. 4. Runtime fragility of the various data layouts in our micro benchmarks

Let us first consider the runtime fragility of compiling, i.e. the effects of changing the compiler setup which consists of the compiler, O-level, and runtime vs. compile time layouts. In Fig. 4 in each subplot we show the median query times, when fixing only the machine, query, and the dataset, but changing the compiler setup and the data layout. The fragility is presented by using box plots, which show the minimum, first quartile, median, third quartile, and the maximum value of the median query times for each data layout. To help us compare the fragility of compiling across the different scenarios, the vertical axis displays the performance overhead of each compiler setup over the best one (displayed till at most 250% overhead; notice that some boxes leave their plot).

The most apparent finding is that the query time of both queries on the char schema is extremely fragile compared to that of the int and long schemas. This is quantified in Table 3, where we show the performance drop between the worst and the best query times, drilled-down along machine, schema, and query. We observe up to a factor 25 difference in runtime. For char we can get factor 3.3 to factor 25 worse by choosing the wrong layout and/or compiler setup. Furthermore, for char there is not only a much larger fragility across the different data layouts as seen in Table 3, but even inside a given layout as well. In the majority of the cases the compiler setup can make a factor 0.5 to 1.0 more performance drop compared to the best layout and compiler setup for Q2 on char.

Table 3. The performance drop between worst and best query times caused by changing the compiler setup and the layout.

Machine	char		int		long	
	Q1	Q2	Q1	Q2	Q1	Q2
Core	6.8	3.3	1.3	1.4	1.1	2.0
Westmere	25.0	3.8	1.9	2.5	1.0	1.3
Sandy Bridge	13.2	3.6	1.6	2.4	1.5	1.9
Ivy Bridge	14.4	3.3	1.7	2.6	1.3	1.7

Let us now investigate how exactly the compiler setup determines performance. In Fig. 5 we can see the query times on the char schema for runtime-layouts (plus row and column). Please note that the query times of compile time layouts are not shown to enhance readability. For Q1 we can see that g++ -O1 and -O2 consistently yield a very bad performance, which is at least 3 times worse for chunk sizes above 8. The worst query times are produced by g++ -O3 on memPAX1 and memPAX2. It is clear that the short-living loops of these two layouts incur a large CPU overhead, yet it is surprising to see that g++ -O3 makes the layouts with chunk sizes not bigger than 16 even more inefficient. Considering the other two compilers, clang++ performs in between the other two, and icpc consistently yields the best runtimes. On the other hand, for Q2 icpc -O2 and icpc -O3 perform the worst for chunk sizes above 2.

4.2   Best Solutions

Our second major finding is not about fragility, but a substantial difference between the effectiveness of the different layouts depending on the machine the

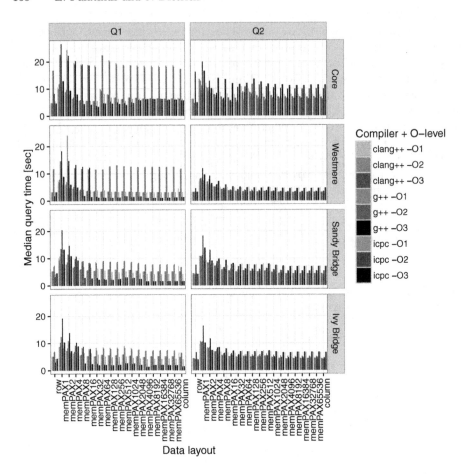

Fig. 5. Query times on the `char` schema across compiler setups and runtime-layouts in our micro benchmarks.

query is executed on. To highlight this we show in Fig. 6 the query times of the best layouts, drilled-down along machine, schema, and query. We can immediately notice the radical difference between Core and the other three CPU architectures. The oldest one, Core, prefers layouts with smaller chunk sizes, i.e. close to row layout. The three newer ones on the other hand prefer larger chunk sizes, i.e. close to column layout. For the latter CPUs we can further notice that the best layout for a dataset is often the one, where the following holds: $k * \texttt{attribute\_size} * \texttt{tuple\_count} = 4\text{KB}$, $k \in \{1 \dots \texttt{attribute\_count} \}$ — which is when the chunk or an attribute's column inside a chunk perfectly fits the memory page: memPAX4096 for `char`, memPAX1024 for `int` and memPAX512 for `long`.

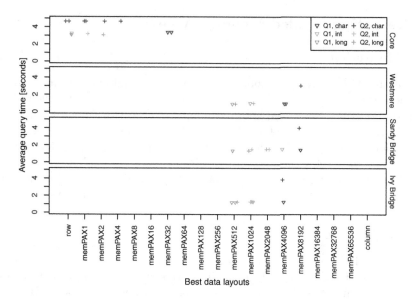

Fig. 6. Best layouts and their query times. Drilled-down along machine, schema, and query.

4.3   Conclusions and Guidelines

We can conclude that when using the int and long schemas, we can focus on choosing a proper data layout only, since the compiler setup is not expected to cause significant fragility. However, for the char schema care has to be taken to choose *both* layout and compiler setup wisely.

Our overall guideline for choosing the best layout is as follows: For servers equipped with a Core CPU it is a safe bet to use row layout, while for machines with the subsequent Westmere, Sandy Bridge, and Ivy Bridge architectures it is just fine to use column layout. For the latter machines we can exploit the schema for some fine-tuning, by creating PAX-blocks with the same size as the virtual memory pages. Having branches in the query is an additional argument for this optimization. The compiler, O-level, and compile time vs. runtime layouts will not change the choice of best layout (see Q2 on int run on Ivy Bridge), but they are to be chosen very carefully for the best performance. In cases like the char schema, for the optimal compiler setup, however, one has to try out all possible combinations, since it highly depends on the target system.

We have also shown how misleading it can be to choose the best solution along means. Take the case of Q2 on char run on Core, where the 6 best solutions are statistically indistinguishable from each other with 95% confidence, yet they differ either in the layout, the compiler, or the optimization level.

5   Revisiting Strided Memory Access

5.1   Motivation

Various size metrics of the memory subsystem are round numbers in binary, or put more simply: powers of 2 in decimal. System engineers have followed this tradition over time. Some well known examples of objects with powers of 2 sizes: cachelines, caches, RAM modules, HDD blocks, virtual memory pages, and even HDFS blocks. Surrounded by this flood of round binary numbers a data engineer feels pressed to develop data structures with similarly "round" sizes. So did we feel, until one day we started to question the optimality of this tradition, and dared to look at memPAX layouts with chunk sizes in between powers of 2.

5.2   Background

One of the CPU events debunking the random-access nature of main memory is the memory bank conflict. To understand this event, we first have to explain interleaved memory. DRAM and caches are both organised into banks. In case of DDR3 there are typically 4 banks. Caches on the other hand can have a varying number of banks, depending on the actual CPU generation. Interleaved memory means that the memory addresses are split among the banks in a round-robin fashion, i.e. membankID = address mod 4, which allows for requests to different banks to be fetched — though not transferred — in parallel, thereby improving the bandwidth utilisation. (See [8, Sect. 5.2] for more details.)

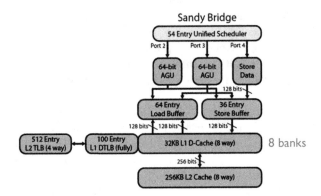

Fig. 7. The architecture diagram of Intel Sandy Bridge. Image source: http://www. realworldtech.com/sandy-bridge/7

In Fig. 7 we can see the part of the Sandy Bridge architecture diagram that is related to the memory subsystem. There are two important improvements over previous generations [3]. Firstly, the Sandy Bridge architecture has two memory read ports where previous Intel processors had only one. The maximum throughput is now 256 bits read and 128 bits write per clock cycle. The flip side of this coin is that the risk of contentions in the data cache increases when there are more memory operations per clock cycle. It is quite difficult to maintain the maximum read and write throughput without being delayed by cache bank conflicts. The second improvement is, that there is no performance penalty for reading or writing misaligned memory operands, except for the fact that it uses more cache banks so that the risk of cache conflicts is higher when the operand is misaligned.

Getting back to memory bank conflicts, the Intel Architecture Optimization Manual [3, Sects. 2.2.5.2 and 3.6.1.3] gives a precise description on this event for the Sandy Bridge architecture: "A bank conflict happens when two simultaneous load operations have the same bit 2–5 of their linear address but they are not from the same set in the cache (bits 6–12)." Thus, in contrast to our expectations, it is actually not beneficial for the performance of load bandwidth-bound code to perform a strided access of addresses with a stride that is a multiple of the cache line size. In that case the addresses will have the same bits 5–0, but different bits 12–6, thus a bank conflict will occur.

5.3 Performance Implications on Tuple-Reconstruction

To demonstrate the effects of bank conflicts on the performance of an application, lets consider Q1 and Q2 executed on Sandy Bridge on `char` fields, compiled with `g++ -O2`, and the chunk sizes being provided at compile time. Let us take a look at the query times for all chunk sizes [measured in tuples] between 2 and 1024, considering multiples-of-2 chunk sizes as well, in Fig. 8. The black symbols on the left show the query times for row layout, while the ones on the right show the query times for column layout. The red line shows the query times for powers-of-2 chunk sizes, while the blue line shows the runtimes for multiples-of-2 chunk sizes, which is more fine granular. This exemplifies the details that can get overlooked when not performing a fine-granular exploration of the parameter space. Interestingly, there is a periodic spike in the query time, with a period size of 64, which happens to be the cache line size. Recall, that when executing Q1 we have to reconstruct the tuples for computing the aggregate value. As we have two attributes only, the stride of the memory access equals to the chunk size multiplied by the field size. Thus, for `char` fields the stride equals the chunk size. From the above discussion we know that a strided access of memory addresses with a multiple of 64 stride should result in a bank conflict.

Therefore, we have decided to validated this claim by letting VTune find the hardware events responsible for the spikes in the query time. We have taken a sample of the experiments, those with a chunk size between 448 and 512. Both endpoints of this interval are multiples of 64, and where the query time has its spikes. We have measured all existing PMU events and looked for those that have a linear correlation with the query time. We have found out that out of the ca. 200 PMU events available for Sandy Bridge, only three correlate significantly with the query time:

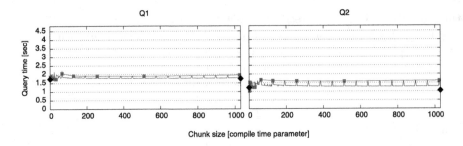

Fig. 8. Query times of Q1 and Q2 executed on Sandy Bridge on `char` fields, compiled with `g++ -O2`, and the chunk size being provided at compile time. (Color figure online)

DTLB_LOAD_MISSES.STLB_HIT: data TLB load misses that hit in the second level TLB

HW_PRE_REQ.DL1_MISS: hardware prefetch requests that miss in the L1 data cache

L1D_BLOCKS.BANK_CONFLICT_CYCLES: memory bank conflict in the L1 data cache

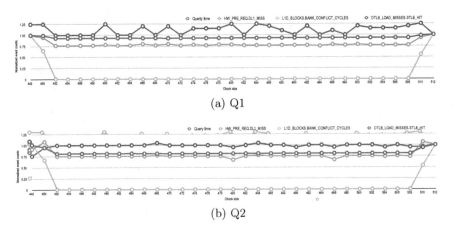

(a) Q1

(b) Q2

Fig. 9. PMU events of Q1 and Q2 executed on Sandy Bridge on `char` fields, compiled with `g++ -O2`, for chunk sizes in $\{448, 450, \ldots, 510, 512\}$.

We have plotted these three PMU events and the query time in Fig. 9, normalised to the respective values measured for chunk size 512. As we have the same spikes in the query time for the two endpoints of the chunk size interval, the normalised query times equal 1 at these points, and are below 1 for all other points. We can see that the memory bank conflicts in the L1 data cache have a very strong linear correlation to the query time. Basically, both the query time and the latter metric have only 3 different values. The query time is the lowest when there are no L1D bank conflicts at all, and it increases together with the metric just next to the chunk sizes where the spikes are, and reaches its maximum together with the metric. The other two events also show a strong correlation, however, they do not drop to 0 inside the considered chunk size intervals.

As we can see in Fig. 8, for Q2 choosing a memPAX layout which is not a power of 2 improves the query time by approximately 20%. This is definitely a significant improvement in the spectrum of what can be expected from data layouts. Q2 is a typical example of tuple-reconstruction, and thus memPAX layout can also be used for improving the tuple-reconstruction part of more complex queries.

6   TPC-H Experiments

Real world analytical workloads are significantly more complex, than our micro-benchmarks. They have a wider schema with different attribute types, and the queries use more expensive operators as well, including aggregation and joins. In order to investigate the runtime fragility of more complex workloads, let us consider the TPC-H benchmark [10].

6.1   Experimental Setup

We have implemented Q1 and Q6 of the TPC-H benchmark as hand-coded applications written in C++. These two queries are single-table queries touching only the Lineitem table. We have implemented two variants of the Lineitem table: one matching the schema described in the benchmark, which we will refer to as *uncompressed*. The second version, on the other hand, is a *compressed* table. We have applied some compression schemes to the Lineitem table, as explained in Table 4, using the information in Sect. 4.2.3 "Test Database Data Generation" of the TPC-H Standard Specification [10].

Table 4. The compression schemes applied to the TPC-H Lineitem table

Field name	DDL-compliant data type	Compressed type	Encoding	Reason
L_LINENUMBER	int32_t	uint8_t	domain	in [1..7]
L_QUANTITY	int64_t	uint8_t	domain	random value [1..50]
L_DISCOUNT	int64_t	uint8_t	domain	random value [0.00 .. 0.10]
L_TAX	int64_t	uint8_t	domain	random value [0.00 .. 0.08]
L_SHIPINSTRUCT	char[25]	uint8_t	dictionary	random string from list Instructions
L_SHIPMODE	char[10]	uint8_t	dictionary	random string from list Modes
L_COMMENT	char[44]	uint32_t	dictionary	random text [10,43]

6.2   Runtime Fragility

We show the runtime fragility of the various data layouts for Q1 and Q6 in the
TPC-H benchmarks in Fig. 10, for both the uncompressed and the compressed
Lineitem table. For the uncompressed Lineitem table, column layout is the clear
winner in terms of performance. What is more important, is that it also has the
lowest fragility across the different compiler setups, and for Q6 it has almost no
fragility compared to the other layouts.

On the other hand, for the compressed Lineitem table column layout is not
a clear winner. If we consider the median query times inside a given layout
— depicted by the strong dash inside the boxes — for Q6 column layout is
significantly worse than the memPAX layouts with larger chunk sizes. There
is one very interesting difference when comparing to the query times on the
uncompressed Lineitem table: the layouts of the compressed Lineitem table are
much less fragile, as for Q6 the boxes are 2–5 times narrower than that of the
uncompressed table.

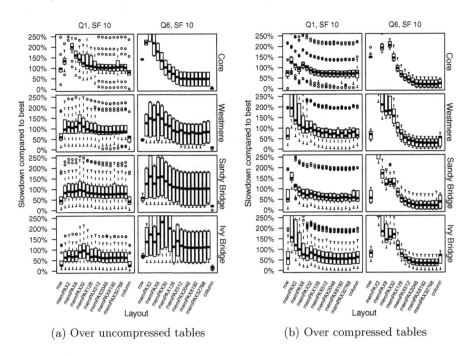

(a) Over uncompressed tables   (b) Over compressed tables

Fig. 10. Runtime fragility of the various data layouts for TPC-H queries

7   Conclusions

In this paper we have identified various sources of query time fragility – implementation factors that can change the performance of a query by factors in an
unpredictable way. We have investigated the fragility of both micro-benchmarks

and complex analytical benchmarks. We have considered the CPU architecture, the compiler, and the compiler flags as important factors. We have introduced the memPAX layout and compared its fragility to column layout and row layout.

We have shown that when querying tables with 1–byte integer columns a very high fragility is to be expected, in our case leading to a performance drop of up to factor 25. In case of more complex schemas and queries the inhomogeneity of the schema has a direct effect on the fragility. Applying dictionary- and domain encoding to the columns have reduced fragility by 50% to 80% in our experiments on the TPC-H benchmark.

We have found a use-case in query processing where using powers of 2 is always a suboptimal choice, leading to one more cause of fragile query times. We have shown how to choose the chunk sizes of the memPAX layouts to improve tuple-reconstruction costs by 20%.

Acknowledgments. Research supported by BMBF.

References

1. Ailamaki, A., et al.: Weaving relations for cache performance. In: VLDB 2001, pp. 169–180 (2001)
2. Boncz, P.A., Zukowski, M., Nes, N.: MonetDB/X100: hyper-pipelining query execution. In: CIDR, vol. 5, pp. 225–237 (2005)
3. Intel Corporation: Intel 64 and IA-32 Architectures Optimization Reference Manual
4. Grubbs, F.E.: Sample criteria for testing outlying observations. Ann. Math. Stat. **21**, 27–58 (1950)
5. Grund, M., et al.: HYRISE: a main memory hybrid storage engine. PVLDB **4**(2), 105–116 (2010)
6. Jain, R.: The Art of Computer Systems Performance Analysis. Wiley, New York (1991)
7. Jindal, A., Palatinus, E., Pavlov, V., Dittrich, J.: A comparison of knives for bread slicing. PVLDB **6**(6), 361–372 (2013)
8. Patterson, D., Hennessy, J.: Computer Organization and Design, Fourth Edition: The Hardware/Software Interface. The Morgan Kaufmann Series in Computer Architecture and Design, 4th edn. Elsevier Science, Amsterdam (2008)
9. Pirk, H., et al.: CPU and cache efficient management of memory-resident databases. In: ICDE 2013, pp. 14–25 (2013)
10. TPC-H Standard Specification. http://www.tpc.org/tpc_documents_current_versions/pdf/tpc-h_v2.17.1.pdf
11. Welch, B.L.: The generalization of Student's problem when several different population variances are involved. Biometrika **34**, 28–35 (1947)
12. Zukowski, M., Boncz, P.A., Nes, N., Héman, S.: MonetDB/X100-A DBMS in the CPU cache. IEEE Data Eng. Bull. **28**(2), 17–22 (2005)

Author Index

Printed in the United States
By Bookmasters